SWIMMING WITH SEALS

VICTORIA WHITWORTH lives with her
daughter in the north of Scotland. She is
a novelist and academic who explores the
culture and society of Britain in the Early
Middle Ages, focusing on death, burial and
memory. She is the author of *Dying and
Death in Later Anglo-Saxon England* (as
Victoria Thompson); *The Bone Thief* and
The Traitors' Pit (as V.M. Whitworth);
and *Daughter of the Wolf.*

Also by Victoria Whitworth

Daughter of the Wolf

SWIMMING WITH SEALS

Victoria Whitworth

HEAD of ZEUS

First published in the UK in 2017 by Head of Zeus Ltd

9 7 5 3 1 2 4 6 8

A catalogue record for this book is available from
the British Library.

ISBN (HB) 9781784978372
ISBN (E) 9781784978365

Typeset by Adrian McLaughlin

Printed and bound in Great Britain by
CPI Group (UK) Ltd, Croydon CR0 4YY

Head of Zeus Ltd
First Floor East
5–8 Hardwick Street
London EC1R 4RG

WWW.HEADOFZEUS.COM

For Kristin and Seamus, Archie and all the cats.

You know why.

'You never enjoy the world aright,
till the Sea itself floweth in your veins'
—THOMAS TRAHERNE, *Centuries of Meditations*

ACKNOWLEDGEMENTS

I have accrued vast debts over almost twenty years of visiting Orkney followed by nearly a decade as a resident. Just about everyone I know has fed something into the mix, and for each name I acknowledge here there are others whose words have lodged in crevices of memory so deep that I no longer remember who said them or when. For this I must apologize. General thanks are due to the Orkney Ranger Service; the Whale and Dolphin Conservation Society and the many experts whom I have badgered for information on marine mammals; and my academic colleagues in Nordic Studies and Archaeology at Orkney College, University of the Highlands and Islands.

More specific thanks are owed to many people:

Katie Thompson, Jessica Haydon, Cathy Thompson and our happy memories of Nairobi.

All my cousins, but especially Clive, Becca and Alex for permission to use the poem 'Travelling' by their mother, Barbara Lacey, which appears on p. 260.

Tom Muir, visionary and storyteller, for feeding my selkie obsession and having faith.

Anne Brundle: may we all be missed so much.

Mark Edmonds and Jen Harland, for shelter, inspiration and marine anecdotes.

Donna Heddle, for giving me the job and throwing me into the deep end.

Alex Sanmark, for landscape and the gender agenda, together with Anna Paaso: soulmates and partners in crime.

Lynn Campbell: so funny, so kind; you make being Orcadian into a performance art.

Kiersty Tams-Grey: words fail me.

Donncha MacGabhann, for many things, but particularly for the gift of Kells.

James Graham-Campbell, without whom I would know very little about the Westness brooch or the Broch of Burgar treasure.

Anouk Busset, for the *clapotis* and the *ressac*.

The Orkney Polar Bears, especially Helen Clarke, our Mama Bear; Anne Gascoigne, Barbara Bailey, Sam Dudley, Becky Ford, Alice Lyall, Yvonne Gray, Amy Liptrot, Kim Dearness, Donna Stephenson, Maya Tams-Grey, Ragnhild Ljosland, Lotty Romaniszyn, Miriam Landor, Lucy Stansfield and Peter Fay; and my London mermates, Jo Smith and Kitty Fedorec.

Tim Morrison and Kim Burns: so much more than just my students.

Eleni Ponirakis, Elaine Treharne and Alice Jorgensen, who I hope will approve my ransacking of *The Wanderer*.

Joe, who likes what salt water does to me.

PROLOGUE

This book had its origins in Facebook posts. I got into the habit of composing them while swimming almost daily over several years at the Sands of Evie in the West Mainland of Orkney, constructing little prose-poems, paying attention to details of weather and tide and wildlife, enjoying the challenge of describing the same activity in the same place in language that was just fresh and different enough, day after day, year after year.

Reading the responses to these posts from friends both within and outwith Orkney made me realize that I was falling into the trap of taking Orkney for granted. This enchanted archipelago had become my new normal. Having the beach to which I so arrogantly refer as 'mine' in these pages reflected back to me in my friends' eyes also showed me anew the extraordinary riches of this little patch of land, sky and sea.

Although the narrative has as its backbone the experience of swimming repeatedly – obsessively – at the one beach in Orkney, it also draws on my experiences of childhood in North London and Kenya; of looking after my ageing parents in London, and my mother's death; and my marriage, pregnancy and early motherhood in York: all of which happened before we moved to Orkney.

A word about structure. There is little chronological linearity, and this is intentional: memories are raw, messy things, triggered by stray associations of smell and touch; often disconnected; always fallible. In my mind's eye I see this book in the form of a necklace of beads of varying age, shape, size, colour and raw material – the kind of necklace the Viking Age woman buried at Westness on Rousay wore to the grave she shared with her baby. The narrative, the string holding my beads together, is an account of a single swim, which took place at dawn in late January 2016. I didn't know it at the time, but I was in the last weeks of my familiar life. Along that linking string, the chapters are laid out, each with its own story to tell. Some of the original Facebook posts separate the chapters, like smaller beads. I have taken the dates off them but otherwise there has been no editing: they were written between 2012 and 2016, and in every season, but reading them now they seem like postcards from a dreamlike time and space, detached from the conventional calendar.

In the copy-editing process, my attention was drawn to the way that the book varies between metric and imperial measurements. On examination, there is a consistency to this variation: I find I naturally use imperial in personal, subjective contexts and metric in scientific, objective ones. Intrigued by this, I asked friends what their experience was, and found this kind of 'bilingual' practice to be universal, with some people adding other examples, that they think in Fahrenheit for high temperatures and Centigrade for low ones, or that they normally cook with metric weights but always bake in pounds and ounces. Given that the unstable and embedded nature of knowledge is one of the themes of the book, I have decided to retain my original usage.

More than anything, this book is a love letter addressed to Eynhallow Sound, the land around it, and the creatures who live in it. Especially the seals.

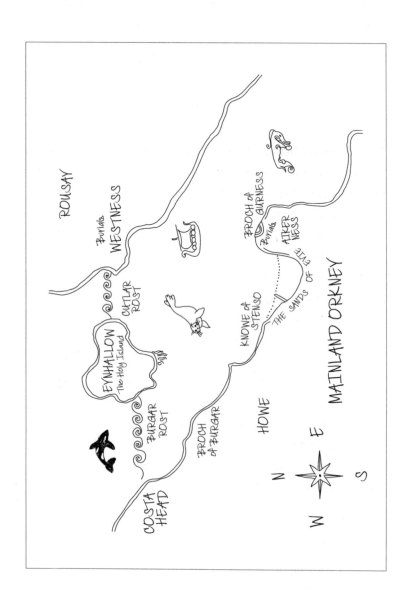

Some swims are harder to put into words than others. This one was liminal; grey veils; the boundaries thin between worlds. Air 10 C, motionless, mizzly-drizzly. Last night's full moon made for a low, low tide at 3.30 this afternoon, no sign of yesterday's swell but a flat grey surface merging imperceptibly with mist and smirr and sky. Rousay and Eynhallow barely visible. Few birds around, the occasional peep of oystercatcher and ululation of curlew. One hoodie crow hopping jerkily about the ebb, pecking at the middens of kelp. The water feels cold. It is so still and quiet that I do what I rarely do alone in winter dusk, and swim out to the nearer of the two buoys that mark the lobster creels. A curlew flies in great loops overhead, crying continuously, and I think of the souls of the dead in *The Wanderer*, coming back as seabirds. I spend a lot of time underwater, staying down as long as I have air, in a deep green world. The shallows are littered with scallop shells, and I dive for them repeatedly, gathering half a dozen to take home. Badges of Santiago: they suit my pilgrim mood.

I have a routine, winter and summer alike, one which I find deeply comforting. I park outside the grey-harled loo-block, leaving the car unlocked and the key in the ignition (it's only polite when parking in spaces that a tractor might need to negotiate to leave the keys in so the farmer can shift your car if necessary). I go into the Ladies' in my flip-flops and robe, and I leave them there. I make a little mat from paper towels so I can stand on it when I come out of the water later and strip off – I don't want to leave a wet sandy mess behind me. Then, wearing only my swimming costume, I walk down to the beach.

My bare feet curl away from each cold surface in turn: first the chilly tarmac of the little car park, recently resurfaced by Orkney Islands Council; then the ruts and puddles of the grassy track that leads from the car park, bending to the right, around the dilapidated hut long abandoned by fishermen and down to the beach; and finally the sand itself. Depending on the state of the tide, this walk from car to sea, which I do almost daily, and sometimes more than daily, can be fifty or a hundred yards. On a fine summer's day, it's effortless pleasure. In a howling January gale, it's a battle worthy of epic.

Today is January, but there's no gale. We have had a week of blasting south-easterlies, bringing endless rain, but a lull has arrived at last. There are breaks in the cloud, and no more than a stiff breeze. The sun has not yet risen, but the slow winter dawn of the 59th parallel means that light has been seeping from the south-east for a couple of hours already, and the sky is a lumpy, uneven grey, with shifting hints of the blue beyond. To my right, to the east, where the waters of Eynhallow Sound are cluttered with more islands – Egilsay, Wyre, a glimpse of Eday – there is a vaporous blur of peach and apricot cloud.

Over the last few years this beach has become my world. Revisiting it in all weathers and seasons is a compulsion, one I can only struggle to understand. Partly, I come here because of the compressed riches of its archaeology and wildlife, its visual beauty and the overwhelming sensory stimulation: the stench of rotting seaweed, the shrieking of the gulls, the wind cold on wet skin, the bitter-salt brine in throat and sinuses. It's my bolthole: where I come to escape the pressures of work, the domestic grind, all my aches and pains, and the slow-motion misery of a failing marriage.

The Sands of Evie lie at the heart of a bowl of hills and islands, in the parish of Evie, on the northern shore of Orkney's West Mainland. To the uninitiated eye the vista is barren, treeless, sparsely inhabited, raw, wild, as though time and humanity have had no effect here. Orkney has a powerful minimalist appeal in our clutter-obsessed culture, an allure which I felt profoundly when I first came here, nearly thirty years ago, and which I have learned only slowly to see beyond. The truth is that the landscape in front of me has been written and overwritten many times across thousands of years, scraped back by forces of geology and weather as well as human activity, revised and inscribed again. Standing here, shivering slightly, bracing myself for the water, I am overlooked by Neolithic and Iron Age sites; cemeteries where Picts and Vikings buried their dead; the ruins of twelfth-century churches and chapels; an island where a saint was martyred; another with a castle built by a giant; a third which was said to belong to the supernatural Fin-folk, a sinister Orcadian twist on mer-people, one of whom snatched a human woman from this very stretch of sand where I am standing now, while her husband's back was turned. The hills are thick with peat laid down in the Bronze Age, divided by drystone dykes built with rocks the crofters cleared as they carved out their livelihood, those fields drained and regularized by the improving, imperious Victorian lairds. Along the skyline the latest in turbine technology turns in the same wind that is making me shiver. *Viewshed* is a concept popular in archaeology, a way of understanding the landscape phenomenologically, experientially, from the perspective of the people using it. A viewshed consists not of what is there, but what can be seen. The viewshed from this beach encapsulates the whole of Orkney in microcosm.

But there is more to this space than that which can be perceived directly. Whole worlds lie hidden underground, under sand and under sea. Robert Rendall, poet, scientist and Kirkwall draper, knew this beach better than anyone. In his 1960 memoir *Orkney Shore* he compares standing on the foreshore and gazing at the sea to being 'in flight over Europe, looking down over a cloud mass that spreads out to the entire compass of the horizon, there is little to remind one of the varied terrain that lies beneath – sandy dunes, rough hillside, rich alluvial soil, wide forest lands, each with its own flora and fauna...' He reminds me of the complexity of even a small patch of shore. Where I swim, the shells that turn up most are limpets, top shells and winkles, occasional scallops, sometimes little cowries. But the other end of the Sands of Evie, the easterly end, is a very different ecosystem from my familiar west, although only a few hundred yards and a stretch of rocky shore divide them. It's much shallower: you have to wade a long way out before it's deep enough to swim, and the flat sands are thick with razor, trough and auger shells, all rarities up this end. It's dislocating to think of that parallel molluscan world. Rendall thought so too: 'At the back of my mind, whenever I walked across a sandy beach, came the thought that beneath my feet was a dense unseen population living its own life undisturbed by the world of air and only becoming active when the tide was up.' Rendall specialized in molluscs, and their hidden lives, but there are other creatures to contend with as well, bigger and more obvious but equally mysterious. Thousands of birds, resident and migratory. The seals that haul out on the Eynhallow skerries, whose singing comes wavering across the water. Cetaceans – Orkney waters have been particularly busy over the last few days: a school of herring has swum into Scapa Flow, and two humpback whales and a minke have arrived in its wake, glutting themselves in the inshore shallows. A pod of orcas has joined them, rare visitors in the winter.

There's change over time to comprehend too. First the Picts built their houses and then the Vikings buried their dead over there at Gurness, in the collapsed ramparts of the Iron Age broch tower. Across the water on Eynhallow, I can see a house first built as an Arts and Crafts holiday cottage, now a base for the University of Aberdeen's long-term study of fulmars. South along the shore from that there's a medieval stone ruin around which Victorian crofters constructed their now-vanished houses. The earliest accurate map of Orkney, part of an atlas of Scotland published in Amsterdam in 1654, shows many of the landmarks I can see now: the hill of *Cofta*, looming darkly to my left; *Alhallow*, the heart-shaped island between Mainland and Rousay which I know as Eynhallow; and the headlands of *Akernefs* and *West Nefs*. These names are Scandinavian, though, not Scots; and they were already seven or eight centuries old when the Dutch printers first pinned them to the map.

Some things we do not know, and never will. What names the Picts used for these same landmarks, before the Norse-speaking Vikings arrived in the ninth century and renamed everything, is anyone's guess. The Iron Age dwellers in the broch towers must have called their structures something but it wasn't *broch*: the word may look Celtic (like *loch*) but it's ultimately Norse, the same as *borg*, a fortress.

The sand slopes away from me, at first a dry jumbled palimpsest of old boot- and paw-prints, then a fine smooth surface made largely of crushed shell, today thickly strewn with lumps of ravaged kelp scattered across the beach like bodies in the aftermath of a battle. Woven in among them is the wreck of a lobster creel, a mass of rusty iron and tattered net. I step awkwardly on my now-freezing soles from patch to patch of exposed sand. In among the slithery tangles of kelp are hundreds of limpets and top shells, fragments of red and purple sea urchin exoskeleton and shed crab shell, little white lumps of coral. The tide is low and ebbing, the breakwater exposed, and there is a steady suck and drip of water from the massed seaweeds growing on it, as the waves lap and splash around the margin. Half a dozen oystercatchers take off in peeping protest as I come closer. Further down the beach, towards the Knowe of Stenso, a solitary heron ignores me. I pause, just where the dark trace of the last wave is soaking back into the sand. Two hundred years ago this beach was an industrial workspace for the processing of kelp into potash, a backbreaking enterprise in which seaweed was burned in slow fires, polluting the air with arsenic-rich smoke, tended by the crofters for the profit of the lairds. Today it's a place of recreation, dog walking, sandcastles in the summer. But for me it's also still a place for processing, for emotional and spiritual alchemy.

This sea and these islands, the wind pimpling my skin, the spray on my right cheek, these are palpable presences in the here and now, transforming me physically. They also reach far back in human and pre-human time. But more than that, they extend sideways into parallel universes, counterfactuals: making me ask how history might have been different; how my own life might have taken other paths. And the sea and islands are also metaphors, scientific, religious and literary, forcing me to think about the nature of knowledge, how the past was understood in the past, the relevance of theories about what it means to be human. Swimming here makes me question everything I have known, in the face of time, danger, loss and death. The quest to find the right words to encapsulate this place is taking me on a long and winding journey.

I walk to the edge of the water, and hesitate.

The display on my car's dashboard has told me that

the air temperature today is two degrees Celsius, and I'm guessing the water is about six. I don't have any way of verifying this: I dropped and broke my thermometer in the loos a few days ago, and the new one I have ordered online hasn't arrived yet. But after several years of swimming through all seasons I am learning to judge the water by other means than the mechanical. The speed with which the blood leaves my hands and feet. The force of the gasp expelled from my lungs when I launch out. The strength of the icy grip on the back of my neck. The shock of cold on my scalp and face, indistinguishable from pain.

This is the hard bit, the forcing myself into the sea, with the wind-chill wicking the heat fast from my shivering skin, in the face of the knowledge that the water will steal my warmth up to twenty-five times more quickly. I must project my imagination up and over this barrier, anticipating the thrill of swimming, which I *know* will come, even if I cannot now feel or believe it. Delayed gratification: Freud's reality principle in action. To keep walking into the water now is an act of faith in the most literal sense: a formula to which one can resort when belief is being tested, or in the face of temptation; an express and willing assent to a truth which transcends immediate experience.

I am an academic specializing in the history, art and archaeology of north-west Europe in the early Middle Ages; I am also a terminally flawed and failed Catholic, married to a very devout one; and my mother was a psychotherapist, specializing in the dynamics of large groups in her earlier work, and later becoming a hospice-based counsellor working with the dying and their families.

She was not quite a Freudian; and I am certainly not one; but we talked about Freud a lot, and I find him a useful point of reference, even when I disagree profoundly with both his working and his conclusions. Therefore, thinking in a mishmash of these cultural references comes naturally to me. And yet at the same time I know they are metaphors; that our knowledge of the past (including our knowledge of our own pasts) is unstable; and that psychoanalysis turns faith inside out, exposing how we use it to bolster ourselves against fear and neurosis. I have grown away from faith, as a hermit crab outgrows its borrowed shell; but like the hermit crab who's not yet found a better option I still lug it around, clinging to the illusion of protection it affords me.

'We're not here to find answers,' I tell my students every year. 'We're here to ask better questions. There's no such thing as a historical fact.'

As well as an academic, I am also a writer of archaeological fiction. Note, not historical fiction, not really, although that is where my novels are usually pigeonholed. But they are set in the ninth and tenth centuries, and they deal with times and places, settings and circumstances and types of people for whom there is almost no conventional historical evidence. Most of my characters are reconstructed not from chronicles and letters but from the coins minted by a Viking king, from skeletal remains, from carved stones, or bronze or silver-gilt brooches. I'm interested in the minor characters, the spear-carriers, the ones who merit only the briefest mention, or who slip entirely between the gaps in history's floorboards.

So, what choice do I have here and now, looking at the landscape in front of me filtered through all the different overlays I carry in my mind, but to do the same thing, to try and find the stories of the people who lived here? I'm listening for their voices, whether they speak in Orcadian or Scots or English, Norn or Old Norse, in Pictish, or Latin, or something else entirely. These hills and shores echo with words uttered in languages known and unknown. I'm listening extra hard for the women's voices, always more elusive than the men's.

The voices I carry in my head are persistent, too. My own ever-remorseful conscience; fragments of poetry and fairy tale; the constant imaginary conversations with people both living and dead. In the Old English poem, *The Wanderer*, the poet describes how in his sleep he has visions of those he has loved, now lost to him; he wakes in confusion to see the wintry waves and the birds; he talks about the *fleotendra ferð*, the floating spirits, and how they always elude him, swimming on their way. He describes them in words that elide birds and memories of the dead, the dreaming and the waking worlds. I first translated that poem when I was eighteen; and I have written undergraduate essays about it, used it to bolster arguments in academic publications, learned it by heart in Old English, chanted it as I walk or run or drive as a way of scaring off the feelings I don't want to have. The first time I ever came to Orkney I thought, *This is* The Wanderer *made into landscape – the wind, the cliffs, the ruins, the restless waves*, although the poem survives in Exeter, almost as far from Orkney as you can be and still remain within the UK's borders: the book which preserves it was bequeathed to Exeter Cathedral library by Bishop Leofric in 1072, and it's been there ever since. I think about *The Wanderer* a lot when I'm swimming here at the Sands of Evie, the floating spirits of my own dead calling in the voices of the wind and the birds.

I pause again, knee-deep now, the breaking surf buffering my planted legs and rocking me slightly, and I stretch my senses outwards, checking for birds and seals, looking for clues to today's mood. I may come here every day, but I have never yet come to the same place twice.

Of course the sea is always, everywhere, moving, but in Orkney this eternal verity is compounded. It's not just the water, but the restless air as well: they conspire in endless movement. The wind governs life here in ways a *ferry-louper*, an incomer, like me can only slowly begin to comprehend. It shapes my body just as it does the land: makes me more Orcadian. Year on year I cut my hair shorter, and my leg muscles get sturdier from ploughing into the gale, step by dogged step. I've given up cycling, exhausted by having to push the bike downhill into a headwind. Every conversation about gardening starts with, *Well, what shelter do you have?* A couple of years ago, one of my MLitt students wrote her dissertation on the role of wind in local politics: it proved a fertile subject, touching everything from the management of AWOL wheelie bins to the placement of wind turbines. After a big gale, the fields are strewn with the corpses of bent trampolines and contorted polytunnels.

Feng shui, the Chinese philosophical system designed to harmonize humanity and environment, means wind-water; and Orkney's feng shui is potent, perennially visible in the flutter of grass, the tearing spindrift and the drama of the sky. I spent most of my childhood in Kenya, and the shifting play of light here reminds me of the shadows of clouds chasing each other endlessly across the East African savannah. The colours too – Orkney's salt-burned, wind-scorched foliage gives the winter hills and fields a brown, brittle edge, like Kenya in the dry season.

Every wind has its own personality, affecting the house in different ways: I've started thinking of an easterly as the *cat-flap wind* – and installing a cat-flap is a classic ferry-louper mistake – while a south-westerly, which makes an unearthly high-and-low whistling in our windows, is the *trowie wind*, named for the fair-folk, the little people, the mound-dwellers. One of the skills a new postie needs to learn in Orkney is how to park at each address depending on the airt of the day's wind: get the angle wrong in the tunnel between shed and house and the van door could be wrenched right off, the letters and parcels carried to Norway on a prevailing westerly. It's a longstanding problem: in the earliest survey of Orkney farmland, from about 1500, we hear farmers protesting that they can't pay their taxes because all their topsoil has been 'blawne to Bergen...'

The wind makes for uncanny weather sometimes, not just wild. A dry fine spell in summer comes to an end – almost always – with a shift in the wind to the east, and the first fingers of fog creeping in, following the contours of the land. The summer fog – the haar – can last for day after day after day, a white blank wall across the whole archipelago, the hill roads unusable, the usually huge skies and horizons brought down to a few feet from your face, the air clammy and palpable. Headlights on full beam at noon. And the wind, which you'd think would blow the haar away, just keeps creating more, as the warmer air passes over the cold waters of the North Sea. It brings on cabin fever; I've heard it called suicide weather. One friend calls it Auntie Mary weather: Auntie Mary arrived for her first visit to Orkney on the day the haar come down, she stayed for a week and it did too, only lifting after her ferry had blundered back to Scotland. She never came back.

Orkney's restlessness inheres in the geology and the folklore as well as the air and the water. Across Eynhallow Sound, on the island of Rousay, there's a standing stone, the Yetnasteen, which is said to lumber down to the loch to drink every Hogmanay. Over to my right, on the headland of Aikerness, there is an outcrop of aeolianite, named for Aeolus, classical god of the wind, where wind-dropped sand is slowly turning to stone, cemented by the calcium carbonate of dissolving shells. The haunting tales about the selkies, the seal-folk who can come on shore in human form, dramatize transformation and exile and irrevocable loss.

This very restlessness had been a powerful attractor in luring me back to Orkney, year on year, before we took the plunge and moved here, experimentally at first – *We'll give it a year*, we said to friends and family, *and see what happens*.

Where's Orkney?

Isn't it very remote?

Is that in the Hebrides?

Will you have to learn Gaelic?

Do they have roads?

Do they have broadband?

What on earth will you do?

And, always, *But isn't it very dark in the winter?*

I have learned to bite back some of the more sarcastic answers, and respond with patience.

Go to the top of Scotland and get a ferry.

When you're here it's London that's remote, irrelevant; Edinburgh marginally less so (but only marginally).

Orkney is north, not west.

It's never been Gaelic-speaking.

The roads are excellent.

And the broadband is better than much of rural mainland Britain.

I'll write and I'll teach, just as I always have done.

As for the winter darkness, it's mitigated by the brilliance of the Milky Way, and the aurora borealis.

No one has ever said, *But isn't it very light in the summer?*

Yet I find the summer nights as exotic, and as challenging, as the winter days. For someone raised on the equator, Orkney's rollercoaster of light and dark is intoxicating. By August I have become drunk and giddy on light, longing for twilight, the gleam of stars in a purpling sky.

There comes an evening, around the time of the County Show, when I find I have to switch on the car headlights in darkness (rather than in haar) for the first time in months, and that little twist of a lever brings a sense of relief, changing pace, Greenwich Mean Time looming on the horizon. A deep inbreath after the long outbreath of summer. The ice cream parlour closes; the B & B owners put their feet up; the islands take off the mask they wear for tourists and settle in to the serious business of harvest homes, muckle suppers, ploughing matches; concerts and knitting circles and reading groups.

County Show, they tell you, *then winter...* It's true, too. After mid-August the sense of being sucked down into the vortex of the dark comes on at speed.

On this particular winter day the dawn tide is ebbing fast. My habitual beach is in the embrace of a sickle-shaped bay, open to the north-west, and within the bay the currents are contained and gentle, usually running parallel to the shore. The old stone breakwater that points north like a compass needle takes some of the immediate force out of the wind-whisked sea. Beyond the headland of Aikerness, however, I can see thick white and dark fast-moving lines and swirls on the sea's surface: even I'm not so stupid as to go into the water from there. Although the gale of the last week has now slackened the wind is still stiff enough to spur little white horses, flickering across from right to left, slapping against and occasionally cresting over the breakwater.

I first came to Orkney in 1988, the summer after I turned twenty-one, after the final exams for my first degree.

I was at a loose end. It was an accident.

I cannot quite believe, looking back to that first of many visits, that I had never heard of these islands – I had been studying the thirteenth-century Icelandic sagas as part of my degree, and *Orkneyinga Saga* must surely have already crossed my radar – but my erratic, expatriate sense of British geography gave me little purchase on the map. My archaeology tutor had laughed at me only months earlier for confusing Leicestershire, Lancashire and Lincolnshire. Ignorant and irritable, I got on a train, and then another. A third in Perth, heading north through Cairngorm. Although I'd been to the Lake District, once, briefly, the idea that Britain encompassed such wild, empty landscapes was new to me. I'd never heard of the Highland Clearances. A fourth train in Inverness. Works on the line meant we were booted off at Dingwall, loaded on to a bus to reboard the train at Brora. I watched the names of the stations switching between Gaelic and Norse, gradually more of the latter. The train finally spat me out at the harbour town of Thurso, clinging to the surf-battered margin between Caithness and the Pentland Firth. I wandered down to the edge of town, wondering what the hell I was doing there, looked north across the water, and saw islands.

What explains the lure of islands? Remote, wild, integral: hard to get to but infinitely beautiful and desirable – islands are their own places. Just to step off the ferry is to achieve something exciting. I've never wanted to give in to John Donne's hectoring 'no man is an island'; and even if he's right it needn't apply to woman.

It was July, grey, wet, cold. The summer ferry from John o'Groats across to Burwick at the southernmost tip of South Ronaldsay was running. There was a bus to Kirkwall, the capital.

I stayed for a week, as long as I could afford. It was like walking through a portal into the Anglo-Saxon and Norse texts with which I'd been stuffing my head for the last three years. *Njál's Saga*, *The Wanderer* and *The Seafarer*, and *Beowulf* and Snorri's *Edda*. I saw the sea beating the storm-cliffs, and the ruins of churches and halls and wartime huts; I exulted in decoding the Norse place-names – Stenness and Stromness, Scapa and Sandwick – and I stood at the Ring of Brodgar and thought about the *eald enta geweorc*, the ancient work of giants. In David Spence's newsagents in the shadow of St Magnus Cathedral I came across *Magnus* by George Mackay Brown, and was blown away not only by the lyrical prose but by the way the novel shatters time in its analysis of power and its abuses, mashing up the twelfth century and the twentieth, mapping the landscape of Orkney on to that of the Nazi concentration camps. I took the ferry out to Egilsay to see for myself where St Magnus had been martyred. The sun and rain came and went; the wind was a constant.

I fell in love, and not only because I had found a world that brought the early medieval North alive for me at last. For the first time since my family had moved away from Kenya I was encountering a landscape that felt familiar. The cloud-shadows hurtled across the hills. The past lurked just under the epidermis of the present. At the Neolithic settlement of Skara Brae it felt as though the original inhabitants had only just left. I sheltered from horizontal rain in the lee of one of the standing stones at Stenness and shared local oatcakes and soft sour Grimbister farm cheese with another tourist, a young Frenchman who pointed out the dark shapes lying in the water of the brackish loch across the road. '*Phoques!*' I stared at him, not understanding, startled by what sounded like a sudden obscenity. And then I saw them. *Phoques*. Seals.

Yesterday the Shipping Forecast website showed Force 10–12 in every single sea area. Today those blasting southerlies have gone, to be replaced by a light but nipping northerly. Air temp 4. Water stiller than it's been for weeks. One shag, one grey seal, both very close – the shag oblivious, the seal fascinated, lingering, popping up and down, giving me the full effect of his deep, liquid gaze. The water feels colder – I didn't take the temperature but I would guess 7. Stayed in for about 15 minutes, lots of time under the water.

Where do you start a story? *In medias res*, in the middle of things, like Homer; or introducing the theme with a fanfare flourish as Virgil does, kicking off *The Aeneid* – 'Of arms and the man I sing'. Maybe a neat little portrait, with just a tinge of what we might read as irony, or maybe malice: 'Emma Woodhouse, handsome, clever, and rich, with a comfortable home and happy disposition, seemed to unite some of the best blessings of existence; and had lived nearly twenty-one years in the world with very little to distress or vex her.' Or a simple statement of beginning: 'I was born in the year 1632, in the City of York.' Take that a step further, and open the book with an account of the main character's conception: 'I wish either my father or my mother, or indeed both of them, as they were in duty both equally bound to it, had minded what they were about when they begot me...' The right beginning encapsulates the narrative: the whole pattern present in a fragment.

Hindsight, as they say, is a wonderful thing.

Maybe this one starts with an ending. My mother fell ill back when I was in my early thirties; I had just finished my doctorate on early medieval death and burial, and was looking for a job in universities in the United States as my then partner was American. My mother's illness and death stopped all that; stopped the person I used to be; put me in a different place; in a cloud, a haar, a darkness.

I have read that you should never make a huge, life-changing decision when recently bereaved, or pregnant. I did both, marrying when bereft and buying a house in Orkney when pregnant, and I regret neither, though there is a lot of unpicking and restitching to do. When you are lost in fog you use your senses differently. It's not just sight that's muffled; sound is also estranged; the dampness of the air and the way the beadlets of moisture cling to your skin make the direction of the wind hard to assess, and if you have no compass then the very concept of direction is also redefined. There's no seeing the sun in haar. The patch of hillside beneath and around your feet is the only thing in colour, and the particularity of each purple bell of heather, each grey-green dendrite of sphagnum moss becomes hugely significant. It's a balancing act: you're newly alive to the micro-terrain, every tiny rise and fall, the sound of each step; teetering on the edge of a peat bank, stumbling into bog. You are utterly alienated from the familiar. Sense of scale is lost. That roar could be the surf at the bottom of the cliff, or just the beating of your own heart.

When the fog lifts at last, you see the old world with new eyes. It has never looked so beautiful, and so uncanny. How did I get here? This isn't where I was when the haar came in. This isn't where I'd planned to be.

The decisions you make while lost in fog have their own coherence; they make sense at the time based on the information available.

Hindsight, as we all know, is a wonderful thing.

After that first visit to Orkney the cold, wet summer I was twenty-one, I was hooked, baited, trapped in a net of longing. I kept coming back through my twenties and thirties, with friends or partners, or on my own. It became a litmus test for relationships: I knew I had no future with someone who didn't feel the lure of the islands, their peculiar blend of Scottish present and Norse past, the volatile sky, the ever-present sea. Life took me elsewhere for a long time, York for postgraduate study, London and Oxford and Leeds for the slog of academic apprenticeships. My mother fell ill. The walls started closing in.

I met the man who was to become my husband less than a year after my mother died, in March 2003, at a party I didn't quite feel up to. We first came to Orkney

in late October, when we were still new to each other.
I was keen to show him my special places, like the Broch
of Gurness. From above, the broch, neatly excavated and
presented, looks as though someone has dropped a pebble
into green water: concentric ripples of wall and rampart.

'It's right on the sea now, but when the tower was first
built in around 400 BC, the shoreline was possibly as much
as forty metres further out. No one really knows what the
brochs were for: they're massive drystone structures, often
compared to the cooling towers of old power stations.
Brochs were architecturally complex, their double-skinned
walls allowing height without too much weight, a stairway
winding between the inner and outer layer of the wall.
Look, the ground floor is internally subdivided and there
are hearths, so people clearly lived here. No windows.
Defence? But it would have been easy to wall people up
and starve them out. And there are so many of them. From
here at Gurness you can see ten more. Up and down the
Evie shore alone we have Costa, Burgar, Grugar, Stenso
and Ritten as well as Gurness. Elite residences? Communal
winter quarters? Look over to Rousay – there's the one
at Midhowe...'

I can hear my excited voice, chattering away to him,
happy and alive with possibility. We sat down to eat our
sandwiches in a sheltered corner of the ramparts, looking
out across choppy Eynhallow Sound to the Rousay shore.
I remember him saying, 'If we lived here we could come
here every Sunday afternoon.'

Significantly younger than me, he was a committed
Catholic who had recently left a monastery and was about

to embark on his own PhD on English literature. I was entranced by his intelligence, his range of interests, his sincerity. I think he was still buoyed up by the courage it had taken to quit the monastery; looking back now I can see how flattened I was, monochrome, two-dimensional in grief. Our energies were closer when we met than at any time since. We were engaged within a few months of our first meeting, and married the following spring. There was a lot I didn't ask, and a lot he didn't tell me. He would probably say much the same about me. But this isn't his story.

When I was four months pregnant we came up to Orkney for a New Year holiday, the first time I'd ever been here in the deep dark of winter. Lying on the sofa in a cottage near Skara Brae, listening to the wind and the sleet, I felt my baby kick for the first time, little burping frog-leaps, like no sensation I'd ever experienced. At the same moment, I felt a pang of bitter grief that my mother, five years dead, would never know my child. That same week we bought a converted stable in the centre of the West Mainland, although we knew it would be a year or two before we could move in to it. That impulsive moment has shaped everything since.

Last night was clear, frosty and windless. This morning the south-easterly had brought the haar, and the thermometer had risen by 10 degrees C. The wind and the swell cancelled each other out, the sea was wild and choppy yet strangely flat – still smacking me in the face, filling my nostrils with brine, the wind wicking the heat out of my wet head. One little seal bobbing up and down in the shallows, playing tag with me. Hundreds of swooping gulls.

I cannot remember learning how to swim. Just swimming anecdotes, vignettes. The time in France when I was a cheeky four-year-old bobbing in the pool and my fully dressed father, standing on the brink, thought it would be funny to put his foot on my head, and fell in with a swamping splash. I have a vivid memory of the dripping banknotes from his wallet pegged to the line, but I could have made that up.

Another summer: standing with him sideways-on to the waves in Cornwall, holding his hands and jumping as each wavelet came rushing in.

The old open-air pool on London's Highbury Fields, with the creaky wooden half-doors of the changing cubicles that gave directly on to the poolside and the cold, chemical water.

Swimming was always a joy, but when I was pregnant it became a drug for the first time. A side-effect of the closing months of my pregnancy was plantar fasciitis, one of those conditions you never hear of till it strikes home. The plantar fascia are the flat bands of collagen on which you tread, and if they go, everything goes. By week thirty-six I couldn't walk to the end of the street. I didn't know, then, what was happening. It would pass after the baby arrived, surely. *Surely?* My husband knew, vaguely, that my legs hurt, but I told neither the GP nor the midwife. I didn't want to make a fuss, and the tongue-clicking and gloom that seem to be the inevitable fate of women who put off their first baby till they're forty had already pissed me right off. I was aiming for a drug-free home birth: complaining about anything might jeopardize my chances.

Instead I swam in the York council pool daily, endlessly: seventy, eighty, a hundred lengths, simultaneously rejoicing in freedom and dreading the return of gravity and impact. This, I thought bitterly as I hauled my waterlogged and chlorinated carcass up the metal ladder, is either a demonstration that God is not only male but a sadist, or – more likely – the proof of Elaine Morgan's aquatic ape theory: no biped would ever evolve this mode of pregnancy on land. No competent civil engineer would come up with this blueprint. All the stresses are in the wrong places for efficiency.

There is a growing corpus of scientific evidence about the adaptation of the human body to water, exploring both our extraordinary evolutionary capabilities and the ways in which time spent in water is beneficial not only for mental and spiritual well-being, and for injuries, but also for many chronic ailments, even for dementia. Of all the great apes, we are the only ones adapted to life in another medium. Is this merely one more aspect of our nature as opportunistic, niche-exploiting, fiddling monkeys, or does it tell us some deep truths about human origins?

Ever since I first encountered Elaine Morgan's aquatic ape hypothesis, in my teens, I have been enchanted by it. Her books, *The Descent of Woman*, *The Aquatic Ape* and *The Scars of Evolution*, revived the fascination I'd developed with human origins growing up in Kenya in the 1970s. Morgan's theory suggests that our hairless bodies, our subcutaneous fat, our prominent noses, our upright gait, ability to dive deep, sweating and weeping, even male-pattern baldness – all unique among our nearest relations – stem from the ancestral hominid going through a semi-aquatic stage before returning to the land. Scholars of early hominid evolution say there is no direct evidence; that the theory attempts to explain away too many of the unusual aspects of the human package; that these quirks have other good evolutionary explanations.

But they don't, not really: most of the 'other explanations' have just as little basis in evidence, or are hopelessly mired in cultural specificity, or gender prejudice. *Bipedalism emerged because a male needed his hands free to carry the provisions he brought to his female and their young, rewarded in his turn by the female's devoted monogamy.* Well, maybe. This sounds more like a nostalgic vision of the 1950s than a serious attempt (in 2010) to explain the evolution of forest-dwelling *Ardipithecus ramidus*. Did we really lose our fur as a way of keeping cool, either in the forest or on the savannah, and then develop fat that clings to the underside of our skin as a way of heating up again? Other animals with blubber need it to keep themselves warm in the water.

Part of the allure of Morgan's work is that, as well as exploring the idea that we are a semi-marine mammal, she also puts mothers and children in the middle of the story. As she says acerbically, the survival of the baby is at the heart of evolution. What possible advantage, she asked, could a primate gain from losing her body fur, that natural climbing frame for her baby? Why do only marine mammals have plump, buoyant breasts? (And she nailed the ludicrous idea that women evolved breasts because men would fancy them – talk about confusing cause and effect.) Move over, man the mighty hunter, in favour of mamma the mighty gatherer, baby clinging to her back and the thick hair of her head as she stands upright supported by the warm shallow waters off the East African coast, bracing one leg as the agile toes of her other foot pluck up edible shellfish. A new species coming to birth, with the sea as midwife.

I wrote to Elaine Morgan when I was eighteen, a gushing incoherent tribute to the first challenger I'd ever encountered to the idea that men drive evolution and women just come along for the ride. She replied almost by return of post, a friendly handwritten letter in which she said that I – as a fellow student of Eng. Lit. – would understand the obstacles she had encountered in her quest for recognition by the scientific community. How dare a mere creative writer claim that accepted scientific dogma is 'demonstrably nonsense'?

There is a wonderful illustration in *The Aquatic Ape* that shows land animals on the left and their water-dwelling equivalent on the right: lumbering, hairy, quadrupedal, morphing into sleek hydrodynamic silhouettes. On the left something half-bear, half-weasel; on the right a seal. On the left a chimp; on the right a woman powering through the waves. She looks like me; white, with shoulder-length hair, solid muscle, a functional swimming costume. The aquatic theory is dismissed by some within the field as pseudoscience; I badly want it to be true. More than that: I want to reclaim it as an origin myth, with the sea as my Garden of Eden. I assert kinship with hippos, walruses, manatees, seals, orcas, polar bears: all the other land mammals who have gone some or all of the way back to the water.

As it turned out, the only difference giving birth made to my health was that my own needs slipped even further down the agenda.

Every morning came with burning, aching feet, especially the heels. The pain ebbed during the day, if I moved cautiously, but walking any distance brought it back. I was trapped, longing to get out of the echo chamber of the house, climbing the walls, weeping as I sat there with a sleeping baby on my lap, my computer just beyond arm's reach, the book I needed in the next room. Being unable to write felt like being gagged. No, worse: as though I had opened my mouth and screamed as loudly as I could, only for no sound to emerge.

'… you must give this voice to me. I will take the very best thing that you have…'

'But if you take my voice,' said the little mermaid, 'what will be left to me?'

'… have you lost your courage? Stick out your little tongue and I shall cut it off.'

If I did go out I clung to the pram like a Zimmer frame, limping from bench to bench, all the way across York to the Starbucks tucked in the back of the big bookshop to meet a friend, my soles on fire, skewers stabbing up my shins. *Smile, latte, fine, fine, all fine.* And then back again.

> Every footstep felt as if she were walking on the blades and points of sharp knives, just as the witch had foretold, but she gladly endured it. She moved as lightly as a bubble as she walked beside the Prince. He and all who saw her marvelled at the grace of her gliding walk.

I trapped myself in silence, calling it courage. Nobody knew about the frustration, the weeping, the pain. Life now was all about my daughter, and she was wonderful. There was no time to swim, no time to write. It didn't matter. I didn't matter. We went to a Steiner toddler group; I was great at breastfeeding; we used cloth nappies; I spent time with other middle-aged, over-educated, high-achieving first-time mothers. We were all in shock, in our different ways. Few of us were brave enough to admit it.

I am capable, now, of asking the obvious questions about undiagnosed post-natal depression. But at the time I lied to everyone. I didn't think of it as *lying*, of course. It was *coping*, *muddling through*, *putting a brave face on things*. Anything less would be an admission of failure, and I've never been good at that. 'Stop being such a perfectionist,' my mother said to me when I was revising for my A Levels. 'I'm not a perfectionist,' I snapped. 'Everything I do is crap.' She pulled out a chair and sat down next to me. 'Darling, what do you think perfectionism *is*?'

What response did I anticipate if I confessed that I wasn't coping? The same things I'd heard from older women all my life. *Don't be so picky. You'll never get married at this rate. Lower your expectations. Welcome to the real world. Making a rod for your own back.* Never, in those words, from my own mother, but she was one of a tough, war-baby generation. Besides, she was dead by then.

Then came the move to our converted stable in Orkney, in 2008. Nothing changed, except I was now stuck in the country and had no friends nearby. My husband was still working on his doctorate, so he had the attic – the old hayloft – containing the desk and the books for his workspace, and I wrote, when I could, on a corner of the table in the living room. I hobbled around, limping the half-mile to the Harray Stores for milk, walking wincingly from car park to church for Mass on Sunday. I was moving less and less, getting stiffer and heavier and less happy by the day. It was a glimpse into the abyss: if this was life in my early forties, old age was going to be unbearable.

At last I admitted to myself that this was not normal, that it was not tolerable, that I needed help. After ticking me off for not coming sooner, the nice foot specialist at the Balfour Hospital in Kirkwall explained what he called 'the cumulative effect of repetitive microtrauma'. All those years of walking to the library in frivolous sandals, slap-slap-slap on the hard, flat surfaces, a heavy bag of books slung lop-sided from my shoulder: my feet had been in no state to cope with the extra burden of pregnancy. He described the plantar fascia as wound too tight, like blinds around rollers in the balls and heels of my feet. If I had left it much longer, he said, the swollen collagen would have started to calcify, forming lumps of bone within the soft tissue of the heel. That would have meant an operation, one with a poor record of success. He prescribed exercises, and handed me rolls of adhesive tape with which to strap up my feet every morning, to give the support which the plantar fascia were not providing. He told me not to stand, not to walk, not to run. I smiled and ducked my head in acquiescence, thinking, *So easy with a toddler*. I was not to wear flip-flops or Birkenstocks, nothing I needed to grip with my toes.

He said, 'This is going to take a while.'

The white strapping turned grey within hours, stuck to my socks, looked hideous in sandals. The tacky residue it left on my skin meant I could no longer walk barefoot on the beach unless I was prepared to spend hours afterwards picking at my harled and sandblasted feet. Swimming in the pool was fine, but I needed to bind my feet again straight away afterwards, so that I could hobble to the car. I stretched out my Achilles tendons with the religious fervour that I could never quite muster for the rosary my husband wanted us to say daily. The doctor was right; it did take a while.

Years.

But in the end the burn and ache began to ebb. I can walk again, and I can even run, though I'm wary: the tissue of my soles is printed through with the memory of pain, like the words in a stick of rock.

The air temperature at the beach was 4 degrees C; the water probably twice that. The sea as still as I have ever known it, the tide far
out, the sand sludgy with weed. No seals, but one low-flying heavy-
winged heron. Land dark, sky bright with the last of the sunset.
Cows booming from their byres on both sides of Eynhallow Sound.

In Hans Christian Andersen's 'The Little Mermaid', the
nameless heroine renounces her ability to swim in return
for life on land and a chance – no more than that – at love.
She also has her tongue taken away, and although she can
walk on her alien legs every step is agony. Her feet bleed.

I taught a course on children's literature to trainee
primary school teachers a couple of years before we moved
to Orkney, in which the students and I traced stories back
not to source – that's impossible – but back up the flow,
looking at their shifting forms and patterns, how they
reflected changing social norms and expectations. There
are fifty students: forty-nine of them are female. All the
students have seen Disney's *Little Mermaid*; none of them
has read a translation of Andersen's 'Den lille havfrue',
although Andersen is on their cultural radar. They have
no knowledge of the history of fairy tales, and very little
awareness that stories come in alternative versions, few of
which have what we might call *a fairy-tale ending*. Most of
them are startled enough by learning that Cendrillon goes
to three balls not one, never mind about the mutilated feet
and pecked-out eyes of Aschenputtel's stepsisters. They are
shocked by Red Riding Hood eating her grandmother's

flesh and drinking her blood, and by the wolf's demand that she strip herself naked; unnerved by the prince's casual rape of the still-sleeping beauty, who wakes to find herself pregnant.

It is the unfamiliar, un-Disney ending of Andersen's 'Little Mermaid' that perturbs them initially, the idea that the right girl fails to win the prince. Being rewarded by transformation into a daughter of the air with a chance at virtue and Christian salvation seems a poor substitute. The idea of an immortal soul, and heaven, is culturally alien to most of the students. The bloodiness of the little mermaid's tongue being severed and the agony in her feet appal them, as does the prince treating her as a household pet, and the way she smiles and dances for him, concealing her pain.

They note – and I agree – that the ending of the story feels tacked on. It's as if Andersen had flinched away from the tragedy his narrative demanded at the last moment. They nod and sigh when I tell them that the moralizing idea that the daughters of the air will suffer less or more depending on whether children are good or bad was a later revision. Andersen isn't technically a 'Victorian', he's too early and too Danish, but it's the word the students use. They view the story's muddling of sex and religion with distaste; I suspect them of wanting to give Andersen a smack.

It's a great class.

Ten years after teaching 'The Little Mermaid', I am reading it again, no longer shocked by her pain and self-sacrifice in the way that I was as a young woman teaching younger women. It seems to me now that these things come with the territory. I ponder the resonances between the little mermaid's terrestrial experience and my own: the choice of silence, the painful steps, the smiling-smiling-smiling. The damage that women are capable of doing to themselves.

How are you? How's marriage? How's motherhood?
Fine, fine. Everything's fine.

(A storyteller and therapist friend once told me that FINE is an acronym for Fucked-up, Insecure, Neurotic and Exhausted.)

Andersen's story also makes me think about my own marriage, the clash of worlds it embodied. When we met, I wanted so desperately to believe that this person could provide that which I lacked, and I suspect he felt the same. Our worlds seemed to intersect in so many meaningful ways. We were both happy to spend every weekend poking round old churches. His knowledge of medieval theology and liturgy was an inexhaustible source of inspiration when I was writing my first novel, *The Bone Thief*, with its sweet, shy, introspective clerical hero. A year after our marriage I was received into the Catholic Church, in a move that shocked many of my friends. New and exciting, a tough moral universe, none of the well-meaning Anglican compromise. It also provided a fascinating insight into a different kind of history of England, a narrative of persecution in which Elizabeth I was a villain and poor silly Mary Queen of Scots a kind of saint. I thought if I just worked hard enough I could create a garden, a walled and secluded fertile space, in which we both could flourish.

I tried, but slowly, sneaking under the threshold of awareness, the knowledge came to me that I could not make him happy. I was failing, faking the role of a good Catholic wife and mother less and less convincingly. I could never seem to communicate that I wasn't failing on purpose. That lack of faith in one God, the Father almighty, maker of heaven and earth and all the rest of it, wasn't for want of trying.

I had been brought up with an ambiguous relationship both to religion in general and Christianity in particular. My parents had first met in the early 1960s at a dinner party organized by Mensa, the society for people self-diagnosed with high IQs. In the Mensa Members Register for 1963/4 my father lists atheism, computers, politics and chess among his interests; my mother just describes herself as an Anglican and a psychiatric social worker. My father was separated, with a son and a daughter in their teens: he didn't want any more children, but my mother refused to marry him unless children were at least a possibility. Though no longer a regular church-goer she always took the religious impulse very seriously and had an ongoing, slightly sentimental, love affair with High Anglicanism: Cranmer and George Herbert and the Authorised Version. She was drawn towards the Quakers but she couldn't stomach pacifism: some battles couldn't be dodged. 'We had to fight Hitler,' she would say sadly, resigned to the inevitability of evil. She and I developed a private tradition of sneaking off to Midnight Mass at St Margaret's Westminster, that bastion of the Established Church, with the chimes of Big Ben a hundred yards away marking the transition from Christmas Eve to Christmas Day. My father, in contrast, was reluctant to set foot in a church, even as a sightseer – 'he's worried,' my mother hissed to me once, 'they might *get* him.'

I have read a lot about atheism by writers who have a triumphalist, sneering approach, more or less explicit. Religion is a con trick, they imply, imposed by manipulative powerbrokers – bishops and kings in the Christian Middle Ages – and adhered to by wish-fulfilment-addicted fools. There may be truth in this. But I want to read more by atheists like myself, who feel the tug of faith and yet cannot believe. Not long before he died even my godless father, crippled by strokes and almost blind, told me what a comfort he thought faith would have been to him in the aftermath of my mother's death nearly a decade earlier. He and I were closer in that moment than at almost any other time in our lives.

Faith is such a charged word. It has so many positive associations: I have always wanted to be faithful, not an infidel committing all kinds of infidelities. Faith is so close to trust, and I've never found trust easy either. Not long after I arrived at my boarding school we had to do a trust exercise which involved falling back into the arms of another student. I couldn't do it; I was simply physically incapable of leaning away from my toes, rocking on my heels, letting the weight of my head and shoulders pull me backwards, and going past the point of no return. Faith is tied up with loyalty too, and here we get into the semantics of unquestioning obedience to the *loi*, the law. The triple vow taken by monks and nuns consists of poverty, chastity and – hardest of all – obedience. It's not that I don't understand the theory: I can remember – in one of the periods when I was performing such a good simulacrum of Christianity that I had us all fooled – I can remember arguing that perfect obedience is perfect freedom. 'Thy will be done,' we say in the Lord's Prayer, in the words of Mary when she learns of her pregnancy. But now I think it's just another way of dodging blame.

We who lack faith and long for it are the children out in the snow, noses pressed to the sweet-shop window; the would-be club-goers, dressed up and ready to party, turned away at the red velvet rope by an implacable bouncer for lacking the one vital accessory. I have known so many wise and thoughtful Christians, people whom I admire from the bottom of my heart. I have experienced such overwhelming emotion before an icon of the Virgin Mary; lit candles at Anglican and Catholic and Orthodox shrines; shouted 'Christ is risen' at midnight while Holy Saturday turns into Easter Sunday as the lamb roasts and children throw fireworks in Greek mountain villages. I still reflexively cross myself if I hear of a death on the news, dip my fingers in a stoup of holy water, bob my knees as I pass the altar.

But no traction results, the cogged wheels don't engage, there's no miracle for me.

And maybe that's good, because there's a dark side to faith, one that's missed by the people who say, 'Faith must be such a comfort.' We've talked about hell. If I've understood, it's not brimstone and pitchforks and BDSM devils, it's an eternity spent in the awareness of God's love and the knowledge that you have consciously chosen to reject that love. It's a full understanding of all the pain you have caused and all the damage you have done. It's total self-knowledge and public humiliation – there's an Anglo-Saxon sermon which describes souls at the Last Judgment as being like clear glass, with every little sin on show. I think of an aquarium, all the warped and dark thoughts, words and deeds swimming in suddenly clear and spotlit water. But what sort of god rejects someone for an honest inability to believe? This god has a clipboard and biro: he's ticking his boxes, tallying my errors, marking me down, shaking his head at my wilful failure, my inability to love enough. His eyes are genuinely sad. His penalty is the withdrawal of approval.

I don't want to sit this god's exam, even if heaven is the reward for passing. I'd rather dissolve into nothingness, in the way the little mermaid was supposed to, burst like a bubble, lost in the anonymity of a thousand million other bubbles on the crest of the waves.

The little mermaid and the prince are an impossible story, lovers who cannot naturally survive in the medium the other breathes, as alien to each other as frog and princess. My husband and I had so much in common, but there were fundamental incompatibilities, lethal off-shore skerries that only became visible once the emotional tide began to retreat. I was in love with medieval Christianity – not just the patterns and structures of theology, but the architecture and the music and the poetry. He mistook that love for faith, and to a lesser extent – to my shame – so did I.

I was in love. We see what we want to see.

But I'm a historian, and a novelist: I need to understand medieval Catholicism if I'm to have the faintest hope of getting under the skin of the people about whom I write. My husband introduced me to the modern Church. He challenged me on many of my most deeply held beliefs, on abortion, homosexuality, women's claims to the priesthood. He was much better informed. I was ashamed to realize how little I knew about the teachings of the Church, the law of the land, or the hard facts. I had no idea, for example, that more babies are aborted every day in the UK than come up for adoption every year. I knew almost nothing of the technicalities of abortion procedures. But maybe it never occurred to him that, even after I knew the facts in all their distressing detail, I would still assert a woman's right to choose; I would still ask awkward questions, and claim that doubt has its own validity. It certainly never occurred to me that my doing so would be a problem. But there is no halfway house when creatures from two different mediums meet.

I began to perceive, in terror, that honesty about my lack of belief would mean the end of the marriage.

This unwanted knowledge sat for a long time in a dark corner of my mind, like the stain of damp in the corner of the room that keeps reappearing no matter how many times you bleach it, treat it, paint or paper over it. At some point, you move a big piece of furniture into that corner and pray no one notices, but it's still there, still spreading. You can smell it.

Any marriage whose very survival is predicated on dis-honesty has already ended.

I just got out of the sea. Air temp 7, sea 13 (felt WARM!) Heavy rain, very high tide, breakwater almost completely submerged. I went in the water to the west of it, was aware there were seals around, in the shallows, dark moving shadows, their backs occasionally breaking the surface. One popped up the far side of the breakwater, maybe 8 yards away, selkie (grey seal), lovely dapple-grey throat and chest. We gazed. He sank. I shifted round. And there was a seal right behind me, maybe 6 feet away. NEVER been so close. I yelped – I couldn't stop myself. He gave me a long liquid reproachful look and sank calmly, none of the usual 'Ooh, you're not a seal!' splash-flurry. Then they resurfaced just beyond the breakwater – three of them, all selkies – and lay on the surface for a while, rolling a little, swimming a little but mostly just bobbing on their sides, raising an occasional front flipper, crooning from time to time. Happy, relaxed, looking over at me sometimes. I felt privileged, safe, protected even.

Danish *hav* (*havfrue*, sea-woman, mermaid) is cognate with Orcadian *haaf*. In the Scandinavian languages and Icelandic *hav* or *haf* just means sea or ocean, but here in Orkney it has the more precise connotation of the deep or open sea, as opposed to the inshore waters. The grey seal, the *selkie*, is also the *haaf fish*. Mermaids as such are rare in Orcadian tradition, although both land and sea are swarming with otherworldly creatures. Grey seals are said to be able to take on human form, and there are many stories of sexual union between a true human and a selkie. The selkie-wife stories, in which a man wins a bride by stealing the selkie's sealskin when she is in her human form, are the best-known, but there are a host of others. Selkie-bride stories do the job of mermaid tales in Orkney: the *haaf fish* filling in for the *havfrue*. Both narrative traditions are about terminal incompatibility, yearning for the impossible, exile from one's true home, true self.

What has the little mermaid's prince done but look pretty and enjoy extraordinary privilege? Why should he deserve this passionate, physical, imaginative young woman? And why does Andersen so insist that she is *little*? She is a woman for most of the story, not a child.

'The Little Mermaid' is also a tragedy of mistaken identity. The mermaid loves the prince primarily because he reminds her of the marble statue of a handsome boy salvaged from a wreck to adorn her garden. She has a vision of what love ought to look like, and no reality is strong enough to shatter it. The prince cannot love the mermaid because his heart is already given to a girl he glimpsed just once, whom he believes rescued him from drowning. The tragedy is compounded by the fact that the rescuer he dreams of *is* the mermaid, but he cannot recognize her, and has no idea who she truly is.

As my students perceived, the narrative slips uneasily back and forth between erotic and religious modes. It is so tempting to read it through the lens of Andersen's own complex and unhappy sexuality; and to note that he wrote the story in 1836, the year his dear friend Edvard Collin got married; but the story has poetic insight at its heart that transcends context-specific gender politics. It explores the stubborn compulsion of the mermaid, with her random, hormone-fuelled, inappropriate erotic fixation. In the first part of the story she is so active, wilful, desiring, contrary. So powerful, but with such a tenuous grip on social and biological reality, the epitome of a teenage girl. How does she imagine she and the prince will have sex, with their incompatible genitalia? And, of course, they don't: she becomes a woman and achieves the right organs but at the cost of being able to tell him what she wants, and how she feels. Her body becomes the locus of pain not pleasure. And she ends a virgin.

Jungians have had a field day with this story, suggesting that while the mermaid may be the main character, it is really the story of the prince. He is the *animus*, the masculine principle, associated with daylight, the upper regions, the sun, strong warm colours, life. The mermaid, in contrast, is the feminine *anima*: a creature of water, death and the dark. He cannot be healthy and complete unless he acknowledges and is reconciled with his *anima*. He is the conscious, she the subconscious. In this reading the mermaid and the human princess who looks so like her are one character, both embodying the female principle, and the story has a happy ending as *animus* and *anima* retire to their couch in the shipboard tent of purple and gold to consummate their marriage. The broken-hearted mermaid throws the masculine dagger into the feminine sea, which turns red, representing both death and the loss of virginity, as though they are one and the same thing. This reading, eloquent though it is, annihilates the mermaid's autonomy. She only exists to allow him to achieve wholeness: and I can't bear it.

Andersen should have had the courage of his original vision. She should have turned into foam. Simply to dissolve, to let go, to become one again with the elements, without an immortal soul, without even a grave: why should this be a tragic ending? But instead the mermaid's grandmother speaks wistfully of the human soul:

> ... which lives forever, lives after the body has been turned to dust. It rises up through the clear, pure air beyond the glittering stars. As we rise out of the water, and behold all the land of the earth, so do they rise to unknown and glorious regions which we shall never see.

The old mermaid queen has no more experience of those regions than does the poet of *The Wanderer* when, at the end of a bleak poem which dissects all earthly consolations and shows how they fail, he offers the trite consolation of the heavenly home, the one foundation. And yet they sound so sure.

I wish I knew where they get their conviction from.

I went for a run up the track soon after sunrise – a vision of islands: Rousay, Eynhallow, Gairsay, Eday, glimmering in the hazy sea – larks, wrens, lapwings – then down for a swim at the Sands of Evie. Lots of eider ducks. I swam out to the end of the breakwater, then turned, and there was a seal between me and the beach, maybe four yards from me. Usually they look startled and splash off, but this one –

a small common seal – just swam steadily, watching me – I could count every whisker, see the whites of its eyes. Then it dived, and surfaced a bit further away, with a friend. They stayed about 30 feet away the whole time I was in the water, tracking my zigzags, watching me with hopeful puppy eyes. Young ones, I think. Very curious as to what I was up to. The eiders kept up their gossipy chorus of disapproval throughout.

Over my two decades' dreaming of moving to Orkney I envisaged long walks along the cliffs, birdwatching, playing on the beach, creating a garden, exploring the hills, getting to know the archaeology intimately. Even swimming in the sea, in the summer of course, when the water is less cold, less wild; though only if I can find a beach where I feel safe.

But in many ways life here has turned out to be no different from life anywhere. Bills still have to be paid. I am trapped, sedentary and deskbound in ways I never foresaw. Both my employed and my freelance work involve long hours at the keyboard. We live around fifteen miles equidistant from both Kirkwall, the capital, and Stromness, Orkney's second city. It's not a long commute compared to what I was once used to, but nothing's in walking distance, and far too much time is spent in the car. For several weeks either side of Christmas I drive to work in total darkness, sit hunched over the computer in artificial light, and return home in the dark again.

Nor did I foresee the way my body would mutate into an alien weight I hauled around after me: those painful feet, the shoulders set in concrete, the stabbing pains in the small of my back, losing the knack of sleep, the relentless wave of tension headaches eroding the shores of joy and sanity. It was as though I'd moved into an unfamiliar house in which all the doors jammed in their frames, the banisters wobbled under my hand, the roof leaked; always stubbing my toes on the furniture, banging my head on sloping ceilings. Marriage, I told myself. Middle age. Motherhood. The human condition, right? No big deal. Keep muddling through. Stiff upper lip.

An image haunts me, of a lobster entering a creel, beguiled by the bait; turning to leave only to find it's the wrong shape, all bristling claws and wild antennae, to fit back through the narrowing, netted tunnel. A friend tells me of the anger felt by Orkney's lobster fishermen when they haul up their creels only to find them empty: that a seal has broken in and stolen the bait, rendering the trap useless. I listen, and nod, keeping my facial muscles quiet to hide what I'm really thinking. The seal may not know it's saving the lobster, but that doesn't make the salvation any less real.

We have already been living here for three summers when I first start swimming in the sea regularly. I need more exercise: I am still hobbling from the plantar fasciitis, and the swimming pools have very limited opening hours.

It's Helen's idea. This being Orkney we know each other in several contexts – we have both worked in local tourism and are connected with the college; our daughters go to the same tiny school. Her background's in marine biology; she's a great person to go rock-pooling with, and I have always admired her practical energy, the glow she has about her. She and Barbara, whom I first meet as another mother of young children, whom I get to know better as a rangy, feral thrill-seeker, have come up with the project of swimming off the slipway in the little harbour nearby at Tingwall every Saturday: the Tingwall Polar Bear Club! Why not? The idea gains traction, around half a dozen of us come along regularly; it becomes the high point of my week, both the plunge into summer-cold water, and the flasks of tea and the companionable blether which come afterwards. We meet in the car park by the little shack that houses the ferry office, gather on the slipway, walk down the weed-slick slope into the sheltered harbour. We swim around the pier and the rocking fishing boats, climb out again on the rusting rungs set into the concrete. My back unlocks; the cold water is bliss on painful feet. After a few weeks of this I find I'm standing taller, breathing more deeply; long-disused nerves and muscles stretch and furl in the dark, reaching after sunlight, oxygen, water.

Then Helen suggests a swim in each of Mainland Orkney's thirteen parishes. This is an entrancing combination of the ambitious and the easily manageable – even land-locked Harray has its lochs. It's an adventure with purpose and momentum. I see new corners of coastline, venture into waters that a few months earlier I could not have imagined becoming my territory. We splash in the shallow freshwater Loch of Skaill – we were warned about leeches but never encountered any. We let the rapids whoosh us under the arches of the Brig o'Waithe on an incoming tide rushing through a narrow channel described in 1529 as 'very dangerous … where many perish'. We take our cars down tracks I didn't know existed, to swim from shingle, or rocky headlands, or coves studded with red and green sea anemones. Orkney looks so small on the map, but it turns out to be vast; layer upon layer of secret places are folded into that apparently open, treeless, feature- less landscape. My confidence grows. The weeks go by. September turns into October. The water is still warm by Orkney standards – thirteen, fourteen degrees Celsius – but I know it won't be for long.

Someone mentions a rule of thumb they've been told by an Australian friend, that you should never swim in open water unless the combined temperature of air and water is above forty degrees Celsius. We laugh, a little envious but mostly self-satisfied, superior: you might achieve that in the south of England, but on the warmest summer day here the aggregate is unlikely to exceed the low thirties. Come the winter, the old hands tell me, even in largely frost- free Orkney, we could easily be swimming in combined temperatures of ten. Eight. Five.

Time to get a wetsuit. The swimming club – now expanded into the Orkney Polar Bears – has people who know the sea much better than I do, serious snorkellers, scuba divers, sea-kayakers, many of whom swim in varying amounts of neoprene all year round and swear by it. I have never so much as fingered a wetsuit, but clearly it's the new must-have accessory. Already by December the water is down to eleven degrees – the threshold between mere 'cold-water swimming' and '*extreme* cold-water swimming'. Not everyone wears a full wetsuit – some keep to their swimming costumes, just adding neoprene socks and gloves; others wear rash vests – but I'm a neophyte, not acclimatized like them.

However, it's not as straightforward as I thought. The dive shop in Stromness has nothing in stock that will fit me, and I'm reluctant to buy one online. The unwillingness of companies to ship goods of any kind to the Isles is a perennial gripe, and I anticipate a prolonged and wearying back-and-forth as I try to find one that suits me. More importantly, the grotesquely over-long wetsuit that I do try on is terribly uncomfortable. I'm reminded of a comment I once heard from a boyfriend, about how sex when you're wearing a condom is like trying to pick your nose with rubber gloves on. This is the marine equivalent. Surely the point of swimming in the sea is to be as close as possible to the water. The Lycra of my Speedo is more of a barrier than I would really choose, never mind this clumsy exoskeleton. But this is not mere discomfort – it verges on phobia. I'm shocked by the power of my revulsion. It's as though some stranger has his hands around my throat, and the wrap-around embrace of the neoprene gives me the shivers, the texture, the way it squidges between my fingers.

Still, it's going to get cold. It's going to get *really* cold. I need to get over my squeamishness and buy one from somewhere.

Just not this week, though the temperature is still dropping.

Nor next week.

Nor the week after.

I keep forcing myself into the water, promising myself that next time it won't be so hard, that I'll have one of these magical garments before long, and then I'll be able to swim through the winter.

But – and almost before I know it – I have done. Saturday after Saturday, I grit my teeth and wade in, and kick off, and it's never as bad as I think it's going to be. We're into March, then April, and I've gone on swimming, Saturday after Saturday, and now the water is beginning incrementally, infinitesimally, to warm up again. Seven, then eight, then nine degrees. It's as though I've crossed some invisible border, undergone a rite of passage. I look much the same, but I've changed. People start to call me *tough* and *hardy*, and I find this very strange: it's a persona I seem to have sidled into without really noticing. But, unlike the wetsuit, I can wear these words in comfort.

I'm beginning to feel at home, and that's a strange sensation. Polar Bear dips are wonderful, chaotic, communal experiences. In some ways, we're a random bunch; in others we're a distinct demographic. Overwhelmingly female, few under thirty-five, all with a stubborn streak and a sideways take on the world. Some are very fit, runners and rock-climbers; others (like me) chafe at a deskbound life. Everyone brings something different to the party.

I love these Saturday mornings, and yet I find them hard. Like all social situations, it's full of anxiety. I find banter challenging – yes, English is my mother tongue but though I'm fluent I'm not idiomatic. I went to international schools in Kenya; few of my childhood friends were native speakers; and I've never really grasped informal English. A friend who's a historical linguist finds my command of the language fascinating – no regional accent, and the only slang I use unselfconsciously is the odd bit of 1940s idiom picked up from my mother. *Aggers* for *agony*, as in *Gosh, my new shoes are aggers*. When I first came back to the UK at almost sixteen, to boarding school in Hertfordshire, I found the speech of my age-mates incomprehensible. *Can't be arsed. Can I scab a fag? I skived off maths... Haven't done that for yonks*. I'm left floundering, always a pace behind, trying to read facial expressions for clues to meaning, pretending to laugh at jokes I don't get.

I feel stupid, wary, always on the edge. There are rules I don't know, unstated conventions I've never learned.

There's another problem, one I'm barely aware of myself. Being in a failing relationship seals you off from the social world. People ask cheerily, casually, after my husband. *How is he? What's he up to?* I gape at them, feeling as though I'm stuffed, under glass. I have no idea how to answer.

But it's different in the water. There's not much scope for banter when a choppy wave is smacking you in the face, when you're gasping for breath, when you're in a group strung out over a hundred yards of surf. Our common language is the shock of cold; the sting of brine; the reddened skin; the shivering that won't stop.

Organized sports were torment at all my schools, but in the sea, for the first time, I get an inkling of the non-verbal bonds that are forged between team members. We are linked by our desire for cold water; we're united against the disbelief or awe or disapproval or mockery that comes from observers. We laugh at ourselves, but secretly we're proud. It's intoxicating, being an insider: I can't remember feeling this way before.

I begin to see my place in the world differently. The week revolves around Saturday mornings: the queries and suggestions that emerge on our Facebook page around Tuesday – *Where are we going this week?* – and gain traction and definition until consensus is reached: *What's the wind/tide/current doing? Easterly, Force 6 – how about Bay of Skaill? High tide's at 9 a.m. Does anyone else need a lift from Stromness? Any orcas been spotted? Who's bringing the cake?*

A new world of knowledge is opened up to me: I become acquainted with websites like magicseaweed.com, aimed at surfers but their panoply of information – water temperature, wind, swell – all becomes part of my armoury. I watch with fascination as projected Atlantic depressions mass in a threatening, widening gyre off to the west of Ireland, and learn how to plan swims in response.

And I learn to relate to other sea-creatures, not just the human Polar Bears.

Eynhallow Sound this morning was like a lake in a volcanic caldera, a ring of dark hills, topped by equally dark storm clouds, but above the sky was blue, cloudless. Tearing southerly wind blowing straight into breakers coming in on a very high tide, scattering spray back across the swell. Many shags, gulls, plover. I stayed in my depth and was still swept off my feet. Looked up one mound of rising wave straight into a seal's nostrils: they were having as much fun as I was.

When I first started swimming in the sea it was always a shock to hear that deep-lunged snort, sometimes only a few feet away; to see the dark head of a seal rise from the water: the huge eyes, alert nostrils, water dripping from whiskers and beading on sleek spotted fur. Seals gaze in a way that suggests intense curiosity. They are predators, with sharp teeth and strong jaws. But I rapidly grow comfortable being with them in the water. They're in their element, and I'm their guest. I never swim towards them, and although friends who are scuba divers report the seals coming close, mouthing the swimmers' flippers, allowing – even enjoying – physical contact, my seals are warier. Seals are confident when fully immersed, more cautious when bobbing on the surface, shy and easily spooked when hauled out on the rocks. I've never felt any threat, though if one comes too close for its own comfort and dives with a sudden, shocked thrust of its body, the thud of the displaced water is a visceral reminder of their strength and mass. And sometimes, when there are five or six of them, and they're feeling self-assured, diving and surfacing ever closer, I have to remind myself that they don't hunt in packs.

The seals are everywhere along the Orkney coast, sunning themselves on the rocks, or sleeping nose up in the shallows, or swimming along, following you as you walk by the shore. The best way to summon them is to take a dog down to the beach: the German word for common seal is *Seehund*, sea-hound, and the seals seem to recognize the affinity, popping up from the water, coming into the shallows, their eyes wide and fascinated. The two indigenous species are the common or harbour seals, and the grey seals, although occasionally exotic visitors like bearded seals come down from the Arctic. The grey and common seals haul out on the rocks together: from a distance it is hard to tell one from the other, and it's often said that *grey seals are common and common seals are grey*. But the more time you spend with them, the easier it is to tell them apart, even from a glimpse. The common seals are cuter, smaller, snub-nosed. Their nostrils converge, in a heart shape. When they lie on the rocks in the sun they lift their heads and tails at the same time, as though doing V-sits in the gym, working on their formidable abdominals.

The grey seals are much larger and more dignified. They have ponderous Roman profiles and haunted eyes. It is the grey seals who give rise to the selkie stories. It is they who are the *haaf fish*, creatures of the deep sea. They have souls. The common seals are 'only' animals, the *tang fish*, creatures without souls, named for the shallow-water weed among which they hunt crabs. Common seals can dive down as far as fifty metres, and keep under for ten minutes at a time. They stay in the sunlit zone, which extends to about 180 metres, but grey seals have been recorded diving to 400 metres, well into the gloom, cold and pressure of the twilight zone. They can remain submerged for an hour. Common seals forage up to sixty kilometres from the beaches on which they haul out; grey seals have been recorded 145 kilometres away from the shore.

Common seals are impressive enough. Grey seals are hard-core.

Seals are not the apex predators in these waters, not

by a long way. That honour goes to the orca, and orcas, unlike seals, definitely hunt in packs. No matter how often we Polar Bears reassure each other that *no wild orca has ever attacked a human being*, if I were to spot a dorsal fin in the distance I'd be leaving the water as fast as I could flounder. An orca's open mouth is a metre across, its teeth up to five centimetres long.

A Shetland sea-swimmer shared a story recently; she'd been swimming in her usual patch when she noticed a crowd of people on the shore, pointing at her, waving. *I swim here every day*, she thought, *what are they fussing about?* They'd spotted what she had somehow missed: the dorsal fin of a male orca – as high as a tall man – speeding fast in her direction. He dived, only a stone's throw from her, and the onlookers were convinced that she would be eaten. She didn't realize what was going on until a pulse of energy in the water made her look down. The orca was only a few feet below her, sussing her out. Before she could react, he swam away.

Still, despite the heart-race, the throat-lump, the adrenalin-rush, I can't help thinking, even here and now wading into their territory, that there are many worse ways to die than in an orca's jaws. No doctor, no drugs, no long slow decline of power or personality. Observers of big cats hunting down gazelle in the Kenyan savannah have noted how, despite the fury of the chase, in the last moments the prey animal appears resigned, calm, just as a kitten stops fighting when its mother picks it up by the scruff, or a sheep enters a quasi-catatonic state when the shearer pulls her into a sitting position, or a shark turned over on its back goes into tonic immobility. Human survivors of attacks by wild animals have reported something similar: in the jaws of the beast there is no panic, no struggle, only an eerie calm. Shock, perhaps. But I imagine also that Freudian Thanatos, the death wish, comes into play. All our lives we fear the thing under the bed, the shape behind the door, the spider that scuttles out from the skirting board, the creature that lurks in deep water, the vengeful god.

Thanatos, the joy of consummation: *Here it is at last.*

As a very small child, before we moved to Kenya, when we still lived in the tall narrow house in North London, I was dreadfully afraid of wolves. My terrors were the wolves of fairy tale, skulking and devious, monsters of teeth and red wet tongue, whose only thought was to devour children. But they were real wolves, too. My father used to take us to Regent's Park to see the bits of London Zoo which could be viewed from the park without paying. He wasn't really a cheapskate, he had his moments of flamboyant generosity, but he was always looking for an advantage, some way of beating the system. The wolf enclosure was one of the most accessible: those leggy grey creatures through the wire fence, running among the trees. When I expressed my terror, my mother would ask in frustration whether I really thought the wolves were capable of escaping from the zoo? Would they *really* make their way to Islington, more specifically into my bedroom, and eat me? Out of all the little girls in the world? To which the only possible answers were *yes*, *yes*, and *yes*. The knowledge was self-evident to me, embedded in some deep part of the hominid brain.

My mother thought it was 1970 and London N1, but I might as well have been an Australopithecine child, four million years ago, on the Plio-Pleistocene grasslands of East Africa, knowing full well that the noises in the dark were made by what the palaeontologists call the *hypercarnivores*: giant lions, leopards and hyenas. This is where the nightmares are born.

Once we'd settled in Nairobi my fear of wolves ebbed in the face of a developing passion for wildlife. I got used to a suburban garden in which the pepper tree by the back door was full of caterpillars with poisonous bristles, the Cape gooseberry bush harboured a boomslang, baboon spiders lurked in tunnels on the lawn, *siafu* – army ants – marched through the grass in Napoleonic columns. I ignored the caterpillars, and backed cautiously away from the boomslang; my father rushed me to hospital once with a nasty spider-bite, and the mighty-jawed *siafu* got into my little sister's hair when she lay down on the lawn, though I was more distressed by their devouring a whole litter of our rabbits' babies. At school, we were taught two alarm drills: the fire bell, for which we went outside; and the lion bell, for which we came in. We never had a fire, but there were lions on the rounders field once, and the wardens from Nairobi National Park came in a green Land-Rover with a cage on the back to retrieve them. The nightmare that the wolves had once embodied retreated in the face of the waking world and these manageable dangers.

But being eaten by an orca would be to meet that nightmare face to face, to look it in the eye and name it, to say, *I know you*. Surely there's virtue in this. I talked it through once with Yvonne, another Polar Bear, a poet, while we were at the Sands of Evie, swimming at a summer-leisurely pace out to the buoys that mark the lobster creels. We further speculated that there would be other advantages to this death. No funeral expenses. The satisfaction of providing a good meal for a species that is threatened, if not yet endangered. We'd make the front page of *The Orcadian*. A worthwhile contribution to scientific understanding of orca behaviour. Nonetheless, as we rounded the buoy and started our way back, we agreed that we would rather the orcas held off at least until our children had left secondary school. And we were both swimming rather faster, and looking over our shoulders more often.

I knew nothing about orcas when we first moved here. It's an obsession which has moved in on me gradually, fuelled by that occasional glimpse of a dorsal fin, the arcing back, the flick of flukes, and by the realization that globally we are coming to a better understanding of these extraordinary beings. I track the different communities through the Facebook pages of the scientists studying them – rejoicing to learn that Granny of the Southern Residents J pod is still going strong aged 105 (and grieving to hear of her death, just as this book went to press), swimming up and down the western coasts of North America; delighted when I see that Mousa, one of our local matriarchs, has a new baby; sorrowful to hear that for yet another year the little Hebridean community is calfless. I am beyond intrigued to learn that orcas are not only matriarchal, they are menopausal. The females lose the ability to reproduce aged around fifty, just as we do; but they go on being the power in the nuclear family and the wider pod. Both sons and daughters stay with their mother for life, and young male orcas work as nannies for their younger siblings and cousins.

But – let's be honest – they are also really, *really* scary. Writing in the first century AD Pliny describes orcas in the Mediterranean attacking other whales when they are calving. His usually precise language breaks down under the strain: 'its image cannot be properly represented or described other than as an immense mass of flesh with fierce teeth'. 'Carnis inmensae dentibus truculentae' – all hiss and click and the tap of tongue on palate, as though anticipating the monster breaking the surface. Olaus Magnus's map from the 1530s shows the *orcha* (*sic*), looking like a marine triceratops with fangs, attacking a whale, a *balena* (which also has teeth), just to the west of Orkney.

They will pursue a grey whale and her newborn at such a pace that the calf cannot stop to feed, and finally eat the baby when it is starving and exhausted. In Argentina they intentionally strand themselves to pluck sea lion pups from beaches. Off San Francisco a solo female orca took down a great white shark: rammed it in the gills to stun it, flipped it over into tonic immobility, ate its liver, left the rest for the swarming gulls. They'll kill a sperm whale, and only eat its tongue. Do I really want to enter these creatures' realm?

This is not a book about *overcoming* fear of predators, or cold water, or the dark – or death, which is the shapeless thing that lurks behind all these masks. The word with which I am grappling is *reclaiming*, as land is reclaimed from the sea. Awareness of death cannot and should not be overcome, and I am learning as I voyage on through middle age that I don't want to overcome it. What I want to do is map it, colonize it, rename it, make it my own. That dark thread, the panic, the sense of the scree slipping beneath my feet, the lurch, the visceral tug, the undertow; these are utterly woven into the fabric of self. I do not want a map that is all rich pasture and well-watered uplands, bright expanses of sand and sunlit shallows. I need access to the shady side of the valley, the crevasse, the depths where light never reaches, where monsters lurk. Reciting the names of the levels of the sea reclaims them for me, makes them into a meditative technique for taking consciousness down into the depths:

Sunlit zone.

 Twilight zone.

  Midnight zone.

   Abyss.

And, underlying the abyss, there are the deep-sea trenches, the *hadal zone*, named for Hades, lord of the underworld, the god who stole Persephone/Proserpine and conned her into giving up her freedom in return for six seeds of pomegranate, until her mother the earth goddess Demeter came and haggled successfully for Persephone to live half her year in the sun, half in the darkness. Our technical, scientific language has potent myth lurking just under the skin, like the fine fan of facial muscles that underpins and gives power to human expression.

Reclaiming. Giving myself something to stand on.

Gaining an understanding of why, every time a loving friend tells me I am *strong, clever, confident, beautiful*, I lurch and stagger internally. Over the years the pressure of trying to achieve the expected standards – both external and (much more dangerous) the hopelessly high ones I set myself – has become impossible. I am never aware of what I manage to do, only of the yawning gap between vision and reality, and I live in permanent terror that someone will notice. The strain of maintaining the façade: scaffolding and pit props holding the stucco and sash windows in place while behind all is rubble, fly-tipping and fireweed. My relationship with reality has become ever more tenuous: going into cold water shocks me back into myself and what really exists, here and now. What really matters.

This is not a book about overcoming the fear of the dark. This is a book about meeting that nightmare face to face in the waking world, looking it in the eye and naming it, saying, *I know you.*

Cloudless lapis-lazuli morning for the Feast of the Assumption, slight breeze. Air temp 10 degrees C. The water was very still, a reticulation of golden light flickering over the sandy sea floor. One hermit crab trundling along in a top shell from which most of the surface had rubbed away so it was a nacreous, iridescent shimmer of movement. One white crab smaller than my big toe. Terns perched on the buoys, calling to each other. Female eiders bobbing in the distance. A grey seal asleep in the shallows, sometimes rocking gently, nose to the sky; sometimes asleep on his belly with head and back out of the water. I could hear him breathing – swam quite close but either he didn't notice me or was too blissed-out to care.

Quite soon, the Saturday-morning swims stop being enough. I wake every dawn with the salt water tugging at my consciousness while I'm still drifting up from the midnight zone of dream. The craving for what the water provides – shock, numbness, struggle – has become as pervasive as gravity or magnetism, incessant as heartbeat. Days without a swim are like withdrawal, real pain.

The Polar Bears only meet once a week, though; and I can't make every Saturday. My daughter is in proper school now, and weekends have become ever more precious. I have deadlines to meet. And I know there's a duty I'm dodging: I should be making time for my husband, finding a way to bridge this gulf between his island and mine.

But none of these voices shouts louder than the call of the sea.

What's more, although I am coping with, even enjoying, the social aspects of being a Polar Bear, I find I want to swim alone. I need to take private ownership of this astonishing experience, this new relationship between my body and the sea. I look at the strand and the waves with different eyes now, proprietorial ones: there is nothing to stop me claiming the water for my own, whatever the time of year, the Beaufort scale, the temperature.

I'm afraid to, though, and I can't work out why. It's not

the thought of the seals, or even the orcas. I've been an
Orkney Polar Bear in all four seasons now. I've swum
enough around these shores to have a repertoire: to know
which beaches, like Evie, are safe, as long as you pay
attention; which bays, like Skaill, have rocks which are
concealed at high tide; which headlands, like the Point of
Ness, have strong currents. I have a better tolerance of cold
water, and a good understanding of my body's response.

I am learning how to get warm again.

Nonetheless, I am reluctant. Too shy even to propose
midweek swims to others, I wait until Helen or Yvonne
or Anne suggests it, and then happily go along. But
left to myself I look at the sea longingly, imagining the
passionate shock, the buoyancy, the briny sting; and yet
at the same time my breath shortens, and my shoulders
tighten and hunch, as though something or someone is
compressing me into an ever-smaller space. It's like being
back at a school disco, gazing at those who are brave
enough to dance, finding it impossible even to imagine
peeling myself away from the wall and crossing the gulf to
join them.

I don't understand this fear. It's different from the reluc-
tance to put a warm body in a cold sea which we all still feel
at times. I remember being with Anne at the Point of Ness
in Stromness one wild wintry day, looking at the waves
dragging the shingle, the pewter sky and the distant trails
of snow showers across Scapa Flow, and the tearing current
only a little way out. *Oh God,* I thought, *do I have to?*
She caught my eye, read my mind, and smiled complicitly.
There was a glorious, giddy schoolgirl moment of sheer

naughtiness, evading the inner monitor, the vision of bunking off, the possibility of getting away with it. *We don't have to do this... I won't tell if you don't.*

But peer pressure is a very powerful force, even *in absentia*. We screwed our courage to the sticking-place, and swam anyway; and it was wonderful, a rollercoaster romp, letting the current carry us round the point and then wrestling it to get back to the beach. The seals were enjoying it as much as we were, only a few yards further out but in the full force of the tidal stream that gives Stromness its name, letting it whirl them along, then swimming forcefully back to do it all over again.

This anxiety I feel about swimming on my own is quite other, as powerful in calm mild midday as in a dusk of gales and rattling rain. Something else is going on: this is about my inner ecosystem, not the outer world.

I'm such a good girl. I've been brought up to be such a very good girl.

For, firstly, my mother was born in 1927 to a dynasty of career soldiers and empire-builders, and thus her life was shaped by war and rumours of war. Utility boarding school, mother in London driving an ambulance, father an officer in the Egyptian desert. She looked after her little sister; she made do and mended. She was presented at court in May 1945, at Queen Charlotte's Ball, where – we used to pester her for the story – the ranks of white-clad debutantes curtsy to an enormous cake that represents the queen. After all the years of rationing the sight of the shimmering, white-glazed confection was almost more than the massed eighteen-year-olds could bear. On rising from their curtsies, however, they saw a lady-in-waiting opening a little door in the side to take out plates of dry sponge made with powdered egg. The cake was made of cardboard.

But she already knew how to live with disappointment. At the age of three she had been chosen to present a bunch of flowers to Princess Beatrice, Queen Victoria's last surviving child, on the terrace of Osborne House, on the Isle of Wight. Little girls' expectations of princesses – even in those just-pre-Disney days – were high. But, on seeing her, my mother exclaimed loudly, 'That's not a princess, it's an old lady in a black dress.' I've a newspaper clipping showing a mass of dark looming adults, a white-clad, bemused-looking toddler centre stage.

Lower your expectations. Bite back your real thoughts. Do what you're told. Keep smiling.

For, secondly, I am also an older sister, my place in the sun always under threat from a bright, beautiful, adventurous usurper coming up fast in the inside lane.

For, thirdly, childhood in Kenya was constrained by the knowledge that this was not our home (though it felt like home, and London fast became entrancingly alien, with its grey skies and red buses); that we were guests (I typed *gusts* by mistake just there – *blow-ins, ferry-loupers*); that all British people would be judged by our behaviour.

For, fourthly, my father's weapon was cold anger. He liked his daughters amenable. There was no margin for error. I could see that my sister was the pretty one, so I had to be the clever one. My mother thought their having met through Mensa was a huge joke, if faintly embarrassing, whereas my father took it with deadly seriousness. He had a red book

full of brain-teasers and he would pull it out and test us –
*Who can count backwards from twenty, rotate the shape
to match the example, spell antidisestablishmentarianism*
– setting us against each other, never mind that my sister
was two years younger. The humilation, when she won, was
appalling, the bottom fell out of my world. (I never stopped
to think what it was like for her.) I had to hide the ways
in which I was less than perfect because of the withdrawal
of approval, the way his blue eyes would go hard and very
pale when he was disappointed in me. I grew to hate having
my photograph taken, not from vanity – or not only from
vanity – but because it showed me all the ways in which I
fell so far short of any ideal.

For, fifthly, I get my notions out of books.

At a conference once I heard someone give a paper on
the experiences of nuns in France in the seventeenth and
eighteenth centuries, focusing in particular on the ways in
which the novices were educated, and how they internalized
the demands of their confining lifestyle. One anecdote
in particular has stuck with me. The speaker described
the layout of a convent, completely enclosed by a high
wall. The only way in or out was via a massive gatehouse,
which was built over a long tunnel (in my mind it stretches
to infinity) with gates at each end, like an airlock on a
spacecraft. The nuns spun, wove and embroidered fine
linen; tradesmen and farmers brought supplies. The nuns
put their handiwork into the tunnel, and closed the inner
gate again: the merchants opened the far gate to collect the
goods and take them to market. The farmers brought bags
of flour, carrots, salt, through the outer gate and left them

in the tunnel; when they had gone the nuns came out and collected their food. There was no need for the nuns ever to go beyond the tunnel into the town, or the townsfolk to enter the mysterious bounds of the convent. More than merely the breaking of a house rule: to have allowed such trespass would have been a sin.

And then one night the convent caught fire. The townspeople flung the gates open, shouting for the nuns to escape through the tunnel. But the women couldn't bring themselves to do so. Their fear of infringing their code was stronger than their fear of fire. They all died.

I would like to think that I remembered the episode wrongly; or that the speaker had misread the historical records; or that the records lied. That maybe one young novice who had not yet had the survival instinct beaten out of her, or some wise old sister who had reserved a corner of her conscience for herself, overcame the conditioning and bolted for freedom.

I try to fool myself that I would have been the nun who survived.

I wonder about the sisters' motives, and their feelings. Did some of them try to enter the tunnel, and others hold them back? Did they all try, but feel an unseen power block their way? Were they brainwashed, or truly devout? Did they fear for their dignity? Were they too proud to be seen singed and screaming by the townspeople?

Am I allowed to do this, to take these steps across the sand and heaps of storm-torn daberlack and walk into this water, alone, in the gale, in the cold, in the dark? Am I letting the side down? Who's going to be angry with me?

What's the worst that could happen?
There's only one way to find out.

Beautiful serene swim this morning, no seals, but shags and plovers and oystercatchers and curlews under a pink and blue pre-sunrise sky, and half a bright-silver moon, big rolling swell, and I found a lovely sea-worn piece of Victorian china with a transfer print of green weeping willows.

I'm standing half in the water, half in the air, a hybrid, a mermaid, a tiny node on a vast nexus of forces, visible and invisible. *Wind. Tide. Current. Neap. Ebb. Slack water. Air pressure. Swell. Moon phase. Water temperature.* Over the last few years these words have become like a litany, new helpmates that shove the old patron saints aside.

In what airt is the wind?
   Still south-easterly, so the Sands of Evie are
   comparatively sheltered.
How much further out will the tide go?
   Far – it is the dark of the moon.
Which way is the current tugging?
   From west to east, to judge from the angle of
   the rope tethering the nearest buoy.
I read the signs, looking for the parameters of safety and danger, in the way a Roman augur might have looked for meaning in the flight patterns of birds.

Wind and water may have become my new spirit guides, but they have not quite displaced the human saints of this landscape. If we listen for the voices of the past around Orkney's shores, the saints' are among the loudest, even if echoed and distorted in complex acts of ventriloquism. Their narratives tug at me in part because so many of the early saints of Britain and Ireland were on a quest like mine, to find their perfect island hermitage. The stories also appeal because so often there is a touch of humour, affection – a groundedness.

Three monks from Ireland, two old and one young, set out to the north in their tiny wicker-framed boat to find an island. They took little with them, but the young one could not bear to leave his cat. After some days sailing they spotted a rocky outcrop among the waves; they moored their coracle, and clambered out to pray for a sign that would indicate whether this was indeed to be their hermitage. The two older men were focused on their devotions, but after a while the young monk glanced at his cat. 'Look, brothers, my cat is fishing! Surely this is a sign from God?' But the older monks said, 'It is in the nature of cats to fish,' and went on praying. A little more time passed, and the young monk looked around again. 'Brothers, my cat has caught a fish! This must be a sign.' But, 'It is in the nature of cats to catch fish. Return to your prayers.' A few more minutes went by, and the young monk was distracted by a delicious smell. He turned once more to see that his cat had gutted and spitted the fish and was now roasting it on a fire. And by this even his hard-hearted brethren were convinced.

I spend my working life trying to decode the texts and objects, the stone carvings and the archaeological footprints left by these people: not just the saints but the folk who made them saints, the kings and queens, the bishops and nuns and farmers and housewives and dairymaids. My research centres on death and burial: how corpses were treated; how the survivors used ritual and monument; what they imagined happened to body and soul at death, and afterwards; and how they turned these ideas and practices into art and literature. It's all about transformation, change, loss, coping.

But the saints are so much more than dead bodies or old stories or distant holy figures: they are intensely rooted in place, bound up with identity and everyday need. In the twelfth century, a Norwegian servant girl prayed to St Olaf, King and patron of Norway, but our St Magnus, only newly martyred and relatively unknown, appeared to her instead. She stared at him in bafflement. 'Don't worry,' he said, 'Olaf's too busy just now with all the other folk calling on him, but I'm Magnus of Orkney, I'll help.' A micro-narrative, medieval flash fiction, that gives us a hint of how the bishops and earls of high medieval Orkney might have used the cult of St Magnus to extend their influence over areas of Norway whose residents felt their own overlords were neglecting them.

A Catholic litany starts with the big ones, the universal saints: *Holy Mary*, the angels, the disciples, martyrs and popes, bishops and confessors and doctors of the Church, monks and hermits and – finally – other women, the tortured virgins like Lucy and Agatha; descending at last to the little, and the local. If I were to come up with a litany for the Sands of Evie there are four names it would have to include: St Columba, St Tredwell, St Magnus and St Rognvald.

And I'll add St Cuthbert of Lindisfarne to that list. Cuthbert never came to Orkney, but like the earliest churches in Orkney his monastery was a daughter house of Columba's Iona, he knew all about islands, and like me he forced himself into the cold North Sea. The eider ducks which coo and tut along the Evie shoreline are known south, in Northumberland, as *cuddy ducks*, St Cuthbert's ducks.

If I were looking for an early church in which to chant my litany I'd sail across to Eynhallow, the Holy Island. The stone building just visible on the left side of the island is a ruined Romanesque church, from Orkney's great age of church-building in the twelfth century, maybe a monastery – surely holy enough to merit the island gaining such a label. The island has a Norse name (of course): Eynhallow comes from Eyin Helga, meaning the Holy Island, a name it shares with Lindisfarne and Iona. But there's an oddity: although the words are Norse, their order – noun-adjective, island-the-holy – is Celtic, providing one of the very few linguistic hints that the incoming Vikings may have spoken to the Picts while they were taking over their land and renaming everything. The Norse word order would have given us *Helgay*. And that *in* fascinates me, the Norse definite article – *eyin, **the island**, not just *ey*. *The* Holy Island, not just any old holy island. Chances are good that there's a seventh-century Pictish monastery lurking somewhere on the island, though there's no material sign of it: maybe it underlies the twelfth-century Norse ruin.

A mild south-easterly – waves breaking crest-on to the breakwater with wild streaming spray, sea surface very choppy but little swell. Today feels lighter – only 10 days on from the solstice, and heavy overcast, but the planet's axis feels to have tilted away from the thick inspissated gloom of mid-December. I was keeping a weather eye out for dorsal fins, but saw nothing more predatory than two eider ducks and a drake, and a few gulls.

St Columba, *pray for me.*
St Cuthbert, *pray for me.*

Columba and Cuthbert are often paired in scholarly conversation. Their island monasteries, Iona and Lindisfarne, flank Britain like the pans of the scales held by St Michael for the weighing of souls at the Last Judgment. Iona is the higher, the lighter of the two, floating free of the western coast of Mull, whereas Lindisfarne is tethered to Northumbria by its tidal causeway. Iona is also older, founded by the Irish exile Columba in the 560s. The Pictish kingdoms of eastern Scotland, including Orkney, were converted at Columba's behest. It was to Iona that Oswald, the Irish-educated King of Northumbria, sent when he needed inspiring men of God to enthuse his nominally converted people in the early seventh century; and thus Iona's daughter house of Lindisfarne was conceived.

But that paragraph I've just written doesn't even begin to capture their charisma.

Columba is a hero from epic, his every recorded deed larger than life. His story reads as though he should have had a career like one of the Irish superheroes of legend, Cúchulainn or Fionn mac Cumhaill, a member of the king's warband, battling gods and monsters, except that Christ got in the way. When in Pictland Columba made the River Ness safe for swimmers by driving away a man-eating monster.

Cuthbert's energy is gentler. A shepherd boy from the Scottish Borders who had visions of angels. One of nature's hermits, he only reluctantly took up the administrative burden of a bishopric. Like me, he sneaked out of the house when he hoped no one was watching, to go down to the beach. Though he only went into the sea up to his neck he stayed in much longer than I do, singing psalms all night. Otters came to him afterwards and warmed him.

Back in my early twenties, when I was roaming around looking for somewhere to invest my energies – teaching English in Athens, tourist-guiding in London, anything that kept me mobile, flexible, independent – I had no intention of being an academic. There was a big world out there. But the early Middle Ages kept pulling me back, so many beautiful objects, so many stories, so many unanswered questions. When working as a London Blue Badge Guide and taking my foreign visitors round the sights I had to be careful. Left to myself I would have lingered so long in the British Museum's Anglo-Saxon and Viking gallery that we had to skip the Parthenon marbles; or speculated interminably on what Westminster Abbey might have looked like in the eleventh century when the visitors really – understandably – wanted to know about the Gothic splendours and royal tombs in front of them. They wanted to know about what they could see; I was haunted by what was lost.

One evening in 1992, at a friend's party in Highgate, I found myself sharing a sofa with a nice young man. I don't remember how we got there, or where the conversation took us, but I have a very clear memory of my earnest voice, slightly slurred with wine, trying to explain to him the difference between St Cuthbert and St Columba, and why it was so terribly important. Not long after that I gave up the struggle and applied to York to do an MA in Medieval Studies.

Saints are lenses: ways of looking at particular times and places and their relationship with the transcendent and the eternal. They give the abstract a human face. Columba and Cuthbert help me to think about the ways in which Christianity converges on pagan Pictland, including Orkney, in the sixth and seventh centuries, from the English south and the Irish west. Columba and Cuthbert engage with the natural world; they challenge warlords; they are pioneers of a new faith, carving out a living from a hostile, uncomprehending world.

Columba went to tiny Iona as an exile from Ireland, but his monastery became a political powerhouse and a key creative centre in the seventh and eighth centuries, producing fabulous metalwork, stone sculpture and manuscripts. The Viking tide swept over Iona in the ninth century, though, just as it did over Orkney; and only scraps survive. Far and away the most famous of these bits of flotsam is the great gospel manuscript, the Book of Kells. In my working life I spend a fair bit of time teaching and writing and thinking about the art of the Book of Kells. But I go there for escape as well: it's like plunging into a parallel space/time, letting the artists' wonderland logic work its spell. Especially now that all 680 pages of the manuscript are available online: it's so easy to take a deep breath and dive, drifting from folio to folio, following motifs… There are lots of fish swimming through the intertwining kelp-forests of Kells. And mermen.

Columba looks monsters in the eye, and they flee. The Book of Kells is full of monsters, and teeth, and menace. It makes you face your nightmares.

There are no monsters in Cuthbert's story, but he is the patron saint of otters, and of those who need warming up after being in the sea for too long. (I made up that last bit, but it's true now. You can footnote me. It's in print.) And his contemporary St Ronan of Iona is the patron of seals, his name, rón-án, means 'little seal'.

Both sunrise and wind notably more easterly this morning. High thin cloud. Frost white on grass and windscreen, roads slick, flooded fields skimmed with ice. The tide was high, only a little swell but a strong roll and drag to the incoming waves tugging me out towards Eynhallow and the Atlantic. The oystercatchers have started to flock and peep again. One black-backed gull riding at anchor. One unsinkable shag. I thought that – yet again – there were no seals. A little sad, I started swimming with great energy, several lengths' worth of breaststroke and crawl, zigzagging, heading out past the breakwater – swimming FAST – and had to slam on the brakes to stop myself crashing into a common seal who popped up only a couple of yards away. We both laughed, retreated, bobbed up again, swam companionably side by side for another five minutes or so.

St Magnus, *pray for me*.
St Rognvald, *pray for me*.

The saints of *Orkneyinga Saga*. This complex narrative, spanning centuries, justifying the claims of Orkney's jarls and giving them mythic origins, was almost certainly not written in Orkney, or by an Orcadian. Its very existence reminds us how embedded the people of Norse Orkney were in their wider world, and that their world was not Scotland or Britain, but the North Atlantic. Iceland and Orkney were part of a cultural continuum.

The greatest export of medieval Iceland was its literature. Praise-poets, scholars and historians thrived in that fertile volcanic landscape and scattered across the wider world of the Norse diaspora, singing the fame and recording the deeds of kings and jarls and heroes from Newfoundland to the Bosphorus. No king counted unless he had an Icelander in his retinue; and after the conversion of the Norse world to Christianity the poets adapted their word-hoard and stayed in business. Poems and histories were to medieval Iceland as silver jewellery is to modern Orkney: high value and easy to export. In around 1200 someone – probably the jarl, or one of his circle who wanted to please him – commissioned an Icelandic expert to create the saga. Our saga-smith knew Orkney well enough that you can navigate the modern topography, Penguin Classic in hand.

Magnus turns up everywhere you go in Orkney, this man of blood who (the saga-writer claims) took the gospel so seriously. He was killed on Egilsay, just visible over there to my right, by his cousin and rival Hakon. *These islands aren't big enough for the both of us.* Magnus tried everything he could to save his neck – *exile me, imprison me, blind me, but don't kill me.* The saga-writer insists that this was not cowardice but a noble attempt to keep the sin of murder from his cousin's hands. Hakon paid no attention, and got the cook, a handy man with an axe, to butcher him.

Magnus had the last laugh.

We have a lot of material about Magnus: two versions of St Magnus's saga, as well as *Orkneyinga Saga*. St Magnus Cathedral in Kirkwall was built as his shrine. He unites Orkney, Presbyterian and Episcopalian as well as Catholic. Uniquely – bizarrely – the cathedral belongs to no Christian denomination, but to the people of Orkney, and is run by Orkney Islands Council. Its incumbent is a Church of Scotland minister, but when floods closed the Catholic church for a couple of years the congregation from Our Lady and St Joseph was made welcome in the cathedral, and an area at the east end given over to the celebration of the Mass for the first time since the Reformation four and a half centuries earlier. Father Ronnie, the octogenarian priest who cared for Orkney's Catholic population when we first moved here, was convinced that the archipelago remains such a wonderful place to live because St Magnus still holds it cupped in the palm of his hand.

There are three chief places in Orkney connected with our holy jarl. Egilsay where a round-towered kirk marks the site where he was killed and first buried. Birsay in the north-west of Mainland, the site of the first cathedral, where his bones were first translated. The twelfth-century cathedral in Kirkwall, where he now resides. Land and water separate these sites, but if you climb high into the Harray hills, in the West Mainland, there is one spot from which all three St Magnus-kirks can be seen. That too was a place of pilgrimage, a watershed in the hills where the parishes of Evie, Rendall and Birsay meet, a suitably liminal setting for contacting otherworldly powers.

I love the word *translation*, from the Latin irregular verb, *fero* – one of the first words you learn, *fero, ferre, tuli, latum* – I carry, to carry, I carried, carried. *Transfer* and *translate* both come from it, both meaning to carry across. We could so easily say the saint is *transferred*, but no, the process of moving the bones to an ever more holy and prestigious grave is given this analogy with language. When Cuthbert died in 687 he was all alone on his hermit island of Inner Farne. His monks collected his body and took it home to Lindisfarne for burial, and he was translated into his first shrine eleven years later. Further translations took him to Chester-le-Street and where he is now, in Durham. Columba's bones were divided in the ninth century and translated from Iona to Kells in Ireland and Dunkeld in Scotland – all his shrines are now lost. Magnus and Rognvald were finally translated into hiding at the Reformation: secret graves in pillars in the cathedral, as though in some Gothick romance. The American writer Archibald MacLeish defined poetry as 'that which is lost… in translation', but the opposite is true of saints: the successive translations of saints' bones take them further away from the prosaic and mundane, the ordinarily human; translation imbues them with ever more poetry.

St Magnus is said to be present in the white spear-thistles which flourish in Orkney. They grow along the route the saint's body was carried when he was translated for the second time, moved across the West Mainland from Birsay to his new shrine in the purpose-built cathedral in Kirkwall. Ghost thistles, tall and delicate despite their weapons, their petals looking as if they are already thistledown, not fully of this world: just right for that warrior-trained jarl-saint who sat on deck and read the psalms while arrows whistled past his ears during a sea-battle off Anglesey.

But Magnus isn't nearly so interesting as his flawed and fully human nephew. The sandstone cathedral in Kirkwall was founded by the most attractive man in the whole of the Norse world (he certainly thought so), the real hero of *Orkneyinga Saga*: the poet-warrior Kali Kolsson, who took the name of Rognvald when he became Jarl of Orkney. Rognvald is the name by which he is generally known, but I think of him in two guises: Kali the man, and Rognvald the saintly construct. *Kali* is also the Swahili word for fierce, dangerous. Signs at house-gates in Nairobi proclaim *Mbwa Kali* – 'Fierce Dog'. That coincidence of syllables is random, meaningless in academic terms, but the two meanings chime in my brain: they give Rognvald Kali an extra edge, an unpredictability, a gleam of teeth.

We know about Rognvald Kali only from *Orkneyinga Saga*, and the saga-writer knew him primarily by his poetry, which is quoted so incessantly that if a biopic were to be made of Kali's life it would have to be a musical. He undertook a pilgrimage to Jerusalem, devoutly sacking castles and attacking other ships on the way. He also had a fling – or claims to have had a fling – with Ermengarde of Narbonne, one of the most glamorous and powerful rulers in southern France. He dared to compose tough, bloody skaldic verses mashed up with erotic *amour courtois* convention in praise of this patroness of troubadours, one of the women who invented the courtly love tradition, civilizing sex and making it into an art. Among his other talents, Kali was a keen swimmer, and on his pilgrimage to the Holy Land he swam the River Jordan.

Magnus is the big saint in these parts, but he's never seemed real to me. Rognvald Kali remains my true love. I hope he swam for pleasure in Orkney's cold sea, as well as in the Jordan under the pomegranate trees, the olives and the date palms. When I visit the cathedral, it is his pillar on the north side beside which I linger, not Magnus's. Every year, my students fall in love with him. After his death, there was a valiant attempt to have him canonized, as St Rognvald, but his cult never came to anything outside Orkney, and possibly not much even within the islands. The author of *Orkneyinga Saga* claims with great authority that he was canonized by Pope Celestine in 1192, but this is fiction at its purest. No one in Rome has ever heard of St Rognvald. There are no miracles associated with his bones, although the bloodstains on the stone where he was murdered renewed themselves no matter how often they were scrubbed away.

Perhaps Kali-the-man is as much fiction as Rognvald-the-saint; he is just too dashing to be true. The only time he ever did anything graceless was when he caught his foot in his stirrup, in the late summer of 1158. He had been hunting, both deer and an exile called Thorbjorn, across the flow country of Caithness. When Kali stumbled in dismounting, one of Thorbjorn's men fatally stabbed him with a spear.

In many ways Rognvald Kali is the least Orcadian of men: the biggest sin in Orkney is to be *bigsy* about yourself, your talents and achievements. Given his bragging, his self-promotion, his infinite capacity for telling his listeners how great he is as an oarsman, archer, chess-player, killer of men and lover of women, his dubious sanctity comes as no great surprise.

Magnus and Rognvald help me to think about Orkney

in the high medieval centuries, part of Scandinavia, not Scotland. A northern world edgily integrating with the Mediterranean culture of troubadours and courtly love and Crusades.

Kali reminds me that men have other attractive qualities besides saintliness.

Sights while swimming at Evie just now: gulls and terns mobbing a raven; fulmars playing touch-and-go; three fearless shags diving within feet of me; a tern almost landing on my head; indignant eiders; two curious but cautious seals; and (on the beach) a lion's mane jellyfish over 2 feet across.

St Tredwell, *pray for me.*

I've done this out of order. Columba and Cuthbert belong in the sixth and seventh centuries; Magnus and Rognvald in the eleventh and twelfth. Tredwell comes somewhere in between, in more senses than one. The energy and aggression of those four male saints were turned outwards, towards political and spiritual enemies. Hers was vented on herself. No one doubts the historical reality of those men, even if it's a struggle to discern something resembling fact through the fogs of fairy tale and cliché. But, while she has a story, and a ruined chapel on a broch mound by a loch on tiny Papa Westray, Tredwell probably never existed in the solid, sunlit world. She's known outside Orkney by the Latin name Triduana, which means a three-day fast in reparation for sin; and maybe she's just the embodiment of an idea, the voice of conscience, penance given a face, born from a hunger for stories, like Aphrodite from the foam of the sea.

One version of events says Tredwell was an idealistic girl from Turkey who came to Pictland to spread the Gospel, and was rather taken aback when the king made a pass at her, telling her she had lovely eyes. I imagine her with a soulful dark gaze, Frida Kahlo brows, a creamy oval face, dark ringlets escaping round the edges of her veil, like the Fayum mummy portraits painted in encaustic wax in Egypt. Other female saints found a range of solutions when confronted with a similar erotic challenge: Uncumber grew a beard; Frideswide hid in a pigsty; Etheldreda married her king but refused to have sex with him.

Tredwell told the king's messenger, 'Your master can have what he wants.' She went into a dark corner and gouged out her eyes, sending them to the king, skewered on a stick, like olives in a martini. An article in the *British Journal of Ophthalmology*, of all places, suggests she was acting on the instructions of Christ in the Gospel of Matthew, chapter 18, verse 9: 'If your eye offends you, pluck it out.' But did Tredwell really so internalize the idea that women's bodies are offensive merely by existing? She's in a noble line of female saints who got into trouble when they rejected suitors and insisted on retaining their virginity. I'm using the prettified language here of conventional retellings of saints' lives – *unwanted suitors* and so on – but these are really stories about resisting rape. And not merely bodily rape and the loss of physical virginity but the wrenching away of these women's lives from the career path they wanted to follow. We tend to see virginity as an innocence, an ignorance, a lack, but in medieval Christian thinking a virgin – male or female – was an unbroken vessel, strong and integral. In Freud's essay on the uncanny, he equates a fear of having one's eyes gouged out with a fear of castration. Perhaps Tredwell would have agreed with this: I like to think her response to unwanted sexual attention was not a masochistic act stemming from fear of violation, but an assertive in-yer-face battle-cry: *Look how strong I am. If I can do this to my eyes, what will I do to your balls?*

Tredwell, real or not, helps me to think about the consolidation of Christianity in Pictish Orkney, the growing integration of our archipelago into a Mediterranean rather than a merely insular world, and the power of bishops and popes. A flourishing of monasteries, sculpture, literacy, through the seventh and eighth centuries and into the ninth. Papa Westray, Papa Stronsay, Papdale – all Norse names that suggest the presence of Pictish priests when the Vikings arrived in about 850.

But Tredwell also helps me to think about the strength of will necessary to retain integrity. About women's bodies, balanced between the violence they do to themselves and the violence the world does to them. Tredwell is one of many young women drawn by the dark, sometimes fatal, magic of self-harm when the world makes demands of them that they find intolerable. Get in there first and fast, cut, burn, binge-and-purge. Pre-empt the pain, take control of it, use it as a means of release.

When I got down to the beach at dawn it was deserted – empty sky, empty sea. Raining: everything grey, except the beach – when the sand is dry it is silver but wet it is gold. Everything very flat: the sand was rain-smoothed, seaweed-free, very few shells; the sea was flat calm except for the little raindrop-craters. It was so still and quiet, apart from a wren singing from the old fishermen's hut on the shore, and the patter of the rain. But after I started swimming life began emerging. First a solitary male eider, dabbling in the shallows. Then a tern, and a couple of gulls. Two shelducks flew over, and four more unidentifiable ducks bobbing a little further out. Then three seals arrived, swimming fast, popping up and down, one coming closer than he quite liked, and disappearing with a huge splash. All good.

That early hesitancy overcome, I have gone to the other extreme. I now prefer to swim on my own, before dawn and in the deep dusk, in the bitter cold, in the gale, always without a wetsuit, sometimes without a swimming costume. (And, yes, I know what my mother would have said, not about the nudity but about the risk.) Often, in all but the worst weather, there is an intrepid dog-walker or two on the beach, but if I got into trouble there wouldn't be much they could do to help, even if they were to notice me struggling.

Would they plunge in after me? Ring the lifeboat, the coastguard? The signal for mobile phones is poor out here in Evie.

And there might well be no struggle, no panicked scream, no arm-waving. That's not how drowning works. That's not how hypothermia takes you.

But I'm not worried, not any more. In part, this is because I know this beach very well. There are no hidden rocks, no turbulent undertow or unexpected cross-currents. The sand shelves gently, and the breakwater provides shelter, a safety net. I grew up swimming in the Indian Ocean, in waters that held Portuguese men-of-war, stingrays, stonefish and cone shells, all potentially deadly. Nothing like that shares the water with me here. The seals swimming in the bay are curious, friendly, even playful, but they keep their distance and I keep mine. They have impressive teeth, but when you hear of someone being bitten it's usually because they have approached a deceptively adorable new-born pup on the shore. Bull seals battle each other bloodily, but I've never heard of a seal biting a human in the sea. As for the apex predators, I tell myself over and over: *No wild orca has ever attacked a human being*, as though repeating the phrase will transform it into an eternal truth. I suppose I might get my toe nipped by an assertive crab, or my thigh nettle-stung by a moon jelly.

No: the chief danger to me here, the only real danger, is me.

After the initial shock of the water has been overcome, the beauty of this place is mesmerizing. (Despite the *mer* element, *mesmerism* has nothing to do with the sea: it is named for Franz Mesmer, an eighteenth-century German doctor. But Mesmer developed a theory that the human body was governed by tidal ebb and flow, which he tried to treat, to *mesmerize*, with magnetism, in an attempt to replicate the effect of the moon on the sea. There is a deeply pleasing coincidence here, rich potential for folk etymology.) One morning the world may be monochrome in the pre-dawn winter half-light: sky, land and sea all the same streaky grey-jade. The next morning the sky will have cleared, the setting moon painfully bright, the east pomegranate red. This beauty takes you out of yourself. Crab-like, I can feel my old shell cracking open, allowing a new self to emerge, gleaming, soft-bodied, and vulnerable for the first time in a long, long while.

In the dark quarter of the year, the water is first intolerably cold, then stimulating, then numbing and then – and here's where I have to be careful – lulling. Last week, just before the gales hit, I went into the water just after early-afternoon sunset. It was rapid, thickening dark, with tide low and the air quiet, but a big, lazy rolling swell which spoke of weather brewing. Everything was very still. There were no seals, and although orcas had been sighted a few miles to the west the previous day nothing was stirring out in the sound. The water felt pleasant if chilly, and for ten minutes or so I swam around in vigorous circles. Then my energy began to mellow. I wallowed in the water for a while, floating on my back, rolling over and watching the headlights of a car over on Rousay as it negotiated the island's only road. Happy and comfortable, I relaxed to the extent that I almost fell asleep, drifting off like a baby in her mother's arms. For how long I do not know, but something snapped me alert to find that the swell and gentle current had combined to ferry me a hundred metres eastwards. Parallel to the beach, into the curve of the bay; and I had only been carried a little out of my depth. But it was a warning not to get too complacent.

Just got back from the sea. Today was thick and dark, neither quite fog, nor mist nor cloud, but lumps of grey visible vapour under a low overcast, shifting and bumping between the hills and the water. Got into the sea well after sunset, stiff easterly whipping the waves into a rough-house, slap-your-face briny exuberance that left me thrilled and gasping. No birds calling, one solitary gull glimpsed against low murk, no seals, no shags. Stayed in until the sea and the sky were almost indistinguishable charcoal-purple. Car-lights came and went across the water on Rousay. Tide high and incoming, wind pushing the water and me towards the Atlantic. Stayed in 25 minutes, didn't want to leave.

Inattention leading to hypothermia is one danger. Another is the call of the dark. I have a strong urge to swim out into the black water at dusk, and to keep swimming. If ever I were diagnosed with a terminal condition, untreatable cancer or motor neurone disease, this is what I would do. Every time I go into the sea I am rehearsing that moment; a reassurance, not only that the weapon is in my armoury, but also that it is regularly tested, oiled, primed, even if the safety catch stays on.

How do we deal with that longing for the dark running like a hidden current below the frothy surface? Early on in his exploration of the human psyche, Freud offered the *Lustprinzip*, the pleasure principle, as an explanatory mechanism for human behaviour: the idea that we all juggle a complex economy of pleasure and pain, that when healthy we are naturally drawn to the former, repelled by the latter.

Of course we are. But it's not always easy to decide which is which. And how do we draw the line between them?

Freud balanced the pleasure principle with the reality principle: delayed gratification, adjusting your expectations of pleasure to the exigencies of the real world. There's a prim, self-denying snobbery about the reality principle. Forgo the little, easy, cheap kick now in favour of the greater pleasure further down the line. Take it to extremes: forgo all pleasure now in favour of the joys of heaven.

In introducing the third element of Thanatos, the death drive, to his psychic economy Freud allows for the idea that all organisms crave dissolution. Whereas pleasure and pain are united in intensity, Thanatos pushes us towards what John Donne calls 'absence, darkness, death; things which are not'. But I'm not sure I can really distinguish readily between pleasure, pain, and oblivion; categorize them in Linnaean fashion as though they are separate species who cannot interbreed. Standing here waist-deep in the winter waters of Eynhallow Sound I experience intense sensation, but I could not tell you if it was pleasurable or painful, and in fact I now think it's irrelevant. It is overwhelming, and that's what matters. *Overwhelm* comes from a Middle English word meaning *to overturn*, there's no implicit connection with water but the association has been there since the Middle Ages. Overwhelm is a word that seems to go naturally with boats and waves, perhaps because *whelm* also contains echoes of Old English *wylm*, meaning *that which wells up*. The *Beowulf* poet wrote of *ýþum weól, wintres wylm*, the waves welling up in the *wylm* of winter.

Intense sensation can itself lead to being overwhelmed and sinking into oblivion, sensation so powerful that it shorts itself out, like shock. *Oblivion* is a fascinating word: its disputed etymology may come from *lividus*, giving us a dark, blue-black memory, one that has sunk into night. Or it may come from *levis*, smooth, like a surface from which the inscription has been chipped away. The word is replete with a masochistic comfort, a forgiveness even, inherent in being forgotten, in falling out of history and memory. The oblivion that comes after pushing the pleasure/pain boundary as far as you can, when the only way of reconciling the two supposed opposites is sleep.

I think of sinking down through the layers of the sea, through the sunlit zone, the twilight zone, the midnight zone, the abyssal zone, and finally coming to eternal rest in the hadal zone, the underworld, the territory of the winter queen Persephone. All the sea in my viewshed here is sunlit: Eynhallow Sound, carved out a couple of million years ago by a Quaternary glacier, only goes down to around twenty metres. But the island of Eynhallow teeters on the brink. Westward, out in the Atlantic, the water is much deeper and if you keep heading out you will hit the Rockall Trench, which goes down to 3,000 metres, well into the abyssal zone, where there is never any light and the water is close to freezing. The sunlit and twilit zones are comparatively well understood, but below that the sea is still full of mysteries, and the grey seals, which I see almost every day, spend most of their lives unobserved and unobservable, oblivious to my curiosity, in the *haaf*, the deep sea.

I have looked for consolatory meaning in work, in marriage, in faith, in poetry and finally here, shivering and almost naked, in my Speedo, in this liminal place, the waves battering me off balance. I take another couple of paces into the water. Pulses of cold go up my ribs; the muscles across my still-dry shoulders twitch and shiver.

It is one thing to be drawn by the allure of solitude, another to embrace the idea of being forgotten. The sea represents that dark undertow which has always been a gravitational pull in my life, a response to every outward surge. I have often rejected it or left it unacknowledged, hurried past it with my eyes averted as I might some acquaintance rumoured to have committed an unspeakable deed, but it has always been there, like the still stretch of water on a surf beach that alerts us to the presence of a riptide.

I think about my public, professional, social self, the careful construction of identity, passwords and PINs and photocards: the ephemera which we invest with so much value, the things we would save from a burning building. But in the end they're nothing but rubbish. When I cleared out my parents' house I allowed myself to keep two box-files of paper mementoes, one for my father, one for my mother: curling sepia baby photos, yellowing certificates, a wartime diary. The files sit on my shelf like ossuaries: the whole of their long lives reduced to these absurd sheaves of paper.

Cold-sea swimming is the obliteration of self. The chipping away of carefully inscribed personality, the reduction of all my complexity to a bare, forked animal. This very annihilation is addictive. I cannot tolerate swimming pools any more: the water is dead; the chlorinated air unbreathable; the other swimmers too fast, too slow, always in my way. Pools and changing rooms bring me uncomfortably back to a social persona, a self-consciousness of the worst kind, whether my response to the people with whom I am sharing my space is cringing and apologetic, or brusquely *out of my way*.

Even natural or semi-natural fresh water, like the ponds on London's Hampstead Heath where I used to swim with my mother, or the lovely outdoor pools I visited last summer in St Gallen, in Switzerland, supplied with changing rooms and showers and boardwalks, but also thick with weed and fish and ducks: even these have an inert quality about them. I miss the brine and the buoyancy, the pump and throb of the waves, the tide, the knowledge that I could go into this water, here, and end up anywhere.

I miss the battle, the day-to-day unpredictability that means one day's in-driving tide, landward swell and easterly wind make for crazy, choppy cross-waves, and the gulls riding the storm; while the next day is hushed as for a funeral, all silent lull and ebb. Yesterday in the gale the kelp was one continuous mattress across the sand; today it lies in clumps; tomorrow the sand may stretch blank, like an unwritten page.

I miss the awareness that there are creatures in the water that could eat me, even if they choose not to.

Warm salt water doesn't do it for me either. The tideless Mediterranean is like tepid soup – a playground, not a battlefield. Here in cold Eynhallow Sound, where the North Sea and the Atlantic Ocean reach their long wild fingers out to each other as though taking partners in a country dance, my awareness of self is profoundly altered, at once diffusing and contracting. It extends beyond my body, stretching out into wind and tide, my consciousness flowing and tugging this way and that. But my sense of who I am also withdraws deep into the core of my body as my blood leaves first my hands and feet, then my arms and my legs, the heart beating the retreat, commanding a strategic falling-back of the troops to protect my brain and spinal cord, my vital organs.

In the water, there is only *Now*.

Magical swim. Wind brisk and mild, patchy cloud. In the water just before sunrise. To the west a rainbow arching from the wind turbines on Burgar Hill across to Eynhallow – an arch framing the gateway to the Atlantic. It started pink against pink clouds, took on the full spectrum as the sun lifted free of Arwick in a froth of golden cloud. Very active water: tide ebbing westerly, wind southerly, still a big swell from yesterday's gale. A couple of hundred rooks filling the air with their zap-gun calls. Many plover flying low just above the water, sunrise in their wings.

Evie is a dispersed community of under a thousand people, in a few hundred houses, loosely strung out around the main road that snakes parallel to the coast. It is a triangular wedge of land running from the top of the peat-hill to the bottom of the ebb. The primary school has about fifty children. There is an old church, now being converted to holiday apartments, and a new church, and a shop. Evie, like the rest of mainland Orkney's thirteen parishes, was probably laid out in its present form in the twelfth century, to provide maintenance for the new cathedral in Kirkwall and its canons. Evie is subdivided into townships composed of clusters of old farms; I live in Redland, triangulated by the farms of Flaws, Niggly and Quoys.

The Evie coastline runs north-west to south-east interrupted by the promontory of Aikerness, which points north, curving up to the right of the Sands of Evie. In the late sixteenth century it was noted that Evie is a parish 'where whales enter freely'. Apart from my beach, the coastline is formed of exposed slabs of Old Red Sandstone, laid down four hundred million years ago, just as the first lungfish were emerging on to the land.

Evie, like every other old name in Orkney except

for *Orkney* itself, is a Norse word, *efja*, meaning eddy, backwater, swirl. There's another Evie parish – Evje – in Setesdal, in southern Norway. Our local *efja* is that turbulent rost, the tidal stream that divides to pass either side of Eynhallow, where the tide pours in from the Atlantic, compressed by Westness, over there on Rousay, and Costa, here on Mainland, whose cliffs drop over a hundred metres into the sea.

Demographics. Geography. History. Geology. Toponymy. I hold up each of these lenses in turn and scry the view from my beach, seeking for better understanding. Am I so aware of *Now* in the sea because the landscape is so crammed with *Then*?

The first experimental big wind turbine to be connected to the UK grid was raised on Costa, back in 1951.

It blew away.

West beyond Costa there is the open Atlantic, nothing but distant, invisible and uninhabited Sule Skerry between us and Canada. But to the right of Costa's dark hump, the island of Eynhallow blocks the view of the open ocean: no one lives there, either, but they used to. According to local lore Eynhallow used to be part of Hildaland, the hidden land, the territory of the otherworldly Fin-folk; some people say it was invisible then, others that it came and went, but all versions of the story agree that it was an Evie farmer, from Thorodale, who first staked a human claim to it, with salt, some say, or the sign of the cross, and fixed it where it is now.

North beyond Eynhallow looms the dark bulk of Rousay – or Hrólfsey, named for an otherwise forgotten

Norse colonist. The stretch of Rousay's south-west coastline that I can see from here has perhaps the densest multi-period archaeological remains of anywhere in the British Isles. Shifting the gaze to the right along the Rousay shore, the view out eastwards along the sound is blocked by overlapping islands. Spearhead-shaped Wyre. There's Egilsay, where St Magnus was butchered. And just a glimpse, over Egilsay's shoulder, of Eday, where the pier was so damaged by last week's gales that the population of around 150 is effectively cut off for the time being.

Shift south-eastwards, look back on to Mainland, and your eyes sweep across Aikerness and Gurness, an Iron Age broch with later, Pictish houses and Viking burials inserted into its matrix; up to Hammars Hill, where two hundred ravens nest, to the farm above our house, and to Burgar Hill, where there is a loch frequented by red-throated divers. The whole skyline is ornamented by endlessly turning wind turbines of all sizes from the domestic to the epic. And when your eyes return to Costa, whose dark bulk forms the boundary between Evie and the adjacent parish of Birsay, the panorama is complete. I stand at the heart of a natural amphitheatre of hills and islands, like the Colosseum, and this sandy floor is the arena on which I wage my battles with wind and water. An image comes to mind of the *retiarius*, the Roman gladiator who fought almost naked, armed only with weighted net and trident, like Neptune, god of the sea.

The Romans had only a tangential relationship with Orkney, though they claimed its conquest. Late in the first century AD the Roman general Agricola circumnavigated

Britain. His son-in-law, Tacitus, who wrote his biography, asserts that Agricola was the first to prove that Britain is an island, and that he both discovered and conquered the 'Orcades'. Neither of these statements is likely to be true, but he was probably here. Perhaps his fleet came through these very waters of Eynhallow Sound. It's easy to imagine the people who live in and around those eleven broch towers putting aside plough or sickle, coming down here to my beach and watching – hostile, curious, thrilled or fearful, babies on hips and spindles idle in their hands – as the Roman ships go by, much as I watch the Atlantic-bound fishing boats chug past in the early morning, or the lobstermen checking their creels. And Agricola standing in the bow, with the red sails flapping as his helmsman struggles with the prevailing westerly, his ship fighting the wilful *efja*, wind and salt stinging his eyes. A man from the tideless Côte d'Azur, gripping the rail and staring thoughtfully at the massive, tapering towers of the brochs, and the little dark figures on the beach: *What can I do with you? Are you worth it?* Behind his impassive face he does his cost–benefit analysis: tots up men and materiel, the wild waters he has just come through, the hundreds of miles of mountains, the hostile tribes to the south.

The Roman conquest of Orkney had much the same effect as planting an American flag on the moon. The Orcades were at the end of the earth: subjugating them was a powerful symbol to the Romans, even if the local people never noticed they had come under the yoke. But at the Broch of Gurness, over to my right, two fragments of a Roman amphora were found in 1929. It is of a type that had fallen out of use a generation or more before Agricola sailed through, and it hints at a different and more complex interaction. A gift of wine, perhaps, or olive oil, to soothe these troubled waters.

Back in the here and now, in the sluggish January dawn, I walk further out into the water. There are conflicting messages battering me from the ebb that draws me onwards and the current that pulls me sideways. My body is flashing urgent signals that it's too cold, that I've already been in too long, gone in too deep: I ignore them all, much as I would a toddler pestering for sweets at the supermarket checkout. Giving in is not an option.

The frantic, gale-threshed tide of the last few days has churned the seabed and it is much stonier than usual. Normally I am immune to the hi-tech charms of neoprene socks, but today they would have been a welcome protection against this sharp, unstable surface. My bare feet are numbing already, but I keep my awareness in them, spreading my toes, letting my weight settle on the ball, lowering arch and heel, pushing off again from my big toe. Plantigrade: walking flat-footed and upright.

My hands are down by my sides: it takes another conscious effort to force my fingertips to trail the surface. Like the protagonist in *The Wanderer*, that poem with which I have an endless tussly love-hate relationship, I am stirring the rime-cold sea with my hands – 'hreran mid hondum hrim-cealde sæ'. Scholarly editions of the poem will tell you that *stirring with hands* is a periphrasis for rowing, but that's not what the words say. It sounds as though he's getting his skin wet. Knuckles, palms, wrists: the advancing cold sends a shiver up my still-dry arms and across my shoulder blades. Hands and wrists are fine-tuned to temperature, and I theorize that the sooner they're wet and cold, with their thermoreceptors sending alarm signals via my sensory neurons to the brain, the sooner my whole body will adjust to the sea.

SUCH a good swim this evening. 20 minutes – cold and grey, air only 4 C so sea warmer than air. Lots of seals, bright-eyed and curious and curiouser and coming right into the shallows, and a raft of eider ducks, and two swans.

When I had been sea swimming in Orkney for nearly three years, I finally had the chance to visit St Columba's island, Iona. The first thing I packed was my swimming costume.

I was there for a week in late spring, teaching a course about Columba to a group of international mature students. At least half of them were ordained ministers in one church or another, and it was an exhilarating change to have a class who already understood the tenets of Christianity. There's no need to try to explain who Jesus was to this lot, before we get stuck into the minutiae of the Book of Kells. No need to clarify that the Book is written in Latin, to students who can also read Greek and Hebrew. The weather was alternately battering and luminous. Corncrakes grated from every clump of reeds, and the island was swarming with bird-watchers.

We were staying in the abbey, as the course was hosted by the Iona community. Everyone was expected to do their bit with the cooking and the housework: I didn't mind the tasks but I found the mass socializing claustrophobic and escaped whenever I could. A new friend and I curled up in her sitting room with glasses of wine as she told me the gory details of her divorce and how, for all the trauma, her husband dumping her was turning out to be the gateway to adventure. I sat for hours in the abbey's little museum, watching the artificial light of the *son et lumière* playing over the great stone crosses, and then outside, contemplating cloud-filtered sunlight and spatters of rain on St Martin's cross, still in its original socket after twelve centuries. Long walks – or as long as can be managed on that tiny island – over rough tussocky grass to tiny coves. Lots of time for thinking about what was going horribly wrong at home, but at that point I still had my hands over my ears, shouting *shut up, I can't hear you!* at the doom-laden voices in my head.

I asked at the abbey about swimming, and they said to go north, about fifteen–twenty minutes' walk, up to Traigh Ban nam Manach, the White Strand of the Monks. Where the Viking massacre was.

White sand, polished granite shingle, the green tufts of the machair, views over the sound to Mull in one direction, Coll and Tiree in the other.

The first time I went for a dip, and the second, I coincided with another new friend, a member of the Iona community who had been swimming at this beach for twenty years. The tide was coming in across flat sands punctuated by outcrops of rock resembling prostrate dragons turned to stone in their sleep. So unlike Orkney, with its flat-bed sedimentary sandstone. Most of Orkney is four hundred million years old, although the metamorphic outcrop in which Stromness nestles is a billion or so years older than that, once a granite island in Lake Orcadie, lying a little further south of the equator than Nairobi does today. These Iona stones are a billion years older *again* than the Stromness granite, more than half as old as the planet. The sea was fierce at Traigh Ban nam Manach, pinched between the northernmost tip of Iona and an off-shore islet, Eilean Annraidh. The water between is the Caolas Annraidh. The names mean the Island of Storm, and the Strait or Kyle of Storm. Gaelic names are enchantingly exotic to someone used to Norse Orkney.

I am looking at that beach now on Google Earth, marvelling at my own stupidity. Those first two times, I could feel the cross-cutting waves coming in from either side. I could see the rocks. But I could also see David, merrily splashing about. I followed him. The sea was wild and glorious.

The third time I went, I was alone. I'd woken up at dawn feeling heartbroken and numb and the sea was the drug I needed. There were long hours before breakfast, the sky was barely light, and the sea was full, the sands largely hidden. I had dutifully signed myself out in the abbey guest-book – name, time, destination – jibbing a little, reminded of being back at boarding school. The heavens were clear, the air cold. I left my towel and robe above the high-tide line and padded towards the water. I could see the big swell, the waves driving in from both left and right. They didn't put me off. I'd been here the previous day, and the one before that. I was feeling better already, distracted by wind and the promise of sunshine in the paling sky, thrilled all over again by being on Columba's island.

Iona is such a mythologized place, one I had visited in my imagination so many times, that it was hard, in that silvery pre-dawn light, to believe I was really there. The complicated journey from Orkney had been a pilgrimage (fly to Inverness, drive down the Great Glen, ferry from Oban to Mull, bus across Mull, ferry from Fionnphort to Iona) and the fulfilment of a desire which had been brewing for decades. Back at home I had been writing a book chapter about the relics of St Columba, their importance in England as well as Scotland and Ireland, and why I think a stone cross from tenth-century York alludes to his cult.

Columba's bones were lost from here long ago, whether to the Vikings or to the Reformation, or to other churches: there is just a hollow space at the heart of Iona now, beneath a rebuilt chapel where his shrine once stood. I have been struggling for years to understand the iconography of his main relic, the Book of Kells. Holding intense late-night online conversations with like-minded obsessives about the meaning of a single tiny purple cat in the margin. Poring over the digital version of Kells at ever greater magnification, seeing it in pixelated detail that its makers could never have imagined, getting lost in that rabbit hole, that outlandish, carnivalesque vortex. No other manuscript even comes close.

This is the clutter at the forefront of my mind, this May morning on Traigh Ban nam Manach; these are the things that seem so terribly important. Being on Iona at last feels like being in Narnia, Middle-earth, some fantasy made virtual reality. This is not the solid world of pain and death. Bad things can't happen.

The water is cold, but not shockingly so. I wade in confidently, midway between two of the dragon stones, the sand firm, the waves powerful, rocking me back on my heels. Knee-deep, thigh-deep, waist-deep, and I start swimming, still well within my depth. I strike out a little, trying to keep to the mid-point between those jagged rocky outcrops. I'm struggling to remember what the beach looked like at low tide: whether there were other rocks which now lurk concealed.

The water is *powerful*. I have been distracted by the surface movement: the waves coming from two directions, the Caolas Annraidh and the Sound of Mull, interleaving each other like a pack of cards shuffled by a casino croupier; the swell which looks mountainous now I am in the water. I hadn't realized the force of the undertow.

And I should have. I could plead self-indulgent misery, or poncy scholarly musings, or schoolgirl excitement, but there is simply no excuse. Given the bulk of water visibly moving inwards I knew perfectly well as I walked down the beach that the same quantity would have to be moving out again. Every action has an equal and opposite reaction. I had seen the swell beginning to shoal as it entered the shallower, narrower space between the rocks. Confinement forces the incoming waves to slow down, and their dynamism has to go somewhere. A wave compensates by getting both higher and deeper before it breaks, its energy cresting and plunging downward in wild kinesis, dragging and swirling the stones, sand and shells on the seabed, and then pouring back out the way it came, forced down by the next wave coming in on top. The science of describing the behaviour of incoming waves is problematic enough, trying to force their complex, non-linear patterns into neat categories – they *spill*, or *surge*, or *collapse* – but the turbulent eddy after the wave has broken is truly chaotic, and scientific language also breaks down. My brain had been processing all this without giving it enough conscious attention. Time to wake up.

Waves are cascading across me from two directions, but the combined force of the water is flowing back out in one direction only, the one in which I am swimming, midway between the rocks. An undertow – even the most powerful – can only last as long as the next incoming wave, but this is a steady hauling, and even though I am still in my depth I can't keep my footing. I am falling, tumbling, being buffeted, smacked in the face, choked by brine, being pulled mercilessly away from the beach.

This isn't just the familiar shove and tug of undertow. It's a rip current.

And suddenly I am really frightened.

I can't swim against this; it's too strong. Oh, I know the theory: swim to the side of the rip, they're usually narrow. But the rocks are there.

Or let the rip carry you until its force has dissipated, then swim out of it and find a different way back to the beach. But allowing myself to go with the flow would mean being carried into even less familiar water, out towards Staffa and Ulva. I don't know what currents there might be beyond the rocks; there's no one else around; the sun hasn't risen yet.

Maybe I'm not as much in love with oblivion as I thought.

I fight diagonally in a gasping front crawl, my arms ploughing the resistant water. I am making headway, all my attention focused on regaining the sand.

And a lateral wave slams me into the rocky outcrop on the right-hand side of the beach.

I never saw it coming.

It's rough stuff, this Lewisian gneiss; sedimentary and igneous deposits that have been melted and re-formed so often that their original identities have been lost. Among the oldest rocks on Earth, they are part of the crystalline basement that forms the continental crust but is rarely visible, usually buried deep beneath sedimentary layers. Here on Iona though, they break through: the bones of ancient continents.

I am already winded. This collision smacks the last breath out of me. It doesn't hurt, though.

The wave's recoil pulls me away from the rocky surface. I flail, and look over my shoulder to see another mountain about to break, its avalanche of bubbles already toppling.

Slam. The wave picks me up and hurls me against the gneiss, rough as a cheese grater. I am still shocked from the last impact. I slide down the rock with the foaming backwash.

Just now, I would promise anyone anything. *Lord of Heaven, save me. Our Lady Star of the Sea, pray for me. St Columba, hold out your hand.* I am caught in an endless vortex like the spirals and interlace of the Book of Kells, and I have a sudden image of the Book where it is now, in Trinity College Dublin Library, in a darkened room, lying in its glass coffin like the body of a saint.

I am gulped down, sucked into the belly of another great green wave. The swell feels Alpine, Himalayan, as I look up to see it toppling mindlessly down on to me. This time I am dragged along the face of the rock, and I manage to grab, and hang on, my fingers worming frantically into crevices, hauling my bodyweight behind them, a blind survival instinct, Freudian libido in action.

Hand over hand, I monkey-crawl along the rock and on to the White Strand of the Monks. The sun is just rising in the north-east, flooding sand and rock with pink light. I am shaking. There is blood mixed with salt water dripping pink and red, running from gashes that run from wrist to elbow. Classic defence wounds. Blood drips on to the sand and instantly disappears. The fronts of my thighs are also deeply scraped and bleeding. Later, in the privacy of my little abbey cell, when I finally peel off my swimming costume, I will find my abdomen excoriated and raw, although the Lycra is undamaged. How much blood has the pale sand of Traigh Ban nam Manach swallowed, since Christmas night in 986 when the abbot and fifteen monks were cut down here by Vikings?

But that's later.

Just now I am standing, shuddering, wanting my mother, a friend, some authority figure to put an arm round me, scoop me up and carry me home. In the water I struggled valiantly for what felt, at least, like my very life. I will never forget how utterly helpless I was in that moment when the backlash of one wave grated me over the rock while the next green mountain was already building. How much does a wave weigh? (Too much, is the answer.) Then, I was fighting to stay alive. Now, I want oblivion, I want darkness, the black velvet of general anaesthetic. I want to fall asleep in the back of the car and wake in my own bed, some kindly adult having carried me up the stairs.

After a few minutes the blood stops flowing so freely. I return to the water's edge and wash my arms and legs. I put my robe back on, my skin flinching from the roughness of its towelling, and my flip-flops. I stumble the twenty minutes back to the abbey.

Everyone else is still asleep.

The next day I return to Traigh Ban nam Manach. Early afternoon, at the lowest point of the tide. It is a beautiful day. There are other people around, young lovers basking on a dragon rock. Dog-walkers. The sands stretch endlessly. The sea is calm, placid even; it looks warm. I go to the other end, the north-western end of the beach where there is a shelving pool, sandy-bottomed, weedy, opening out to the strait. There are gulls bobbing on the water. Salt water stings my scraped skin: agony, like the school nurse putting iodine on a graze. The sea loves me again. I swim to the end of the pool and look at the fast-moving waters of the Caolas Annraidh, only a few feet ahead.

St Columba, *pray for me.*

A dawn of flat grey calm, the silky surface broken only by two distant, indifferent seals cruising past towards Eynhallow. Such clear water: I could stand chest-deep and gaze at the winkles and burnished top shells around my feet. A hermit crab was playing super-safe, wearing a top shell and hiding in a sea-washed Ponds Cold Cream jar.

I am writing this in the winter, grasping after my memories of summer. An almost impossible task, down here in the abyss, to remember the weeks when you feel as though you're half made of light, when the sun is warm on wet shoulders and the skies are alive with swallows over the fields, terns over the waves. In winter the cold of the water drives me in on myself: in summer I expand to the kindly horizon.

It's June. I've swum out to the nearer buoy, tapped its algae-slimed pate for luck, and now I'm moving in big lazy sweeps, back and forth. The tide is low, and there's an easy swell. The sun has hardly moved all afternoon, and I've lost track of the time: no idea how long I've been in the water. Maybe an hour, maybe more? The summer birds shriek in the sky: only here for the breeding season but they are given local names, held in affection as natives. They're never perceived as ferry-loupers.

This love of birds has come late. As a thrill-hungry child, it was always the big creatures that hooked me, mammals for choice, then reptiles. I still have my battered copy of Jean Dorst's *Field Guide to the Larger Mammals of Africa*, illustrated in glossy colour by Pierre Dandelot and published in 1972; and, judging by the very wobbly letters in which I have written my name on the flyleaf, it was given to me when it was new. Maybe a birthday present? It cost sixty-one Kenyan shillings. My first intimations that precise, scientific language has its own poetry came from Dorst's descriptions. The colour of a lion's mane varies 'from silvery blond through ochraceous and rufous to blackish'. The alarm signal of the Thomson's gazelle is 'a ruffling or a flicking of the flanks'. The droppings of the spotted hyena 'when freshly deposited are green in colour but become pure white as soon as they dry into hard balls of crushed bone'.

But my mother loved the birds, and our frequent family trips to Nairobi National Park and Naivasha at the weekend and further afield in the holidays – Nakuru, Tsavo, Samburu, the foothills of Mount Kenya – were governed by birdwatching. A wild swerve that took the car into a ditch in pursuit of one, not long after we arrived in Kenya, meant that any similar accident became known as 'doing a bee-eater'. We'd stop for an hour at an acacia-fringed waterhole, where, I complained, there was nothing to see – only hornbills, crowned cranes, marabou storks, lilac-breasted rollers, bulbuls, weaver birds... But I was vindicated one day. They had stopped the car somewhere on a shady hillside in Amboseli to ponder the identity of a small brown bird hopping about on the verge. Bored and petulant, I was kneeling on the back seat and looking out of the rear window, as much to assert my lack of interest as to keep watch. My sulks were rewarded by a striped hyena as it lounged nonchalantly across the dusty track behind the car. We'd seen plenty of spotted hyenas by that stage, but this was a first. I yelped, and my parents and sister turned in time to catch a glimpse as its shaggy-maned back vanished into the scrub. I chanted 'I have seen a striped hyena' all the way back to the River Lodge.

The striped hyena 'is not as noisy or aggressive as the Spotted Hyaena. Almost entirely nocturnal, it usually remains hidden by day in dense bush...' We never saw another.

Dorst gives the common English name and the Latin name in the heading for each entry, but below that there is the French, the Swahili and the German – Striped Hyaena, *Hyaena Hyaena*, *Hyène rayée*, *Fisi*, *Streifenhyäne*. Spotted Hyaena, *Crocuta crocuta*, *Hyène tachetée*, *Fisi*, *Tüpfel-* or *Gefleckte Hyäne*. I was learning all three foreign languages at school and I seized avidly on these words, proof that what we were doing in lessons had some meaning in the wider world. Mostly Dorst's descriptions are cool and neutral, but sometimes they can send a chill rippling up your spine.

> The Spotted Hyaena follows pregnant female
> antelope and snatches the freshly born young,
> sometimes killing the female herself when she is

in a helpless condition… it can become bold and
even dangerous to man, attacking human beings
sleeping in the open and causing serious mutila-
tion by biting off the face.

Why didn't that give me nightmares?

Birds only started appealing to me once we were back
in Britain and adjusting to closer horizons, lower skies,
tamer landscapes. What else was there to look at here but
little brown birds?

From Eynhallow I can hear the screaming of the Arctic
tern colony, the sea swallows. These fragile-looking
creatures, each weighing no more than an apple, have
one of the longest migrations of all. Over a thirty-year
lifespan they fly the equivalent of three trips to the moon
and back. They crave light, spending our winter months in
Antarctica and travelling north again to arrive in Orkney
in the spring. So neat and spiky, with their black caps, their
sharp ever-open beaks, their forked tails. They hover over
me and shout: it's as though anger is the fuel that drives
them. They're *pickie-ternos* in Orcadian.

The terns share Eynhallow with the fulmars. A single
bird glides by, up close and curious, dipping its metre-wide
wingspan, swooping past my ear once, twice, three times:
I can see the bead-black eye glinting in the pure white head.
Sometimes the fulmars fly so close to the unpredictable
waves that they have to lower their yellow feet, like a
plane's undercarriage, and regain height with a rapid
paddle against the water. *Foul maa* is a term from Faeroe,
the foul-gull, named for its habit of spewing fish oil

when disturbed. It's said to be the only Faeroese word that has entered English. They look like gulls from a distance, but eye-to-eye there's no mistaking the bull neck and the salt-excreting naricorns on the beak that mark them out as close relatives of the albatross. Out at sea for most of the year, they come to the cliffs to breed and, wings braced, they ride the wind that buffets the Orkney shoreline all summer long. In the 1990s one of the females from the Eynhallow colony was identified, at over fifty, as the oldest known seabird in the world. They swoop past my head on their great stiff wings, close enough to touch.

They share the sky with the gulls, the w*hite maas*. Every bird has a different strategy for evaluating something unfamiliar in the water. A tern hovers low and skreeks; fulmars do their up-close-and-personal inspection; a gull will fly curiously towards my bobbing head then turn abruptly, jinking away at the last moment, reluctant for some reason to enter my airspace.

Higher up, the sinister B52 bomber outline of a *bonxie*, a great skua, pauses for a couple of minutes, wondering if I am worth pursuing. They breed on the northern limit of my viewshed, up on the Rousay heathland. Like the terns and the fulmars, they come back in with the spring, having wintered off the Atlantic coasts of Iberia and Africa. That heavy dark shape always brings a frisson: they'll dive-bomb hikers on the moors who come too close to their nests. They are muggers, kleptoparasites: they attack other birds and make them drop or vomit up their catch. I'm nervous with this one hovering low over me. I lie on my back, kick vigorously with my legs, splashing high. It's a classic prey response, trying to make myself look bigger than I am, more of a threat.

A shag cruises by only a couple of metres away, then suddenly up-ends and dives. *Scarfie.*

Closer to shore a raft of eiders hoots and coos. *Dunter.*

I strike out for the second buoy, the black, cylindrical one, further away but still well within the embrace of the bay, safe from the rosts tearing in from the Atlantic past Westness and Costa. I can feel them though, in the tug and play of the water; I can hear the roar of the surf; see the outline of the waves they throw up. I know I am part of something much bigger than myself. I feel as though I am dissolving.

In their letters, Freud and his friend the French writer and visionary Romain Rolland explored the idea of the *sensation océanique,* the oceanic feeling, the sense of being without boundaries, one's physical and psychic integument dissolving, microcosm and macrocosm becoming one. Rolland, who came up with the phrase, proposed this as the wellspring of all religions.

Freud, typically, rejected the idea that there was any real spiritual underpinning to the oceanic feeling, arguing instead that it was the natural state of a feed-on-demand, breastfed baby, who has no sense of difference between herself (only Freud said *himself*) and her mother; and that when an adult experiences this sense of unbounded, floating integration, she is regressing to a more primitive sense of self, one that should have been left behind at weaning.

Freud also said he had never personally experienced the

oceanic feeling. Why was he so ready to label and classify something he could not comprehend?

I like to say it in Rolland's original French rather than English – *sensation océanique* – for the sake of the onomatopoeia, the complex pattern of sibilants and nasals evoking the hiss and splash of the waves, and the *mmmnnn* of the well-being I am experiencing *right here, right now*, as well as the sense that my consciousness is tugging and flowing with swell and breeze and tide and current, that I am up there in the birds looking down at this strange shape in the water that is not a seal, just as much as I am down here looking up at them, their silhouettes distinctive as signatures against the summer sky.

Rolland suggested that the *sensation océanique* under-pinned all religious experience. Freud rejected the idea: too passive, he said, and *much* too pleasurable. Instead, he sought the explanation for the religious impulse in a quest outside oneself, that pilgrim passion for a land beyond, like the love of islands and deserts that fired the early Church. Religion isn't about satisfaction in the here and now; it has its roots in that longing which St Augustine (Freud's example) thought could only be satisfied by coming to rest in God. *God?* said Freud. *No.* God's just wish-fulfilment, a projection, a divine all-powerful source of ultimate authority on to whom one can dump all one's anxieties and responsibilities. 'God' is an illusion that moves in to fill the space left by weaning, when the baby first realizes she is alone in a threatening world. The oceanic feeling is no more than a neurotic adult's way of pretending to herself that danger isn't real.

But I know the danger is real; instead, I'm looking critically at the idea that danger is important, that loss of identity is threatening. Swimming here is salutary for thinking about the dissolving of boundaries, between self and other, body and world, life and death. You have to cross borders in order to grow and change, step over the *limes*, Latin for threshold or border. Hadrian's Wall was the *limes* of empire: for all the Romans' claims to have conquered Orkney we remain ultra-liminal, over the edge. There are particular Northern Isles words for liminal times and spaces. That ambiguous, tricky time between sunset and true dark: *grimlings*. The hours around summer midnight when orange-green-blue sunset segues seamlessly into blue-green-orange dawn: s*immer dim. Tang* is the seaweed that grows above the low-water mark, in the inter-tidal border zone, while *ware* grows below it. Grey seals give birth above the tideline and their pups have a few days as pure creatures of the land, their fur as white as the fatty milk they drink. But common seal pups must learn to swim almost as soon as they leave the womb: they are born between tides, among the tang, in the liminal space between the masses of weed thrown up the beach by the highest wave and the tumble of winkle shell and urchin fragment left by the quietest wave at slack water, just before the tide turns and starts remorselessly in once more.

I reach the second buoy. Again, the ritual thump on its hollow cylindrical side, claiming the territory for my own. I swim around it, dodging its massive, weed-thick chain. When the surface of the water is at eye-level, my familiar view appears different. The wild rosts flanking Eynhallow stand proud of the horizon: backlit and solid-looking, their surf could be mistaken for distant islands, wavering in the haze. The beach looks far away. Suddenly I feel very small.

I swim again in a circle around the buoy, reluctant to start back just yet. The buoy is something to cling to, just in case.

Oh, hello.

This encounter always triggers the same response: a little twitch, a suppressed gasp, a course of adrenalin. Flush, heart-pound, tremble.

Do you feel the same?

How long have you been watching me?

The seal is perhaps four metres away. A common seal, a small one, young and puppy-like. Only the top of its head and muzzle are visible: dark reflective eyes you could drown in, converging nostrils. We make eye-contact. It sinks lazily and then dives, the arc of its back and its rear flippers briefly visible above the water.

I tread water and hold my breath, but not as long as the seal does. There is no hint above the water of its whereabouts: I imagine it circling me, drifting through the tangles of *Laminaria* with occasional power-thrusts of its hind flippers, eyeing my pale, dangling limbs. Seals see well in the air, but even better below, their underwater vision as acute as a cat's on land, drawing in whatever light is available, although when they dive deep they enter permanent twilight-to-darkness.

Freud dismissed the oceanic sensation because he

thought the ego maintains a clear line of demarcation between itself and the outer world, the dissolution of that border being a sign of neurosis. He only allowed one exception: 'At the height of being in love the boundary… threatens to melt away. Against all the evidence of his senses, a man who is in love declares that "I" and "you" are one, and is prepared to behave as if it were a fact.' Being in love, therefore, is primitive, regressive, infantile – and that's bad. Healthy psyches are meant to shrink into themselves, form a hard carapace, creep into their shells and stay there, build a defence against the dangerous world. That's what being a grown-up means.

The seal resurfaces a little closer, lifts itself a bit higher out of the water, and now I can see the speckle-dapple of the throat, the holes of its ears, the backlit ruff of whiskers around its muzzle and above its eyes, still shedding their sparkling drops of brine. It's assessed me from below the surface: now it wants another look at my face. We gaze into each other's eyes for an endless moment, until I feel a wild vertigo; and then it dives again. What's going on here?

To work out what kind of creature I am, what I'm doing in the water, what threat or food or entertainment I represent, this seal is relying not only on vision but also on its whiskers or *vibrissae*, that braced fan radiating out from its face like rays of sunshine, creating an aura of extended awareness. Around ten centimetres long, they grow continuously; and they are fed by ten times as many nerve fibres as a land animal's. The vibrissae radiate consciousness into the space around the body: twitching, feeling the water flow, picking up information from my every kick and wriggle.

The old consensus was that the seal's own movement in the water overrode incoming movement-messages from other creatures, whether predators like orca, prey like fish or shrimp, other seals, or a curiosity like me. The whiskers were only useful if the seal was still, hiding or lying in wait.

But new research blows this out of the water. Bandage a seal's eyes and put headphones over its ears, and it will still track minute movements of objects, its head twitching left or right as it senses the stirring of the water. A blindfolded seal in the Arctic can find the breathing hole in the ice, dead centre, every time. There is a complex interaction between the movement of the tracked object, the speed of the seal, and the shape of the whisker, which is not only ten times as sensitive as a land animal's, but very different in structure. Seals' whiskers have a corrugated shape from root to tip, bulging periodically like beads on a string, but flattened in section. Whereas a flat, straight whisker would flap, the undulating shape is remarkably stable. Rounded whiskers, like those of a sea lion, create distracting vortices in their wake; the seal's whiskers are more sensitive to movement in the sea than the sea lion's by at least an order of magnitude. The vibration caused in the seal's whisker is precisely attuned to the vortex wake of the creature it is sensing – my friend here will have spotted my erratic breaststroke from a long way off. The seal's whiskers are like an orca's capacity for echo-location: an extra sense which we struggle to comprehend. What can it possibly be like to be attuned to the water and the life within it in the way that a seal is?

Reading the Rolland–Freud correspondence again, my heart goes out to Romain Rolland. He makes himself so vulnerable in his brave letter, describing intimate and powerful experience, offering it to his friend as a gift. *This is what I'm feeling, this is what it's like for me, this is real.* And Freud slaps him down. *I don't know what you're talking about, but you're wrong. Back in your box.* Because Rolland's emotions are inappropriate in Freud's paradigm, they are denied. I'm fighting the temptation to over-identify with Rolland: thoughts, ambitions, emotions offered in good faith, all lost somehow in a vacuum of incomprehension. It's not just poetry that gets 'lost… in translation', love seems to, as well. And good intentions.

If I experience the *sensation océanique* in the water, does that mean I'm neurotic? In love, even? Can you fall in love with the sea, or with the seals? And I wonder whether my marriage would have been happier if my husband and I could have accepted each other as members of different species with alien but equally valid ways of engaging with the world. Can a seal understand echo-location, or an orca make sense of vibrissae?

I stay afloat, waiting for the sleek speckled head to re-emerge. When it does, the seal is much further away, perhaps twenty metres, heading westward. It looks over its shoulder at me one more time, then ducks again. This time it's for good. I wait nonetheless, still treading water. Slowly the dizzy, druggy sensation retreats, my heartbeat slows: I am back in my own skin, looking out through my own eyes.

I am cold, tired, needy, small. The sun stands still in the sky – it could be two in the afternoon or eight in the evening. In high summer, an Orkney afternoon lasts for ever.

I ran three miles – first into the wind, then with it behind me. Then to the sea, glorious sunrise, breakers backlit white-gilt. No one around so once in I slipped out of my Speedo and swam with it bunched up in my right hand. Those few square inches of Lycra do make a difference to the experience of cold... but also to the sensuality of the water. Exhilarating wrap-around ice-champagne. No seals but lots of gulls in the air, shags in the water, ringed plovers along the tideline, hoodie crows hopping and pecking at the kelp. Swimming underwater: a colour for which I have no name, green stabbed with gold.

I'm listening again for the voices that once populated the shores of Evie, Rousay, Eynhallow. A hectoring laird and a well-meaning one, a science-minded poet, a stoical fisherman, crofters round the fire, a pompous minister, the Latin chant resonant within a fine stone kirk, a Norse skald singing his gory dream of battle…

Since 1997 and the re-establishment of the Parliament in Edinburgh, there has been a lot of money available for the promotion of the Gaelic language in Scotland. One of the most successful projects has been the establishment of Gaelic-medium primary schools, and the teaching of Gaelic in English-speaking schools. But Orkney has never been Gaelic-speaking. Scandinavian from the ninth century, the islands only came under the Scottish crown in 1468, by which time Scots was firmly established as the language of power in the royal court. The funds for promoting Gaelic were made available to Orkney after 1997, but have never been taken up. A semi-serious suggestion that Orcadian children would do better to learn Norwegian gained considerable traction. Norn, the Scandinavian language spoken in Orkney, only faded out of use in the eighteenth century. Enough scraps survive for it to be reconstituted, but it is a Frankenstein's monster of a language, cobbled together from spare parts and artificially reanimated. No one has ever seriously suggested teaching the primary school kids Norn. There are hints, though, that Norn had great riches, that the world of *Orkneyinga Saga* rumbled on through the Reformation and into the hungry years of the seventeenth and eighteenth centuries.

In 1761 the English poet Thomas Gray came across some Old Norse poetry in Latin translation, in Thomas Bartholin's splendidly named *Three Books of Danish Antiquities Concerning the Causes of the Contempt of Death by the Danes while They Were still Heathens*. The poems seized Gray's imagination, and he translated them into English. A popular success, their publication is a significant milestone in the re-emergence of awareness of Viking culture in the modern world. If you picture a Viking warrior as a fatalist Odin-worshipper who laughs in the face of danger it's Gray – and ultimately Bartholin – you have to thank.

One of the poems Gray translated was 'The Song of Darrad', a masterpiece of the Norse macabre, which Gray renamed 'The Fatal Sisters'. Darrad, a Caithness man, sees mysterious riders entering a bothy. Through a crack he spies on women weaving on a loom made from spears, strung with human guts, weighted with human heads. As they weave they sing. In Gray's words:

> Now the storm begins to lower,
> (Haste, the loom of hell prepare,)
> Iron-sleet of arrowy shower
> Hurtles in the darkened air.
>
> Glittering lances are the loom,
> Where the dusky warp we strain,
> Weaving many a soldier's doom,
> Orkney's woe, and Randver's bane...

Soon after the publication of 'The Fatal Sisters', a minister in Orkney's northernmost island, North Ronaldsay, hit on the idea of reading it to some of his elderly parishioners, thinking they would be interested in a poem that had so much relevance to the history of their islands. He had got as far as verse three or four when they interrupted him: 'We know this poem,' they said. 'Don't you remember?' When he had asked them if they could sing him anything in Norn, they had sung it. Many times. They called it 'The Enchantresses'. But their version hasn't survived.

I want to be a time-travelling fly on the wall, to watch the faces of the old crofters as they recognize the echoes of a familiar pagan song, read to them by a voice more used to lengthy sermons or metrical psalms. Were they in the church, or in the minister's parlour, or gathered around the hearth in one of the croft houses? The minister – was he smirking and superior, or bouncing and eager to share Gray's poem? When his patronage was so abruptly scuppered, did he blush or bluster?

And why on earth did he never write 'The Enchantresses' down?

In 1761, when Gray came across Bartholin's wonderful book on Danish antiquities, it was already a century old. Bartholin had been a maverick in his medical dynasty: his brother Caspar gave his name to the Bartholin glands, the source of vaginal lubricant in a sexually aroused woman, and both their father and grandfather were noted physicians and anatomists. But Thomas Bartholin's interest in death and corpses had taken him in a different direction, cataloguing rune-stones and ferreting in old Icelandic manuscripts. Discovering the dark magic of 'The Song of Darrad', letting it out of its cage to fly free, until it fluttered to rest in Orkney – and turned out never to have been caged at all.

The North Ronaldsay minister in that story stands in for so many of us ferry-loupers, with our readiness to patronize, our assumptions about this place and its people. Writers about Orkney tend to stress the wildness of the islands, their barrenness, their distance from the trials of modern life. Any article about the archipelago in the national press gets us playing Orkney Cliché Bingo – so many points for references to the wind, to the Neolithic, puffins, seals; a bonus point for every use of the words *remote* or *timeless*. But it's all a question of perspective. Look at a map of the North Atlantic rather than a map of the United Kingdom. In its context, Orkney is mellow, fertile, central. Ground frosts and lying snow are rare. The insular maritime climate makes it one of the most temperate places on the planet, with just four degrees Celsius separating the average winter and summer temperatures. Rainfall is comparatively low but still plentiful; fresh water is abundant, as are natural harbours. Grass and oats and barley flourish.

The first time I visited Shetland, around a hundred miles further north, on the 60th parallel rather than the 59th, with much more jagged geology and acid soil, folk asked me if I'd been there before. 'No,' I said, 'but I've visited Orkney several times.' A roll of the eye, a shake of the head, the smile you'd have got if you'd told a Yorkshireman that you'd often been to Kent. To Shetlanders, Orkney is the south, the soft option.

Turn your map upside-down, and the centrality of the archipelago becomes even more apparent. Set your prow towards Orkney from any of the wind's airts – not just rocky Shetland or Faeroe, but from the peat-bogs of Caithness or the mountains of Sutherland, the much more rugged Western Isles, from Iceland or the Norwegian fjords – and you could be forgiven for thinking that you had stumbled on some snake-free Paradise. Wealthy and well connected, not romantic and remote.

To the untutored eye – to my eye, when I was twenty-one – Orkney does look mythic. Elemental. Moving air, light, rock, water, grass. Cattle an Iron Age chieftain would exult in. Fat sheep. Houses built with stones you might find on the beach. A culture of self-sufficiency, bricolage, make do and mend. A dog whelk on the sand, worn away to reveal its perfectly graded spiral core. Seals barely distinguishable from speckled boulders. Nature stripped to its essential components. Very easy to let your eyes drift out of focus, the millennia fade away like mist from the purple hills; to repopulate Skara Brae with sturdy girls from five thousand years ago, seashells braided into their hair, speaking an unknown language with a recognizable easy lilt, their mothers hunkered round the hearth fires, eating hazelnuts, trout, gannets' eggs. Time feels gossamer-thin, the profiles of hill and cliff eternal verities.

Yet this is romance, seductive but patronizing, editing the landscape to suit a particular tourism and heritage agenda. The complex of Neolithic sites in West Mainland, Maeshowe and Skara Brae and the stone circles, are about the only place in the archipelago from which you can see no wind turbines: to mar the horizon with technology would be to risk losing UNESCO World Heritage status. Farmers mutter and grumble, worried that they will be prevented from raising new barns and byres in the vicinity as well.

Orcadians have looked wistfully back to a golden age of Viking owner-occupiers under Norwegian law that respected their rights, all swept away by being brought into the feudal kingdom of the Scots in 1468. Whether true or not, it's a powerful myth, a shaper of consciousness. Partly as a result, Orkney has a different relationship with England from most of the rest of Scotland.

The Orcadian national narrative is one of oppression by the Scots, with Westminster legislation such as the Crofting Acts of the 1880s bringing some relief. Island politicians play Holyrood and Westminster off against each other with consummate skill. In the independence referendum of 2014 Orkney had the lowest turn-out for Yes in the whole of Scotland.

Ice on the puddles, frost on the windscreen. The rising sun rolling in a near-flat arc along the crest of the hill, and the waning moon low in the west. Clear and almost cloudless. Two herons on the beach, lifting and flapping low over me as I went into the flat but choppy water. The sand has been stripped back by the storms – on the right of the breakwater the underlying rock strata are now fully exposed again. South-westerly breeze (but cold), ebbing tide, beach very weedy. No seals.

It's no surprise that the Scots lairds got the reputation that they did in Orkney. In the seventeenth and eighteenth centuries they were largely rack-renting absentees, and even when in the nineteenth century they were more hands-on and philanthropical they still had extraordinary power. David Balfour owned Eynhallow (and much else), and when in 1851 a mystery disease, possibly typhoid from a contaminated well, caused several deaths he decided his tenants needed to relocate to healthier surroundings, on another, less-marginal island. The four families on the island had been living in an interconnected warren of little houses, and the laird felt these were best burned. (He was interested in public health; the Balfour Hospital in Kirkwall where I got my plantar fasciitis diagnosed was another of his projects.) Elsewhere in Scotland lairds who forcibly moved their tenants and burned their homes got a terrible reputation, but David Balfour's name has a Teflon coating.

As the timber partitions and straw thatch of the Eynhallow crofters' homes went up in flames the skeletons of much older stone buildings were revealed. The site has no known history, but it has been argued – on very shoogly evidence – that it must be one of the recorded monasteries whose location within Orkney are unknown. Earlier generations of scholars read the ruin as a typical Cistercian or Benedictine house – which it is certainly not – because they badly wanted to prove that the outlying corners of Scotland were fully part of the European mainstream. A later generation of interpreters emphasized the unusual layout and alignment of the church and associated buildings, now wanting Eynhallow to manifest a quirky North Atlantic identity. A more recent suggestion is that it is not a monastery at all, but a church attached to a centre for processing the natural riches of the Eynhallow estate, which belonged to the bishopric of Orkney at the end of the Middle Ages. We see what we want to see.

Whatever its original function, the church had long slipped out of consciousness to be reborn as the matrix into which Balfour's tenants could slot their homes, like starlings nesting in a drystone dyke. Eynhallow has been unpopulated ever since they left.

Beyond Gurness, across Eynhallow Sound, you can make out Trumland House on Rousay, built by General Traill Burroughs in 1875 after his return from a successful army career in the Crimea and India. Traill Burroughs spent nearly twelve thousand pounds building Trumland, at a time when a crofter's cottage cost around five. Traill Burroughs is remembered as just about the worst of the lairds, a tiny man with a bullying bellow, determined to modernize Rousay. He owned almost the whole island, and he was deeply frustrated by what he saw as the backward nature of indigenous Orkney farming practices, based on communal subsistence.

All was tolerable as long as the tenants showed gratitude for the laird's improvements – he built a pier; funded an annual Agricultural Show, and a School Picnic, and a Best-Kept Cottage Award; set up the first steamship service (the boat was named for his wife, the *Lizzie Burroughs*) – but when his money ran out, and the rents were raised, any crofter who challenged the laird was harried off the island. Traill Burroughs set them up to fail – his leases said 'A crofter is obliged to keep his buildings in good repair, on pain of eviction' and 'All mineral and quarrying rights are reserved to the landlord'. If he wanted to get rid of someone, he only had to wait till they needed stone to repair a dilapidated wall. But they weren't the fools Traill Burroughs believed them, though, those Rousay farmers: they used the local and national press to publicize their plight just as we would use Facebook and Twitter now.

In the end it was the laird who fled, to die in London in 1905. That serenely rugged green and brown coastline of Rousay was a battlefield for years.

There are quieter voices, too, echoing along these shorelines.

Robert Rendall devoted his life to studying the molluscs of Orkney's coast. He published both scientific and popular accounts of them; and he begins his scholarly paper 'Mollusca Orcadensia' by saying that its publication (in 1956) fulfils 'a resolve made in boyhood'. He was also a poet of the Orkney landscape. His work in English is sometimes brilliant, but mostly competent, hampered by formality and full of well-worn images of nature. But at the same time he was also writing in Orcadian, and his poetry in his native language is extraordinarily powerful. He is a pastoral poet of land and shore and sea, the rhythm of the farming year, and the rise and fall of the tide.

Both his poetry and his scientific writing are embedded in the particulars of place, including my beach: 'For bivalves the best sandy beach on the mainland of Orkney is at Aikerness, Evie.' The shells he records from here are wonderfully named: the Pale Venus, the Fragile File, the Distorted Scallop, the Arctic Rock-borer, the Small Wentletrap (*wenteltrap* is Dutch for a spiral staircase). It was Rendall who accidentally discovered the Broch of Gurness while using the grassy mound as a convenient viewpoint for painting a watercolour: the leg of his stool went down a hole, and he peered in to see a winding staircase (a wentletrap!) disappearing into the dark. He used to wander along this beach, his tweed cap in his hand, filling it with shells. I try to channel him when I do the same, but I don't have his eye, or his knowledge.

In one of Rendall's best-known English poems, 'Angle of Vision', an Orkney man is asked if he has seen the world's great cities, their technological marvels and ancient monuments, and he replies that he hasn't – but he has seen the curved horizon of the Atlantic from the Birsay shore, comparing the sea to the universe, Orkney to the Earth, and the ferocious tides of the ocean to the energies that fuel the cosmos. Microcosm and macrocosm. The horizon, the limit of vision, contracts to become the edge of all there is. Orkney expands to planetary scale, suspended in interstellar waters. There's an irony in Rendall – a man who loved to travel – claiming that the world visible from Orkney was enough – no, more than enough: it contained all that he needed and surpassed everything else he saw. There is also a bitter lesson here, central to contentment on an island. *Don't hanker. Let the horizon limit your desire.*

However, the poem of Rendall's that haunts me is not 'Angle of Vision', but 'The Fisherman'. In this ten-line poem in Orkney dialect Rendall depicts the death of an old fisherman, Jeems o'Quoys, who had spent his life taking his small boat, his yole, out into the wild waters of Eynhallow Sound to fish and set his lobster-creels under the Westness crags; and yet died at home, alone, his little cruisie lamp guttering out with its wick untrimmed. The final couplet describes how his memorial stone was raised to him by his fellows rather than his family. It peoples the exact seascape I am looking at now, both with Jeems and with his *yamils*, his age-mates, perhaps the other fishermen.

The dark, irregular outline of the Westness crags is visible across the water from the Sands of Evie, over to the left, just past Eynhallow. Jeems attains heroic stature in the poem, despite dying what the Norse would have called a straw-death, in his bed.

We have seen what the rosts of Eynhallow Sound can be like, and Jeems ventures out there alone, in his small wooden boat. Although yoles are no longer much used in Orkney, there are always a few moored in Stromness harbour, so their clinker-built, two-masted profile, pointed fore and aft, remains a familiar sight. They are closely related to the Viking four-oared boats or færings in which two men were buried in the ninth century at Westness on Rousay. When Rendall published this poem, in 1946, most yoles had already been fitted with outboard motors. But the material culture of the poem suggests a pre-modern world, not just the yole, but the thatch and above all the cruisie lamp, formed of two boat-shaped iron bowls, one placed above the other, the upper one holding a rush wick and filled with fish or seal oil, the lower catching the drips. The untended wick in Jeems's cruisie is left to gutter itself out: an image not only of solitude but also lack of care. That no one of a younger generation commemorates him reinforces the sense that he is among the last survivors of an old world, one of a tribe who lived and worked close to the elements. The poem's claim to authenticity is strengthened further by the reference in the last line to the 'memorial stane', inviting the reader to imagine the gravestone, even implying that the whole poem is inscribed on it as an epitaph.

I wondered, when I first read this poem, whether I could find Jeems's gravestone, or indeed any material truth behind the poem. Quoys is a common enough Orkney farm name, from Old Norse *kví* – enclosed field; there's one next to our house, another on Rousay. A James Kirkness lived at the Rousay Quoys in 1871: did he inspire the poem? If so, he would have been one of General Traill Burroughs's long-suffering tenants. Kirkness had a wife and four children, but Rendall's poem could mean not that Jeems had no family but that they were too poor to commission a memorial.

As it turns out, there probably never was a Jeems o'Quoys. On closer investigation, for all its bewitching local detail, the seemingly solid narrative of 'The Fisherman' dissipates like the haar. The name Quoys was probably chosen precisely because of that generic quality. Rendall's poem is mapped almost word for word on an elegy by Leonidas, who wrote in the third century BC in southern Italy. Rendall knew Leonidas's poem in Andrew Lang's translation:

> *Theris the Old, the waves that harvested,*
> *More keen than birds that labour in the sea,*
> *With spear and net, by shore and rocky bed*
> *Not with the well-mannered galley laboured he;*
> *Him not the star of storms, nor sudden sweep*
> *Of wind with all his years hath smitten and bent,*
> *But in his hut of reeds he fell asleep,*
> *As fades a lamp when all the oil is spent:*
> *This tomb nor wife nor children raised, but we*
> *His fellow-toilers, fishers of the sea.*

I was shocked when I first learned this – more than shocked: outraged, as though Rendall had somehow cheated me, offering a tempting morsel of Orcadian authenticity only to snatch it away with a mocking laugh. Pulling a fast one, winding up the wide-eyed, gullible ferry-louper.

However, the more I reread the two poems, the more re-enchanted I become. In his reinvention of Leonidas, Rendall gives Jeems o'Quoys a classical dignity as well as his home-grown heroism. 'The Fisherman' also encapsulates another of those hard truths about Orkney, people and landscape alike. There's more going on than you think. Pay attention, ferry-loupers, tourists, journalists. Don't be deceived by that surface simplicity, that reticence. The dislike of bigsiness means that this open, apparently guileless, green landscape conceals a myriad of secrets. That quiet-faced, boiler-suited farmer, with his musical vowels and homespun wisdom? He has degrees in Chinese and Arabic and once worked as a consultant to the Sultan of Brunei, but chances are he'll never tell you, though if you're here for long enough one of his neighbours might. A poem which seems to have been born effortlessly from the foam of Eynhallow Sound conceals a lifetime of learning, observation and skill.

I was in the sea around 6.30. Mist just coming in, sunrise still some way off. Yesterday's brisk southerly has dropped, and the water was still in the lee of the breakwater, but retaining enough energy to be breaking on the sand with a greedy lap and slurp. Several seals coming and going, some lingering and curious. One cheerful little shag cruising and diving and pretending to be the Loch Ness Monster. Curlews, ringed plovers, lots of rooks on the beach. Air temp 10, water temp 12. I felt great swimming but probably spent too long in the water – hard to get warm afterwards.

If I've learned one thing over nearly a decade living in Orkney it's that these islands are no more timeless or unaffected by the modern world than anywhere else; and furthermore that the very idea of untouched wilderness is not only romantic but potentially dangerous. Powerful outsiders – lairds, ecologists, journalists, ferry-loupers – come with their myth of pristine Nature, and try to impose their vision on the indigenes. It's a common enough narrative. As a child in Kenya I was in love with the visions of writers like Joy and George Adamson, Karen Blixen, Louis Leakey, Iain and Oria Douglas-Hamilton, with their narratives of the wild *bundu*, the kindly, modernizing colonists and administrators, coffee plantations, of white children growing up learning bushcraft at the knee of wise Kikuyu servants, of lions forever free, cheetahs and elephants living in a world that ought to be untainted by humanity and modernity. But so much of that is fantasy, Eden-myth, an interpretive framework that relegates or even ignores the local people, their needs, their history and their trauma. If the Mau Mau resistance fighters were ever mentioned in my reading, they were demonized.

We moved to Kenya because of my father's work.

His thing was Systems Management, Time and Motion Studies, the streamlining of inefficient bureaucracy and paperwork. He was a senior manager at British Rail when a request came through for someone to be seconded to Nairobi, to support Kenya, Uganda and Tanzania in their development of national rail networks. Exciting times. But my father's not sure he's the right man. My mother's career is taking off; she's just published her first book, *The Group Process as a Helping Technique*. They've only recently finished refurbishing the early-Victorian house in the Islington square. Their daughters are tiny. His only previous experience of travel outside Europe had come in the spring and summer of 1945, as a twenty-year-old radar operative on a ship repatriating ANZAC soldiers. But when he tells my mother of the offer her face lights up.

Because she's been there before. Kenya is a little golden thread that weaves through her family's story. Her father was stationed there in the 1920s, and she has a revolting relic, a silver picture frame containing a studio photograph of him in his Royal Artillery uniform. The frame is circular, and the base incorporates two gleaming tusks, curved like the crescent moon, each about six inches long. 'They're from the first warthog he ever shot,' my mother tells me, and then adds hastily, 'Granny had the frame made, not my father. Not his sort of thing.' We look at the photo together, and I notice she is smiling. My grandfather looks very young, with large, dark eyes and a sensitive mouth that belie the upright pose and the uniform. He died of cancer more than a decade before I was born, but I know he was her bookish parent, the dreamer, the one who encouraged her to go to university. My mother says, 'He always has his hat on in photos. Dreadfully self-conscious about going bald so young.'

And then her sister's family had lived in Kenya in the early 1960s, just before independence. One of my cousins was born there, and my mother had been out to visit, as had my grandmother Stella, widowed by then. I have my grandmother's diary of her trip, sailing from Rotterdam on 28 January 1961 on the Deutsche-Africa Line, through the Mediterranean and Suez, putting in at Djibouti and Aden, and finally docking in Mombasa on 24 February. Once in Nairobi her days were a social whirl of visits to friends on coffee plantations and lunch in hotels. She is unselfconscious in her daily entries, referring to fuzzy-wuzzies, commenting adversely on native hygiene and disorganization. She made a tapestry chair-seat to commemorate her visit: a warthog, a lioness, zebras, giraffes browsing acacia trees, the flamingos of Nakuru, a couple of Kikuyu huts and in the centre a black woman in a blue dress, carrying a load of firewood bigger than herself.

At the end of the travel diary, however, my grandmother becomes reflective:

Impressions

Overworked African women. Europeans not all first class by any means. Indians the main shop-keepers. No Africans in Cathedral choir and

only 1 Deacon – very few Africans at Easter
service. Is it right to try and Europeanise the
Africans? Is our education what is needed?
European children allowed to be very overbearing with the 'boys'. Could there not be a new
title for 'boy'? Glorious flowers and sunshine.
Too many unemployed and physically handi-
capped people reduced to begging. The Africans
have great sense of humour – much giggling goes
on amongst themselves.

I read this with a sick tightness in my abdomen. I don't
think my sister and I were 'overbearing with the "boys"',
but we thought nothing of referring to adult men with
families in those terms. Kimoho and Timona were 'the
houseboys'; Joseph was the 'garden boy'. Live-in staff were
a way of life, although ours was small – no ayah, no driver,
no *askari* with his cap and rifle. And other things – I had
been playing in the garden with a cuckoo clock and left
it there, and later I spotted it in the window of a room in
the servants' quarters. I went furious to my father but
in an uncharacteristically quiet voice he told me to leave it.
'They have so little.' My parents gave Kimoho a radio, and
he was pulled in by the police and charged with stealing it
– how else would he have such a thing? When I was taken
to hospital with earache it was taken for granted that as a
mzungu I would be seen straight away, despite the waiting
room full of Kenyans.

When we arrived in 1972 Kenya had been independent
for less than a decade. That's an eternity when you're five:

it seems like the blink of an eye now. We celebrated the national holidays of Uhuru and Jamhuri, we even called an independent-minded tortoise Jamhuri (*freedom*) because of the way he would bolt for the bushes, but I never stopped to think much about what it all meant.

When the white men first brought their colonial project to Kenya and Tanzania at the end of the nineteenth century, and set eyes on the vast savannahs, the teeming herds of game, they believed they had stumbled on an unfallen paradise, that the East African grasslands had always been like this. In fact what they were looking at was the aftermath of a rinderpest epidemic. The disease first hit in the 1880s and laid waste the cattle, sheep and goats of the indigenous herding peoples, leading to a devastating famine exacerbated by smallpox. Wild animals died too, in vast numbers, but their populations recovered faster than the human. The rinderpest outbreak had itself been a colonial by-product, first brought in with imported cattle from an eastern port in Egypt or India. Two-thirds of the Tanzanian Maasai people died, a far worse death toll than the Black Death of the European Middle Ages. But that illusory sense of a pristine, unpeopled Eden went on to fuel so much of what followed.

The Kenya–Tanzania border, drawn up in the aftermath of the famine, cuts the lands of the nomadic Maasai in half. The treaty which created it was agreed by British and German diplomats, and the boundary runs in a dead straight line except for a little kink in the middle. It's said that the Kaiser was upset at the prospect of Queen Victoria having two equatorial snow-capped mountains, Mounts

Kenya and Kilimanjaro, and he none, so the cartographers made the line bend slightly to accommodate his whim. The needs of the Maasai didn't enter the discussion. Thinking about this, the sick clench in my abdomen begins to relax, just a little. At least my grandmother *saw* the people in the landscape, putting that sturdy, smiling Kikuyu woman at the centre of her tapestry vision.

We have such a powerful need to believe that our real home is elsewhere, whether we look ahead to heaven or an island hermitage, or back to an earthly paradise from which we have been expelled. Kenya remains mine, not the real crowded chaotic nation of 2016, or even the more stable Kenya of the 1970s, but a never-never land of childhood, of outrageous racial privilege which I barely noticed, of infinite possibility and adventure. Perhaps the sense of a personal lost paradise has got something to do with leaving at adolescence, that door forever barred. I can never recapture that grotesque innocence, and mostly I don't want to.

My mother's equivalent lost world was the Isle of Wight, and more specifically Osborne House, the Italianate palazzo in East Cowes which Prince Albert had helped to design as a summer retreat for the royal family. She was told to give that bunch of flowers to Princess Beatrice because my great-grandfather, Commandant of the Royal Army Medical College and Honorary Surgeon to the King, oversaw the home for convalescent officers which Osborne had become after Queen Victoria's death. Even after he retired, my mother and her sister Barbara had the run of the terraces and the beaches, in what they remembered as the endless summers of the 1930s. Then war broke out, and she turned thirteen, and her grandfather died; and childhood was over. I have a little balloon-backed chair, carved with flowers, upholstered in now-very-tatty green velvet. 'It came from Osborne,' my mother said when she asked me if I'd like it. 'Queen Victoria gave it to your great-grandfather.'

Morning swim: wrap-around sunshine, sea like oiled silk. Lots of seals, so close and the air and water so still that I could hear them snort when they broke the surface. Little auk, pomerine skua, as well as the usual avian dramatis personae. Evening swim – grey and windy, water felt cold going in but soon warmed up – I stayed in for a good half-hour. Ebbing tide and wind combining for a strong westerly pull and quite choppy – great fun. One very curious little seal swimming round in circles.

The Orkney Polar Bear Club has been on the go for around five years now, and according to Facebook we have just over two hundred members (though many of these are scattered across the planet). We have English Bears and Scots, Norwegian, Belgian, Polish, South African. Some people come regularly to Orkney and swim with us while they're here. Others have never yet been, but it's on their wish list. Messages pop up on Facebook from visitors, asking for advice, hoping for company. But the core group includes Helen and Barbara; Peter the GP, sea-kayaker and marathon-runner; Anne from Norfolk who calls herself a grumpy old dyke, a care-worker and tour-guide who knows more about the natural world than almost anyone I've ever met, whose sole concession to cold water is to wear two woolly hats rather than just one; Donna, a dedicated rock-climber from Aberdeenshire; Yvonne, the poet who has spent this summer swimming north of the Arctic Circle to raise money for an autism charity. Becky, Orkney-born to English parents, bright-eyed and insightful, researching the relationships between the incomers who work in renewable energy and the local community, with their much richer knowledge of the local forces of wind and water.

Everyone's welcome.

I'm finding it hard writing about my fellow Bears. If I did this in an academic context I would have to draw up a research framework with a robust ethics component, get it approved by the relevant university committees, design consent forms covering every eventuality, make sure my subjects approve my use of their data, their voices, their experience. As a novelist I can redesign and contort my characters into the shapes I need (though they're always welcome to fight back). This is different: these people are real. *Hey*, I post on the Facebook page, *I'm writing about you, just a little – do you mind?* But nobody seems to. So I'm allowed to say how beautiful I think Helen is with her dark eyes and hair; and how much I value Yvonne's infectious smile, and Lotty's sense of adventure; and that I think Anne should wear sparkly silver eyeshadow more often.

It's worth noting that we have very few Orcadians among the Polar Bears. Not none, but few.

Something here, something I'm groping after, about indigenous and incomer attitudes to the sea.

There's an analogy with the old croft houses. They are perfect little structures, a central doorway dividing two rooms, one for receiving visitors, the other more private. Each room has a window and a chimney, so the result is an eye-sweet symmetry, with an apparently instinctive ratio governing the size of the window relative to the height and thickness of the wall. Roof tiles chipped from sandstone march in a steady progression from large ones at the eaves to small ones up by the load-bearing ridgepole. Local stone and home-grown craftsmanship.

But if you'd grown up in one of those houses, unrestored, poky, the flagstones set directly into the dirt, rooms chilly within their metre-thick walls, those flags exuding moisture when pressure changes before a gale, the wooden furniture rotting from the feet up where it stands on the damp stone, you'd understand the allure of a snugly insulated and double-glazed little breeze-block box. It's we incomers who look at modern Orkney houses – often cheek-by-jowl with the picturesque ruin of a croft, in accordance with the council's one-for-one replacement policy – only to lament their ugliness. It's we who buy the old croft houses to do them up, realizing too late that once you've lined them with plasterboard you've made small rooms into tiny ones; if you leave the stone walls unlined there's nowhere to hide the pipes or the wiring; that the windows are like tunnels; that a long narrow house means no room for a corridor, so the rooms have to lead one into the other.

Traditional Orkney architecture, obeying the laws of the local feng shui, the wind-water, turns its face away from the sea. The low cottages tuck themselves into what shelter they can find, and the deep-set windows in those thick stone walls look inland, and often eastward, away from the prevailing Atlantic westerlies. Until very recently, with the advent of heavy-duty insulation and double-glazing, it was only the lairds, like Balfour and Traill Burroughs, and other incomers who hadn't yet learned what the weather can chuck at you, who built houses that took advantage of the view. If you go back five thousand years you find the people of Neolithic Skara Brae constructing a network of windowless houses connected by tunnels like a rabbit warren, within a rubbish dump that was already old. The Iron Age brochs were windowless, as were the Pictish houses, which were planned like marigolds: circular rooms, like petals, surrounding a central hearth-space. The outside world was to be endured, not enjoyed.

Even now the shiny new leisure centre in Kirkwall has something of this philosophy about it: the pool with its water-spouts and currents, heated and brightly lit, hides behind a vast wall of rainbow-striped glass – a chlorinated, over-heated parody of the cold sunshine cut with horizontal showers outside, and the squally waters of Kirkwall Bay only a few hundred yards away. The leisure complex is the Pickaquoy Centre, named for the field in which it was built. *Quoy*, as we have seen, is a common Orkney place-name element, and *Picka* probably invokes the Picts.

The term *picty-hoose* was commonly used to refer to anything old – even the famous Neolithic village on the Bay of Skaill was first published, in 1931, as *Skara Brae: A Pictish Village in Orkney* – and so it seems probable somewhere underneath the fantasy palace of the sports, entertainment and cinema complex there is an ancient stone building, Neolithic, maybe, or Iron Age, or even really Pictish, which also turned its face away from the sea.

I could stay here for the rest of my life, but I will never be Orcadian, nor will my daughter, who was four-teen months old when we moved here from York. *Seven generations in the kirkyard*: that's what they say you need before you're accepted. The first time I met my dear and much-missed Orcadian friend Anne Brundle, at a conference in England, she told me she worked at Tankerness House Museum in Kirkwall. I asked her if she had always lived in Orkney. She paused, and looked at me twinkling and slightly sideways, before saying, 'We moved from the East Mainland to the West in the middle of the sixteenth century, but we've been where we are ever since.' If you put together two Orcadians who haven't previously met the real shock will come if they can't find the family connection. One of my friends reckons he must have around three hundred first and second cousins in Orkney.

Few people break into those inner circles. When I first moved here and went along to parent-and-toddler groups no one truly local ever made conversation with me. The Orkney-born people to whom I found myself drawn were invariably those whose parents were incomers, lured here for much the same reasons as me but a generation earlier. The other mothers were perfectly friendly, but they were all much younger and had been to school together; and if they weren't blood-kin they were acquainted in detail with each other's extended families. It was the same among the children: incomers gravitated to incomers, Orcadians to Orcadians, even if they were barely old enough to talk.

The same interconnectedness and exclusivity was manifest at the swimming pool in Stromness, where I went three times a week before I abandoned the pool for sea-swimming: the elderly ladies bellowing the most intimate details of confinements, operations, family scandals and legal disputes from behind the closed cubicle doors. People are known by their nicknames, and embedded in complex pedigrees. Suddenly the face-to-face world of the Icelandic family sagas, which I have been studying and teaching for decades, makes sense. Now I see why the saga-writers expended pints of their precious oak-gall ink on those endless details of genealogy and legal niceties, so hard for the modern reader (the outsider, the ferry-louper) to plough through: this is the latticework that supports a functioning insular culture and society.

Our first house, in Harray, was as far from the sea as you get in Orkney, around six miles in most directions, although even so on a still night you could go outside and hear the Atlantic surf beating at the foot of the Yesnaby cliffs, and after a westerly the windows were coated with salt crystals. Harray is the only Orkney parish with no coastline, and there are jokes about the Harraymen and their inability to recognize crabs. The house had been converted from a stable by an Orcadian who had spent his working life in Australia and retired home with his adult son. We found enormous horseshoes in the garden, suggesting that the heavy Clydesdales who drew the plough had lived in our sitting room. Down the road, in the Corrigall Farm Museum, the stalls had been restored with the massive planks rescued from our house, dry dung still stuck to their boards.

The man who had converted our house was buried in St Michael's kirkyard up the hill, and his son had inherited a few years before we moved to Orkney. There had been an old farmhouse, we learned, its crowstepped gables a local landmark. But the son had torn it down and sold the stone and slates. People shook their heads when they learned where we lived. 'He did it,' one neighbour told us, 'to please *her*.'

Her?

'The internet bride from Gateshead.'

Slowly the story began to take shape. The son had been brought up in Australia; he'd never liked Orkney. He'd inherited the conversion and the ruin and eighty acres, but he sold what he could, bit by bit, to fund his wife's aspirations. The house we bought had only an acre and a half of land left. She was responsible for the enormous conservatory, tacked precariously on to the front of the house and lacking proper foundations, the showy, rickety spiral staircase up to the attic, and the whirlpool bath whose jets were a fertile ground for mould. They'd stayed a step ahead of the bailiffs for a few years, and then fled, leaving debts all over Orkney.

Intriguing as this was, it didn't quite explain the raised eyebrows, the twitching mouths that accompanied the news of where we lived. Finally, a neighbour put me in the picture. The son and his wife had had a reputation for hosting swingers' parties, notorious, raucous, booze-fuelled evenings. I hired a carpet cleaner and tried yet again to get the stubborn stains out of the wall-to-wall beige. Not long after that we moved over the hill to the house overlooking Eynhallow Sound. Its former owner was the fragile widow of a civil engineer.

I could write my life in houses. In Kenya they were stone-built, French-windowed, thick-walled against the heat, with parquet floors which Timona polished gliding up and down in sheepskin-soled bootees. The first house in Islington, where my parents lived when I was born, was like a tall thin birdcage, a couple of rooms off each landing, like little perches. The house my parents bought on retirement, in which they both died, was a rambling detached cottage, an oddity in central London. After my mother's death it declined in tandem with my father, window-panes rotting, new leaks in the roof, the brambles advancing steadily on the shrinking patch of lawn, my mother's flowerbeds choked with clover and couch grass.

When I met my future husband, I had a house that suited me perfectly. A late-Victorian worker's cottage in York, near the river, end of terrace, five rooms (sitting room, kitchen, bathroom, bedroom, study). It was a little too close to the river: the first winter I was there, in 2000, the Ouse flooded worse than it had since records began in the 1650s, and my ground floor filled with a foot of filthy water. But we got it cleaned up, and I held a legendary *Après le déluge* party; dried-out and redecorated, it was my functional little machine for living.

But it was too small for two writers.

The first night I met the man I was to marry, at that party in March 2003, he talked about his work a lot. His love of particular poets, his book on a twentieth-century sculptor, and this plan he had for doing a doctorate. He wasn't sure where to go: Oxford was a possibility. I was flattered by the interest shown in me by this attractive man seven years my junior.

My own doctorate had been examined only three years earlier: it was all fresh in my memory – the biggest intellectual adventure of my life to date, and I was flushed with vicarious excitement on his behalf. Finishing my thesis had coincided with my mother's terminal diagnosis, and from then until her death in March 2002 my academic career had largely been on hold. I had spent the year between her death and meeting my husband working furiously to turn the thesis into my book on death in Anglo-Saxon England – gutting my research, jettisoning almost all of it in favour of exciting new material, in the library every hour it was open. Writing about death and bereavement a thousand years ago channelled some of my own furious grief. My husband came along just in time to offer a critical commentary on the penultimate draft, do sterling work on the index, celebrate its submission with me, and then its publication in 2004. In retrospect it seems significant that he didn't know me while I was sweating blood over the writing of the book. He didn't witness the pain and the struggle, just the achievement.

He started work on his doctoral thesis in the same month that we came to Orkney for the first time. I thought then – and I still believe – that he really felt the lure of the islands, that he wasn't just suppressing his own wishes to please me. His thesis and my own writing, and the houses we lived in, are all mixed up together for me, the laboratory spaces in which we conducted our experiments in creativity and cohabitation.

The house I lived in when we met being too small for all our books, we jumped at the chance to move to the house across the street: seven rooms (sitting room, dining room, kitchen, utility room, two bedrooms, bathroom). My husband was doing his thesis, so he had the second bedroom as a study. I camped out in the dining room. I wrote my first novel.

We moved to Orkney in 2008. My husband was still working on his thesis: he had the chilly attic as a study. I camped out in the sitting room. I wrote my second novel. Time slowed. The island became the world.

Moving to the islands suited me, but I wonder now if I were being selfish, over-writing his desires and ambitions with mine. Even in the age of superfast broadband, opportunities are limited on an island. Travel is time-consuming and expensive: no budget airlines fly into tiny Grimsetter and airfares are eye-watering. There's the long-haul ferry, which leaves Kirkwall around midnight and gets you into Aberdeen at six in the morning. Or the shorter ferry journey over to Caithness, and then a weary drive, or an even wearier train journey – four hours chugging south and you're still only in Inverness. Online virtual communities are still no real substitute for meeting colleagues face to face, the casual connections and accidental conversations that arise at seminars and conferences and workshops, the chance meetings that change your life.

Two different flashpoints here – the closing down of those familiar networks; and the challenge of identifying what new opportunities an island offers. Moving to such an intricately woven community as Orkney has made me hyper-aware of dislocation and intrusion. It's hard to find a role. You pick up single threads of complex stories, miss most of what people are saying, know someone by their name but not the all-important nickname. *You must know Davey; he's married to Fiona, Inga's cousin in Stromness – you taught one of Inga's daughters...* It takes commitment and a particular kind of personality to become a strand in this web.

Seven generations in the kirkyard... but if you were to relocate to Orkney now even those seven generations might not be enough to sea-change your twenty-third-century descendants into natives rather than incomers, producers rather than consumers of Orcadian-ness. The logistics of our lives have changed too much. Orcadian identity was hard-forged out of centuries of seasonal necessity and marginal survival, not the luxury of Chilean strawberries and Kenyan green beans available in the Kirkwall supermarkets year-round. You can't become an Orcadian by treating the place as a bolthole from the stresses of the world. Robert Rendall has stern words for those of us who use the shore for mere recreation rather than as a place of work, a source of food or fuel or scientific knowledge: 'Only those can know it intimately who *do* something on it, harvest tangles, catch fish, gather whelks, study nature, or even comb the beach for driftwood...'

Even seven generations of people interacting with Orkney in the way that I do would hardly be enough to produce the knowledge Rendall describes in his portrait of an old fisherman making his way through the rocks of the Birsay foreshore to the water's edge: he 'keeps to a predetermined route – one, doubtless, taken by his father before him, and by untold generations of Birsay fishermen... an invisible contour line... particular crevices that criss-cross the uncertain surface'. On their way home in the dusk, 'familiar reefs are now blurred and indistinct, and the value of the traditional route at once becomes apparent'. This criss-crossing traditional intimacy – so evident in the toddler group and the swimming-pool changing room – is powerful enough on Mainland, with its fifteen thousand people. The smaller islands, with populations between two hundred and five hundred – Eday, Rousay, Westray, Hoy, Stronsay, Sanday – have even more hothouse environments. Smaller still are Wyre, Egilsay, Flotta. Mainland Orcadians have low expectations of the indigenous inhabitants of the outer isles: any report of wrongdoing or eccentricity is met with a nod and a sucking of teeth and an *Isles folk, ken...*

As though Mainland were not itself an island.

But sometimes the tiniest islands bounce back in

unexpected ways. Since 1999 minute Papa Stronsay has been owned by a community of Catholic monks, who have built their profoundly traditionalist haven on a once-abandoned island that was almost certainly an ecclesiastical site before the Vikings ever arrived. Their black-clad figures have become a familiar sight, shopping for groceries in Kirkwall or shuffling through security at Grimsetter Airport, having divested themselves of cingulum, scapular and massive wooden-beaded rosary. In an era of religious decline, Golgotha monastery is thriving: the monks are young; they have just founded their first daughter house. Their website quotes St Columba's words to the Pictish king in the late sixth century:

> Some of our brethren have lately set sail, and are anxious to discover a desert in the pathless sea; should they happen, after many wanderings, to come to the Orkney islands, do thou carefully instruct this chief, whose hostages are in thy hand, that no evil befall them within his dominions.

St Magnus would be proud of them, Columba even prouder.

When I was in the sea at 5.30 the tide was right out. A raft of dunters with many ducklings was pottering in among the weed, and I went nosing close, pretending to be a seal. They didn't mind at all.

Back in my study now – glorious sun and stiff breeze – watching the turning tide come fluttering in over the expanse of sand. There are fifteen ravens sunning themselves on the Flaws byre roof, and Cally Bonkers-Cat is sitting in the window watching their every move.

Orkney is a scatter of islands across a thousand square kilometres of sea. The exact number depends on your definition of island. But it's something like seventy, of which about twenty are inhabited. Not all the islands in the archipelago are part of Orkney. Stroma, just south of Swona in the Pentland Firth, belongs to Caithness. Fair Isle, just visible from North Ronaldsay, is part of Shetland. But Sule Skerry and Sule Stack, the gannet rocks far to the west, are Orcadian.

I have seen Sule Skerry just once, and that was from a place where it should have been impossible. On a crystalline day last September I was walking along the shore by the Point of Ness on the edge of Stromness. I had a visitor with me, my Swiss friend Anouk, another Pictish-obsessive. She had never heard of the ballad 'The Great Selkie of Sule Skerry', and I was telling her the story as we strolled past the ruins of wartime searchlight emplacements and gun batteries, past the seals hauled out on the inshore Skerry of Ness, looking out west through the gateway of Hoy Sound and into the Atlantic. At the same moment we both spotted a grey motionless lump, hovering on the horizon, hazy, best seen with peripheral vision, but undoubtedly there. We looked at maps later, worked out angles, Googled images of the skerry, and were left in no doubt of what we had seen although Sule Skerry is sixty kilometres from Orkney, and supposedly only visible from the top of the Hoy hills.

Some strange refraction, a lucky trick of the light, allowing the impossible.

Anouk teaches me wonderful French words for the sounds of the sea. *Clapotis*: the slap and lap of the water around and beneath the jetty. *Ressac*: the surf, and she tells me she would also use this word to describe the sound of water draining back after a wave has broken on a shingle beach. Matthew Arnold's 'melancholy, long, withdrawing roar'. In English, the technical jargon of hydrodynamics has its clapotic wave, one that undulates regularly without breaking but with great erosive power. But 'clapotic' is not the same as *clapotis*: with the shift of the stress and the hard velar [k] to close it the word loses its mournful, onomatopoeic charm.

The ballad of the Great Selkie tells of a mother singing to the baby at her breast when a 'grim guest' enters, and speaks to her of past, present, and future. He identifies himself as the child's father.

> *'I am a man upon the land,*
> *I am a selkie in the sea,*
> *And when I'm far from every strand,*
> *My home it is in Sule Skerry.'*

And he's a good father, if an absent one; he brings money for his son's maintenance and takes an interest in his care.

In Orkney folklore, young women are constantly at risk from the charms of visitors from the sea, whether selkie or Fin-man. In another story, a widower from the island of Sanday took his boat across to Eday to cut peats, there being none on sandy Sanday. It was a wild night, and he couldn't get home to his daughter. She heard a knock on the door and found a handsome young man standing there, dripping wet. *You wouldn't leave me out here on a night like this.* In the end, she felt sorry for him, and opened the door wide.

Even on the way to her wedding, according to island lore, a nubile woman needs protection against supernatural abductors. At the tail end of the traditional Orkney wedding procession two people swept away the bride's footprints with heather brooms so that no supernatural rapist could track her spoor and snatch her away at the last moment.

David Balfour's tenants on Eynhallow, evicted for their own good in 1851, were not the first population to be forced off the island. The same thing had happened to the Fin-folk, long ago. In Shetland lore the Fin-folk are connected to the Finnish Saami, but in Orkney they are clearly non-human, with trailing fins that they can use to disguise themselves. Their homelands are either islands like Eynhallow, floating or invisible, or a palace beneath the sea.

A young woman – *the prettiest girl in Evie* – was stolen from the Sands of Evie by a Fin-man, when her husband, the farmer from Thorodale, took his eye off her for a moment. They were in the liminal zone, between high- and low-tide lines among the tang, gathering limpets for bait, moving quietly – you can only lift a limpet from its rock if it doesn't know you're coming. He stopped to fasten his shoe, and when he turned round she was already in the Fin-man's boat. It vanished as he watched.

There was no low green bump visible between Costa and Westness in those days. The island still belonged to the Fin-folk, and human eyes couldn't perceive it.

So the husband went to the witch over on Hoy, and she gave him a charm and told him what to do. Just before dawn in high summer he rowed out into the sound with his three sons, and there before them was an island where no island had been before. They rowed right at it, beating off a school of vicious whales, and an assault by seductive mermaids. They landed, and defeated a tusked monster and a giant, and then they scattered the salt all round the perimeter of the island, and the Evie farmer got his wife back. After that Eynhallow was fixed in place, trapped by ritual and conquest, just another island.

Woman and island are both contested space in this story, fertile and desirable, capable of vanishing and reappearing, best under masculine control. The farmer's wife gets in trouble when she strays too near the sea. The farmer takes her back, and stakes his claim to the newfound land of Eynhallow in revenge, making the beach safe again.

The Fin-man in this story is a rapist, a kidnapper, like the men who steal selkie-women's skins; but the stories of women who take selkie lovers are more nuanced. There are various theories of selkie origins: that they are the souls of dead sailors, or, more generally, the souls of the drowned. Or the drowned go to join the true selkies, as in the tale of the man who had heard that you could get yourself a wife by stealing a selkie's coat of fur when she takes it off to dance on the beach in human form, but when he did he found that the distraught naked woman scouring the beach for the lost sealskin was no nubile girl but his own mother, who had drowned a couple of years earlier. He still made her haggle to get the skin back, and she ended up promising her son that if he were to come to the beach on the following night she would point him to the coat belonging to the selkie-king's daughter.

There's no hint that this selkie-princess is also a drowned soul: indeed, she not only comes willingly to live on land, following the man who has stolen her fur, she also converts to Christianity. When she is dying, she asks her husband to take her down to the shore and leave her there till dawn. If her body is still there at sunrise, it is a sign that she is truly a Christian, and he can bury her in the kirkyard. But if her body has vanished then the selkie-folk have reclaimed her. (In the version Tom Muir told me, the husband spends the night in his boat, listening to the selkies wailing. When dawn breaks, he finds his wife cold and dead on the strand, and takes her for Christian burial. But I am at liberty to imagine other endings, ones in which she regains her selkie self.)

Another origin myth for the selkies is that they are the chary angels who declined to take sides when the devil declared war on God. Lucifer and his rebels fell to perdition, but those angels who sat on the fence were also jettisoned from heaven, though still too good for hell. The neutral angels who tumbled on to the land turn into the fairies, the *trowies*; those who splashed down in the sea become the selkie-folk. I love this idea: that the selkies are like me, incapable of the kind of blind faith that God requires; looking at both sides of the question, wary of commitment, endlessly dithering about the intricacies of right and wrong. Until it's too late, and they're kicked out of heaven. But not damned – I hang on to that, as well.

Angels are God's messengers, travellers between the material and the ethereal realms. In Cuthbert's boyhood vision of angels, he saw them taking a dead man's soul to heaven. The selkies as fallen, morally confused angels move into this mythic and psychic space, journeying between the daylit surface and the deep sea, escorting the bodies and souls of the drowned, like a marine version of Hermes Psychopompos, leader of souls, who took the dead of the classical world to the realm of Hades. There's a black-and-white mosaic in the pre-Christian cemetery site under the Vatican showing Hermes leading the chariot in which Hades is kidnapping Persephone. The myth has moved, in this artist's vision, from specific narrative to archetype. Persephone represents every soul snatched by Death, jour-neying to the land of the dark, in need of a wise and kindly escort. The role of the soul-leader, the psychopomp, is not to judge the souls he guides, but simply to ease their passage. Jung saw Hermes as the guide who takes us between the conscious and unconscious states, between waking and the world of dreams. Perhaps the selkies can do that, too.

Fallen-yet-not-evil angels or drowned humans: both selkie origin myths offer ways of thinking about different kinds of being, not quite human, not quite animal. Creatures of land and sea. They're not hybrids in the way that mermaids are: the selkie looks either wholly animal or wholly human, but her soul is something else again. It's as though the first storytellers to draw from the well of selkie-tales knew of all the ways in which seal biology adapts seamlessly between life on shore and in the water. Seals sleep in both media; when on land they sleep in the way that a land animal does, with the whole brain asleep. But when they doze in the sea, rocking nose up in the shallows, they sleep in the way that cetaceans do, with only one half of the brain switching off at a time.

Neither the grey nor the common seal is a fully protected species, although it is illegal to kill them in their breeding seasons, and they are not to be poisoned or shot with big guns. But this doesn't stop the fishermen from putting powerful acoustic devices in the water – known as seal scrammers, but they affect cetaceans as well – or from shooting them with other weapons: the law allows for the killing of seals if they are perceived as a threat to livelihood, and many are shot every year – around fifteen hundred between 2011 and 2015, a third of which were pregnant. So-called 'rogue seals' damage the nets at the salmon farms, and they take the bait out of lobster-creels. Although they are no longer officially culled, the debate has not gone away.

Rummaging in the archives I find a 1981 leaflet protesting the culling of grey seal pups in Orkney. It pointed out the inadequacy of scientific research into their feeding patterns, their social structures and population numbers, concluding, 'Seals are elusive, impossible to follow, and live in another medium.' A found poem, this eloquent sentence, a haiku-like, gnomic statement which reminds me of the Anglo-Saxon wisdom lyrics, with their terse encapsulations of the essence of things:

> *Sweord sceal on bearme,*
> *drihtlic isern.   Draca sceal on hlæwe,*
> *frod, frætwum wlanc.   Fisc sceal on wætere*
> *cynren cennan.   Cyning sceal on healle*
> *beagas dælan.   Bera sceal on hæðe,*
> *eald and egesfull.*

> *A sword must lie across the lap,/Noble iron. A dragon in its mound,/Wise, proud of treasure. A fish in the water,/spawning its kin./A king in the hall,/sharing out rings. A bear on the heath,/Old and terrible.*

I want to add:
'A seal must dwell in the sea,/Elusive, not of our world.'

In the ballad of the Great Selkie, the grey seal is a soothsayer as well as a shape-shifter. He foretells the future for himself, his lover and their child: she will find a human mate, and disaster will follow.

> *An' thoo will get a gunner good,*
> *An' a gey good gunner it will be,*
> *An' he'll gae oot on a May mornin'*
> *An' shoot the son an' the grey selkie.*

Is it murder, to kill the selkies in their seal form?

I went for a run up the hill at sunrise – hares and pheasants and geese and all the Northern Isles spread out in hazy light – Rousay and Eynhallow and Gairsay and Wyre and Eday – and shimmery silvery sea. Primroses by the stream all the way to the top, and the first bluebell. Blessings were counted. Big time. Then to the sea. No seals, but a lone swallow doing a victory roll just above the surf, and looking west to Eynhallow I could see the breakers of the rosts sending up spray like plumes of smoke.

In Kenya I become a water-baby. Sunday afternoons go by in a golden haze beside the pool at the Nairobi Club, that post-colonial bastion of a very particular privilege: *Ladies are not allowed in the downstairs bar until after sunset, and not allowed in the billiards room at all.* Superb starlings peck at the remains of our bar-snacks, their brilliant livery of blue and orange gleaming in equatorial sun filtered by acacias. School holidays are often spent at the coast, borrowing a friend's house or renting self-catering cottages, the endless sands fringed with palm and casuarina, the little pale pink ghost crabs scuttling over the ebb at dawn and dusk. The Mombasa Club has a pool filled with seawater, white-walled and built out into the sea, overshadowed by the square grey bulk of Fort Jesus, raised by the colonizing Portuguese at the end of the sixteenth century. My parents were life members of both clubs – their frayed and dog-eared membership cards are in those box-file ossuaries.

We're often at the coast for Christmas; we travel down by sleeper train: dark wood, white linen tablecloths, heavy monogrammed cutlery. You settle down in the cool thin air of Nairobi, over a mile above sea level; awaken in the steam and sweat of the coastal plain. For Christmas Day itself we'll go to one of the big tourist hotels on Diani Beach for the pool and the bar and the cold buffet. The hotel decorates its hot, shadowed, open spaces with the trimmings of Northern Europe: fir trees and lanterns and cut-out snowflakes. Father Christmas doles out presents at the poolside, he is black, with tiny swimming trunks and a huge cotton-wool beard.

Above all, there is Naivasha.

A couple of hours' drive north-west from Nairobi, winding down from the heights into the Rift Valley. *Nai'posha*, rough waters, in Maa: a volcano-fringed lake, trimmed with the white skeletons of bleached trees that have drowned in the periodic rise and fall of the lake level. Fish eagles sit in their branches and the water resonates with their harsh cries. The edge of the lake is ringed with the long stems and green fans of papyrus. We walk barefoot along the sun-warmed boards of the jetty. In the shallows to either side orange crayfish rattle their claws at each other. Further out, on soggy banks of vegetation, the brown bulks of coypu heave out and splash back in. The water smells wonderful, dark, clean and yet with a faint whiff of decay. Our little open outboard motorboat is moored towards the end of the jetty, and we clamber in, heaving the picnic cold bag after us. It's 1976.

Crayfish and coypu are both invasive species, as is the

tilapia for which my parents will fish while my sister and I swim. The coypu have escaped from a fur farm; the tilapia were introduced intentionally. The crayfish are voracious predators, recent arrivals bred for export but already well established. They burrow into the lake edge, causing erosion.

Our little boat chugs along the fringes of the lake. In the distance we can see the curve of Crescent Island (which is – confusingly to a literal-minded nine-year-old – a peninsula), and beyond it the asymmetrical peak of Longonot. The beaches are black, made of pumice, scattered with obsidian.

Naivasha in the 1970s was already an artificial environment: how much more so now. The lake shore is packed with flower and vegetable farms, supplying the supermarkets of Europe, and the green fields and red earth I remember are now covered with polytunnels. A client supermarket in the UK will email a Kenyan grower daily, with instructions about product and quantity depending on the previous day's volume of sales. In Kirkwall's big Tesco I can buy a packet of green beans picked on the shores of Naivasha only two days earlier. The lake is shrinking, growing over-rich with nutrients from agricultural run-off, matted with water hyacinth (yet another invasive species).

But back in 1976 we can skirt the edge, fringed with long-lashed groves of papyrus, watching hippo and long-tailed cormorants and cattle egrets, before turning the bows towards Longonot, heading for the open water in the middle of the lake. Samosas, and sausage rolls dipped in tomato ketchup, small sour apples, and Cadbury's Fruit and Nut chocolate which is already melting even before the silver paper is peeled away.

The water is cool and black. I have no idea how deep it is. I think of the hippos we have just been watching as they lounged in the shallows, their huge tusks and bloated pinky-brown backs, and I imagine them swimming out into the centre, rising from the blackness below me, jaws agape. 'The water's much too deep,' my father says. 'There are no hippos here.' I tread water, stretch a foot as far down as I can, pointed like a ballerina's, sink myself into the abyss. Nothing, no slimy back, no matter how I reach, and I believe him, imagining the lake to be bottomless, though I know now that Naivasha has varied wildly in depth over the last sixty years, as those skeletal trees attest: as deep as six metres, as shallow as two. Its waters are siphoned off for agriculture: there are only two freshwater lakes in Kenya, and Naivasha's rough waters are at a premium.

When I eat that green bean in Evie, I am taking in nutrients from Naivasha. I proactively seek out Kenyan-grown vegetables in Orkney's supermarkets despite the air-miles quandary, their shocking carbon footprint, because my adult self knows how dependent the Rift Valley economy is on the foreign currency this industry brings in, knowing also that the flower- and vegetable-growers earn good money by local standards, though still only about half what the aid agencies estimate is necessary to meet a family's needs. And I also know that most of the hard labour that has gone into growing my bean is female. Single parents, AIDS widows and grandmothers make up the bulk of the work force. But these are the rational, sunlit arguments: what I am really seeking is a much deeper reconnection with the child I was, craving the same intensity of experience, that ability to exist utterly in the moment. Like and unlike Persephone with her pomegranate seeds, I yearn for the enchanted food that means you can stay for ever.

I haven't been back to Kenya for decades, but it is written in me, not just in my memories but in the elements of which I am composed. I run my tongue speculatively around the inside of my mouth, trying to remember long-forgotten flavours I knew in my childhood, counting my teeth, testing as always the rough edge where one of my incisors is chipped, the gap where a wisdom tooth is gone.

Nairobi (*cold water*) and Naivasha are both very high above sea level, part of Kenya's volatile uplands, the land mass which is tearing itself apart along the Rift Valley. From the air you can almost see the perforations. The earthquakes that set our pendant lights swaying, rattle the ornaments on the mantle; volcanoes; lakes like Nakuru, Natron, Turkana, naturally poisoned with chemicals. The water from our kitchen tap in Kiambere Road, the local milk, the maize meal which makes the greasy *posho* and *ugali* dumplings given to us for lunch at school: all these will have left their isotopic analysis in my teeth. The third molar, the M3, is the last crown to form, and analysis of my surviving M3 strontium isotopes would give a very distinctive profile, pointing to an igneous geology, the trachyte tuffs, the layer upon layer of pyroclastic flow that makes up this fertile soil. Nairobi sits on the edge of a mass of phonolite, or chinkstone, named for its metallic sound when struck. The visible landscape is less than fifteen million years old.

The information from my M3's strontium profile could be cross-correlated with that derived from carbon and nitrogen, hinting at a change in diet. I don't remember minding that we had left London, the big Victorian primary school just around the corner, friends, the familiar tall, thin house. But that tomato ketchup – *Zesto* – it tasted wrong. Too musky. I cared about that. And the milk – it had a sour, smoky edge, and came in green-and-white tetrahedrons, not foil-topped glass bottles. Disturbing, and yet exciting.

Finally, the oxygen isotopes in my tooth would point to formative years spent somewhere warmer, drier. The osteologist who has the few kilos of my dry bones laid out on her table, shaving and filing my teeth for the secrets they contain – she might not be able to point to Kiambere Road, on the way out to Langata. But she could certainly say, *Not from Orkney. Not from anywhere near Orkney.* This one doesn't have her seven generations in the kirkyard.

A sprinkling of snow this side of the sound, more on the slopes of Rousay. The steady northerly wind driving the water into the bay, equally rough on both sides of the breakwater. A few gulls in the pre-sunrise sky, no birds in the water, no seals. Hands and feet went numb for the first time this winter but I still managed to get my head wet.

The water is chest-deep now, stiffening my nipples, clamping my ribs like iron bands. It's time to launch myself, and I push off into the water with a gasp, in the January dawn and the shifting grey-gold light, using a steady breast-stroke, my head above water. Once past the breakwater the choppiness of the water is more haphazard, more aggressive. But the curving arm of Aikerness still protects me from the full force of Evie's tides. This is a sheltered harbour, a good place for visiting summer yachts to drop anchor, and it has been for a long time.

Of all the peoples who have inhabited this shoreline, it is the Picts that fascinate me most. Orkney is identified with the Vikings, in the popular and the scholarly imagination alike. The souvenir shops of Kirkwall are full of Norse runic souvenirs; Historic Environment Scotland shame-lessly flogs plastic horned helmets; and a quick Google search shows that 'Viking Orkney' gets six times as many results as 'Pictish Orkney'. One has to envy the Norse their brand identity, their bravado, their capacity for playing up to their reputation. Scratched on to the stone walls of the Neolithic chamber tomb of Maeshowe they left runic graffiti bragging of their sexual and military prowess, and their love of treasure:

'... Ingebjork the fair widow...'

'Hakon alone bore treasure from this mound...'

'Arnfithr Matr carved these runes with this axe owned by Gauk Trandilsson in the South land...'

But even here there are surprises, details that undercut the macho swagger.

One of the runic graffiti in Maeshowe claims 'Jerusalem-farers broke into Orkahaugr. Hlíf the jarl's house-keeper, carved.' Orkahaugr is the Norse name for Maeshowe, and Jerusalem-farers are pilgrims to the Holy Land, the centre of the medieval world. We know from *Orkneyinga Saga* that Rognvald Kali went to Jerusalem, leaving in about 1150, returning in 1153. Hlíf is a woman's name; she seems to identify herself with the *jórsalafarar*, the travellers to the Holy City, and she calls herself a *matselja*, housekeeper. I like to think the jarl whose house she kept was my Kali.

As well as a woman's name *hlíf* is also an ordinary noun; in the abstract it means shelter, but it's often used to refer to a shield. *Matselja* is another interesting word: *mat* is food, and *selja* means to share out, but the housekeeper's role extended far beyond that of dinner-lady. It was one of the very few recognized jobs for women, and prestigious: the *matselja* guarded access to the household's stores and its secrets. The *búr*, the larder, was one of the few lockable spaces in the farmstead, and the Icelandic sagas often mention it as a hiding place for outlaws and fugitives. Plenty of job opportunities here for an ambitious and competent woman, working for unmarried men and widowers as well as the wealthy who ran several farms. The indispensable Hlíf could have gone to Jerusalem with Kali, shielding him from hunger and thirst and dirty linen all the way through the North Sea and the Channel and the Mediterranean, keeping him spruce in his flirtation with Ermengarde of Narbonne. Maybe she washed his shirts in the Jordan. And maybe like Kali she too swam in the river, though if she did she might have chosen to go down to the bank before sunrise, while the men were still snoring in the tents, the dawn breeze rustling the reeds and tamarisks that screened her from curious eyes. What did Hlíf the *matselja* think of her bigsy, outgoing, accomplished jarl?

In contrast to the Norse, the Picts are so elusive, despite the best efforts of people like me, historians, art historians and archaeologists. They linger in the long shadow of the broch-builders, whose descendants they almost certainly were; and their way of life was wiped out here by the Viking settlements, though whether in peaceful integration or through bloody genocide we do not know. The traces they leave behind are so finely made, even dainty: tiny painted quartzite pebbles; exquisite bone pins; delicate silver jewellery; houses whose footprint mimics the shape of a flower, with a central hearth and semi-circular, radial rooms. Above all it is their carved stone sculpture, both the enigmatic symbols and the elaborate cross-slabs, that draws me back, appealing both to my intellect and to a hunger for beauty. But they left very little written evidence, no manuscripts, their inscriptions on stone or bone often indecipherable, their language gone. How quiet do we have to be before we can overhear those voices?

Elusive though the Picts are, they lived and died all around me here. At Gurness, on Aikerness, towards which I am now swimming: I can just make out the roof-ridge of the site museum. The great tower of the broch went out of use around the end of the first century AD, and its stone was cannibalized for Pictish houses between the fifth and eighth centuries. Their shamrock-shaped homes were inward-looking, walled with stone and roofed with turf. The people who lived at Gurness were literate, or at least exposed to literacy: someone owned a knife whose bone handle was inscribed in the Irish ogham script. The iron blade has rusted to shapelessness, but the handle is still perfect, gleaming where hands have gripped it and use has rubbed it smooth. The inscription reads 'IN... IT... TEMOMN MATS', but no one knows what that means.

A few miles west along the shore from here, at Buckquoy in Birsay, a spindle whorl turned up. A little stone disc like a flat bagel, with a hole in the centre, designed to give balance and heft to the drop spindle. Around the curve of the disc there's another ogham inscription: 'ENDDACTANIM(f/lb)'. This has been brilliantly interpreted by Katherine Forsyth of the University of Glasgow as Old Irish: 'Benddact anim L'.

A blessing on the soul of L.

Was it L's spindle whorl? And was it an Irish visitor who carved the inscription? It may be Old Irish, but both *blessing* and *soul* are borrowings from Latin. An Irish churchman, visiting the Buckquoy settlement, scratching his benediction on to this very feminine object: it's made of local stone; he didn't bring it with him. I'm saying *him* because men travelled more, but it could conceivably have been a literate woman who incised the blessing. And surely L, the owner of the spindle, was a woman – the lady of the house, plausibly an aristocrat. Could she read? Did she understand Old Irish, or perhaps enough Latin to make sense of the words? I can see her, standing with her clump of wool in one hand, twisting the thread with the other, the spindle whorl twirling, activating the blessing like a Tibetan prayer wheel, spinning...

A shallow wooden box, hollowed from a single block of alderwood and carved with abstract, flowing patterns very like those in the Book of Kells and on Pictish stones, was found in an Evie bog in 1885, when the men from Howe farm were cutting their peats and stacking them to dry over the summer. If I turn my head I can just see the hill above Howe. The primroses would still have been in bloom among the brown clumps of heather in peat-cutting season. Someone drives her tusker into the side of the peat bank, feeling rather than hearing the thud of solidity. The box – no bigger than a child's shoe-box – contained bone-handled tools, and punches, and a lump of pumice, all suitable for working leather. If it was originally intended as a toolbox, it must be one of the most beautiful ever made. The carvings segue between breaking wave and flowering vine and wind-stirred barley, a harmonic geometry that both lures and soothes the gaze. The pumice probably came from the beach, having drifted in from volcanic Iceland. The box was treasured: the lost lid had originally been attached with metal strips, but these had been replaced with leather hinges. How did it get into the bog? It would be a funny thing to lose by accident, especially with its contents intact; and it wasn't in a grave – to the perennial annoyance of archaeologists the Picts, whether pagan or Christian, didn't put objects in their graves. Wood is a rare survival: this little box hints at the marvels we have lost.

Knife and box are housed in Edinburgh now – you have to hunt for the box, it's tucked away in the Early Peoples gallery of the National Museum, in a case so dark that if you didn't know the sides of the box were carved you'd never notice – but the little stone spindle whorl is still in Orkney. I can't help wondering what other secrets lurk in the unexcavated broch mounds along the Evie shoreline, the brown banks of peat on the hill, along the strand, in the seabed below me.

For the first few strokes the cold makes it impossible to breathe, and then the pain eases, the iron bands burst, one after another. I have entered the water to the west of the breakwater, the lee side on this day of south-easterly wind. I swim in exploratory zigzags, knowing that this is still the difficult part, the bit when I have continually to tell myself, *You can get out soon, you only have to stay in for a couple of minutes, honour has already been served.* But that's a consolatory lie, a way of tricking myself into believing that the worst is over. In truth I know full well that, in accordance with my own crazy rules, I cannot leave the water until I have put my head right under. Three times.

And I've got to do it quickly. I can feel the back of my neck getting stiff and cold, and I don't want too much disparity of temperature to build up between my head and the rest of my body. It takes some courage though. I stall, swim in a circle, look around me for surfacing seals, take in the view. The winter sun is rising: a glint of purple-orange alights on Costa, shifts over to Westness, catches Midhowe on the Rousay shore: another broch reused by the Picts long after the tower had tumbled.

Pictish culture is best known in the popular imagination for its system of symbols, incised into stone with exquisite draughtsmanship, profoundly mysterious and much reproduced on modern souvenirs and as tattoos. Some of the symbols are animals, easily recognized; others are angular or curvilinear patterns, given such prosaic descriptors as 'crescent and V-rod' or 'double-disc and Z-rod'. These may be abstracted images of real objects, or simply abstract. The art of the twentieth century gives us concepts which help in understanding the complexity of early medieval visual imagery: Cubism, Surrealism, the conceptual. There's nothing so post-modern as the Middle Ages.

The Pictish symbol repertoire is depicted consistently on stones found along Scotland's eastern seaboard from Shetland to the Firth of Forth; pairs of symbols are often added like labels to already-ancient standing stones. Best guess is that they refer to individuals: commemorating the dead, maybe, or recording a marriage, or a gift of land, or a boundary. They pre-date the conversion to Christianity, but the Christian Picts went on using them.

Fragmentary symbol stones have turned up both at the Broch of Gurness and here on the Sands of Evie, at sites only an easy walk apart, separated by a few hundred yards of dunes. The one from Gurness was found in 1935, and it carries the symbol known as a 'mirror-case', a rectangle topped with a disc, flanked by two decorated rectangles. The symbols are scratched, and comparatively irregular. It's odd to have three symbols: they usually turn up in pairs, and this stone may be broken. Perhaps it's a trial piece. Or it may be an exception: we deduce the rules from what survives but we don't know the rules that were in the minds of the makers of these stones, or where and when they were allowed to break them.

Whatever they called that symbol, it wasn't a mirror-case. That's a modern descriptor. The Picts didn't have such things, even though they did – probably – have mirrors.

The Sands of Evie stone is certainly fragmentary: discovered in 1967, it shows the handle and part of the disc of a mirror. Every time I wander along the fringe of the dunes, looking for coral and cowries and sea-washed china, I keep half an eye out for the rest of the stone. In the catalogue of Pictish symbols this one is an oddity: as we've just seen most are either animal or abstract, but this is very clearly an artefact, literally depicted: an actual mirror, albeit of a kind that was fashionable in Roman Britain, centuries before this stone was made. Mirrors are usually paired with combs in the Picts' visual language, and the mirror–comb combination isn't used alone; it turns up next to, and apparently modifying, other symbol pairs. On the Hilton of Cadboll cross-slab from Easter Ross a small mirror–comb combination is carved next to an image of a woman on horseback, and it has been suggested that if – as seems likely – the symbols refer to individuals by name, the mirror-and-comb mark that name as female, *Lady So-and-So*, a hint that women could own land and claim elite status using the same terminology as men. The idea that the mirror-and-comb are specifically female may sound like modern sexism predicated on our own notions of female vanity, but in the seventh century a pope wrote to the Northumbrian queen, Ethelburga, asking for her support and offering her 'a silver mirror, and a gilded ivory comb' as a gift; and of the Romano-British metal mirrors found in context three-quarters were in female burials.

So one of the individuals laying claim to Evie in life or death may have been a woman (or just possibly a mermaid).

There's a mystery here. The metal Romano-British mirrors that survive look just like the ones carved on the Pictish stones, but none has yet been found in eastern Scotland, and they pre-date the Picts by a couple of centuries. Made of bronze, with decorative handles, one face of the disc is highly ornamented, the other polished smooth. Maybe the image of the mirror on Pictish stones also tells us something about their attitudes to the past, to rare, expensive metal objects, and to the Roman-conquered territories to the south. Why are the mirror and comb the only recognizable artefacts in the symbol repertoire?

Did Tredwell contemplate her beautiful eyes in an heirloom mirror like this before she tore them out?

Mirrors were expensive. Carved stones were expensive. Whether or not the mirror and comb symbols are really associated with women, they depict objects of power. But what might ownership of a mirror have meant in the seventh or eighth century? A mirror's a tool for the perception and construction of the self. We have grown so accustomed to being surrounded by our own reflections, not just in mirrors but in shop windows, inverted in the bowls of silver spoons, on CCTV, self-portraits taken on our phones and disseminated worldwide in seconds. But the early medieval world didn't have a concept of the portrait – the specific rather than the generic likeness – nor did it have mirrors that accurately reflected the detail or the colour of the world around them. If you wanted to know whether your eyes were green or brown, you had to ask someone. When St Paul speaks of perceiving God 'per speculum in aenigmate' – 'through a glass, darkly' – it is this kind of mirror he has in mind. Long before Alice went through the looking glass, mirrors were understood as portals to another world, one that not only reflected but commented on our own. Not just objects that helped with personal grooming, they may also have been used as surfaces to scry in, like a fortune-teller's crystal ball.

No metal mirrors have yet turned up from Pictland, but at Midhowe broch, over there on the Rousay shore, gleaming now in the shifting winter sunlight, the archaeologists found a whalebone handle shaped very like some metal mirror handles, a long triangle with a disc at the bottom, whose best parallel in sculpture is the Sands of Evie stone. Image and object together suggest that riddling mirrors were familiar to the Picts around Eynhallow Sound. There was a whalebone comb found at Midhowe, too: perhaps the same stranded cetacean provided the material to make both objects.

Other Orkney stones have a different range of symbols: crescent and V-rod, eagle, double-disc and Z-rod, Pictish beast. The last is yet another mystery, and perhaps the most beguiling of all, although it is one of the commonest. I've used it to mark off the Facebook posts in this book. A long-snouted creature, apparently floating, drifting like a sleep-walker, benignly smiling, a pigtail or crest flowing down the back of its neck, its tapering legs terminating in little curls, a tail hanging down. The other animals deployed in the symbol system are stylized but realistic, and unambiguous: stag or eagle or snake or bull depicted in a few perfect lines. The very consistency of representation of the Pictish beast suggests it was a widely recognized – and easily recognizable – image. But of what? Even specialists don't know what to make of it: sometimes we call it the kelpie, or the dead dolphin, or the elephant. But it can't be a land animal, not with those legs. That benevolent, otherworldly smile is certainly reminiscent of a dolphin, or an orca, but the long, pointed jaws are nothing like the rounded rostrum of a living cetacean, although dolphin and orca skulls are a close fit for the elongated shape of the head. There's nothing else skeletal about the beast, though. Could the pigtail be intended as an allusion to the spray from a blowhole, or a dorsal fin?

Thinking about what the Pictish beast might be makes me realize how trapped I am by my own historical moment. My perception of the underwater environment is constructed by second-hand information about what seals and cetaceans look like, and how they experience their world. In reality, when I put my head underwater and swim for four, five, six long strokes, all I see is a green-grey-blue world, blurry and full of shadows. If I wear goggles it springs into focus, but the Picts didn't have goggles. When I see an orca with my own eyes, I catch a fleeting glimpse of fin and arching back, but my imagination can supply the rest of the creature from photographs, and the documentaries I watch obsessively on YouTube. The Picts couldn't. They salvaged whalebone from stranded animals, but a dead or dying cetacean on the beach is utterly different from the flashing being in the water.

This raises a whole set of new questions about the relationship between the Picts who lived here and their perception of the waters of Eynhallow Sound. They certainly had boats, and must have been skilled in their use – how else would they get to Orkney, or travel around the wild waters of the archipelago? There is even a reference in one chronicle to a Pictish fleet. But they didn't eat fish, despite that rich resource on their doorstep. Stable isotope analysis of their bones suggests little or no reliance on marine sources of food. This is so intriguing. Was there some technological barrier, or a cultural one? Was the sea sacred to the Picts, or taboo? (And what's the difference?) The only realistic marine creature depicted on Pictish stones is the salmon, massive and sneering, depicted with the clarity of a portrait; but the leaping salmon is as much a creature of air and fresh water as it is of the sea.

I'm not sure I'd ever put this in print in an academic paper, but I see the Pictish beast as a guardian sea-spirit, not a dolphin exactly but the quintessence of cetacean. Something protecting those of us who are foolish enough to venture beyond the liminal ebb, to explore the boundaries between day and night, land and sea, salt water and fresh. Its blissful, slightly goofy smile is the expression of a creature that has gone through folly to the wisdom beyond. The beast eludes definition in the way that selkies do; it slips through your fingers; hard to think about, but good to think with; making most sense when seen with peripheral vision.

Amazing ice-storms pile-driving through, plunging the fields into veiled monochrome winter. And then the sun comes back and the white vanishes almost at once, and the world is supersaturated blue and gold and green again. Swim in super-choppy spray-pearled breakers, keeping a weather eye out for hail.

The first time I put my head right under it's a hell of a shock, much worse than the initial forcing myself into the water: I duck and I'm up again, fast, eyes open. I'm briefly aware of the deep streaky-jade world beneath the surface, but much more alive to the rapid penetration of the water through my hair to my scalp, carrying cold with it. The sea makes me *feel* how I am put together. The water may stop at the surface, but the cold carries on, through the epidermis to the dermis, the subcutaneous layers. The chilly shockwave spreads seismically through the hard bone of my skull: the blood vessels in the multi-layered fibrous tissue of my meninges respond rapidly to the onset of cold, insulating my brain and spinal cord from harm. In the twelfth century the French natural philosopher William of Conches named the layers of the meninges the *matres*, mothers, because of the way that they protect the brain. He thought that the sensory neurons, taking information in, stem from the *pia mater* (devoted mother), and the motor neurons, pushing motion out, come from the *dura mater* (hard mother). I am grateful now for this maternal embrace, tough and tender, cradling my cognition from the shock of the cold.

My mother died two years before I got married, five years before my daughter was born, six years before we moved to Orkney. She knew of my obsession with these islands, and we often talked about taking a trip up here together, but we never found the right time, and then it was too late. *What if* transmuted into *If only* when my back was turned.

Like me, she didn't marry until her mid-thirties and she had me, the first of her two daughters, at thirty-nine. Her original professional training was in social work, although she had read Politics, Philosophy and Economics at Oxford: when I asked her why she had become a social worker, not a politician or a philosopher or an economist, she looked at me in some surprise. 'It was 1949. The choices were social work, teaching or nursing.' In her day, you were still expected to give up your university place if you got engaged: make room for some poor woman too unattractive to catch a man. She loathed housework and brought me and my sister up to despise it. She warned me never to learn shorthand or typing, and to this day I peck at the keys with two fingers. Also: 'When you're at a meeting with men, never offer to make the tea.' I try to act on that one, too, and am surprised by how often I need to summon her ghost. But the housework still has to be done.

It never occurred to me, growing up, that I would marry. Adulthood meant getting away from my father and his expectations: escaping from a man, not finding one. Weddings belonged elsewhere; they marked the end of the story, the bride gift-wrapped and given away. Fine if you liked that kind of thing – it wasn't that I was consciously opposed to the institution, or that I envisaged a lifelong partnership of a different kind. I simply felt complete in myself, integral, sealed and intact long after the technical loss of my virginity. Relationships through my twenties and on into my thirties were often fun, but also a distraction, an irritation, an energy-drain. Why did the stimulus of intellectual companionship and sex dwindle into this stifling monogamy? The visceral reaction to threat is fight, flight, or freeze. As soon as friends started thinking of us, speaking of us, as a couple I began to jib, buck, take the bit between my teeth and, eventually, always, bolt. Before leaving one boyfriend I had nightmares of him pruning and pollarding me with garden shears, like the Scissorman in *Struwwelpeter* who cuts off the thumbs of the little boy who can't stop sucking them, leaving bleeding stumps.

Tredwell, with her gory, empty eye-sockets.

I gave up wearing the wedding ring not long after we were married. It was too tight one day and too loose the next, cluttering up my hands, interfering with circulation, dexterity and mobility. Being expected to wear a metal band on a specified joint felt as alien and antiquated as foot-binding or compulsory tight-lacing. You might be happy to wear too-tight shoes or a satin corset when you choose – I wore both on my wedding day – but all day? Every day? For the rest of your life? I kept taking the ring off, putting it down, mislaying it, and was in danger of losing it altogether. So the ring went silently away into a little drawer in my jewellery box, with my engagement ring. I hadn't minded wearing that one, but almost as soon as the wedding ring had gone on to my finger I began to feel a tightness under my sternum which has never really left me. Certainly putting the ring away was no solution.

I agreed to take my husband's name in part because I already had my doctorate, I'd been overjoyed to relinquish the clunky title of Ms, to dispense altogether with a gendered identity; and it never occurred to me that anyone would ever address me as Mrs. But we would fill in forms as Dr and Mr, and back would come the completed paperwork addressed to Dr and Mrs. It felt like a slap across the face. *Get back in your box*. The algorithms governing load distribution on the thirty-six-seater planes that fly in and out of Orkney's airport at Grimsetter are programmed to calculate weight difference based on gender, so I am in their system as Mrs. The local authority which manages the college, despite having numerous highly qualified academic staff, regularly writes to me as Mrs. I am sure no insult is intended, but every time it feels as though those passionate, engaged, formative years of working on my PhD thesis are being deleted from my CV. I am being assimilated, digested, depersoned. Forcibly regendered.

The disquiet set in from the start. At our wedding, my brand-new father-in-law steered me towards his wife and his mother, women I barely knew, shouting, 'Let's have a picture of all three of you together.' Three women, all labelled with the same name. My barely suppressed nausea should have told me straight away I'd made a mistake. The hugeness of the promises I'd just made began to bear down on me before we'd even got to the reception. The traps into which we wander are so often of our own making.

I changed my surname after marriage in part because I'd never felt particularly attached to my own father's very ordinary name, and I knew it would please my husband and his family. But now the dull, abandoned syllables of my maiden name smell like the first hint of rain after drought. I think of being that name again, and my mouth starts watering as though I were parched and imagining sucking lemons.

I also changed my name because I wanted to forge a new family in the aftermath of my mother's death, for both parents to have the same name as any children we might have. But I know now it takes more than a coincidence of syllables, and that my child would love me just as much if my name were different from hers. I flinch when I hear families being referred to collectively, *The Smiths*, as though they were all stamped out identical with the one gingerbread cutter. Ragged edges trimmed off and eaten. Dead black raisin eyes.

I felt that I was being pressured to pass, to masquerade as a successfully married woman. None of this was my husband's fault. I waded into this current with my eyes wilfully shut: no one to blame but myself if I got swept away.

It's no coincidence that the crisis in my marriage coincided with my compulsion to swim in the sea. I must be careful here; hindsight is wonderful in part because it is misleading: it gives you the illusion that all roads had to lead to the here and now. And I must not mistake causation and correlation: just because two distribution maps show the same pattern it doesn't mean that the data-sets stem from the same underlying root. But I watch myself running to the sea as I would to a lover, sneaking out of the house in the half-light, throwing myself into the water, seeking extreme sensation. Afterwards I creep back in, sated with guilty pleasure, take a scalding shower and scrub the evidence from my body.

The blanking out of self, the pleasure/pain boundary, the making myself wholly vulnerable: cold-sea swimming has taken over that part of my identity I once identified with sex. The house is cold too, but arid, like a high desert, like the far reaches of space. There is nothing to breathe. My husband and I steer around each other, polite and brittle, planets on different orbits, creatures too alien to understand each other's needs. In most fairy stories the prince is driven by passion to kiss the unconscious girl, or the princess is angry with the cold-skinned frog; they communicate strong emotions to each other, and in the *dénouement* they are transformed by love. But he and I have fallen too deeply under our respective enchantments to communicate, and the stories that lure me now are the ones in which the protagonists find their way out of the cage. Reading the Grimms again, it is now not the rude, ungrateful princess with whom I identify, that spoiled girl who breaks her promises and throws her devoted frog/ lover across the room, but Faithful Heinrich, the prince's follower, so grief-stricken by his master's transformation into a frog that he had the blacksmith fasten three iron bands around his ribcage. It was the only way to stop his heart from breaking.

How different things are in the sea, in which every inch of my skin tingles and thrills, where I am tossed and buffeted, taken to new places – out of the *comfort zone*, as the pedagogical jargon has it, into the *learning zone*, touching on the margins of the *panic zone*. The salt and cold saturate me, the waves throw me around, my sinuses and throat sting with the seminal taste of brine. Sure, I can't breathe freely here either, but instead I gasp, gulp, splutter, always something exciting, always something new. The sea is a reliable lover: always there for me. The sea is an unreliable lover: one day it may kill me.

And the seals give a human face to the sea. No wonder they are always the sexual partners of the humans in the selkie stories, rather than the spirit guides or magical helpers or existential threats. The best-known stories may be those of rape and conquest, of a man stealing a woman's freedom and her access to the sea, but Orkney is also rich in tales like that of the Great Selkie of Sule Skerry, stories of lovers from the sea who fulfil a human woman's needs. The story sometimes has a tragic ending; sometimes, but not always.

There's that tale about the proud young woman on Stronsay, one of the north isles. She was rich and she was beautiful, and she was in love with the big handsome lad who did the grunt work on her father's farm. Mucking out. Hauling. Silage. Slurry. She couldn't show her love, so she suffered in secret, and took it out on the lad with the edge of her tongue. But the day her father died she told him to get himself washed and brushed, off with his boiler suit and on with his Sunday clothes, because she was going to marry him.

It was the scandal of the year. But the marriage didn't make either of them happy. It turned out he was as stubborn as she was, and he didn't like being pushed around. After a few years of him ignoring her and refusing to eat or drink with her and never coming to her bed, her love for him died. But she was full-blooded and restless, longing for a warm body next to her, so she went down to the ebb, kilted up her skirts and waded into the water, and there she wept seven salt tears into the seventh wave of the salt sea. They were the only tears that proud girl ever shed.

Up pops a handsome bull selkie, saying, 'What's your will with me, fair lady?' And their children were born with hands like a seal's prehensile flippers, webs of skin between their fingers.

We're not told what the human husband thought of this arrangement. In telling her story the Orkney antiquarian Walter Traill Dennison changes her name, he says, 'because her descendants are still living among us; and if any of them should read these lines, let them not think that aught offensive was intended. If the lady was their ancestor, she was also a near relative of ancestors of mine.' In one version of the story she is Brita, in another Ursilla. Her real name has been left to fall through the gaps, in case her grandchildren are as prickly as she was. I wonder where exactly Traill Dennison thought the potential offence to her descendants lay: in the adultery, or the seal strand in their DNA?

Brita/Ursilla was too proud publicly to admit the mistake she had made in marrying the man she did, but not so proud that she wasn't going to find herself a workable solution.

Selkie women are proud, too: that surely is part of their charm. They are as unselfconscious as children, dancing on the sand, and the Peeping Toms who steal their skins cannot bear their unlicensed beauty. The selkies are not dancing naked to delight the male gaze: their only audience is each other, their motive the sheer joy of being alive, wind and salt and moonlight on bare skin. Even to say they are naked is a misnomer: they cannot be naked because they never wear clothes, innocent as Eve in Eden. The sealskin is not a garment to hide the shameful body or to assert status or even to keep off the cold: it is their true sea self; just as the human skin is their true land self. The sobbing of the selkie-woman when she realizes her skin is gone, and then her abject pleading when she realizes that a man has taken it and plans to keep her from the sea: these are always part of the story. She is forced to knuckle under, choose slavery over death, even when she already has a husband and children in the sea. She is always a dutiful wife and a good mother.

She has to learn that nakedness is shameful. What did it feel like to put on clothes for the first time, to force your feet into shoes? My own skin flinches, newly aware of the dead, alien weight of wool and linen and leather.

How can her husband live with himself? Does he look at her as she gazes at the sea with the salt water welling in her eyes, and feel a pang of remorse? Or does he hug to himself in secret glee the knowledge of that soft bundle of speckled fur tucked behind the boarded ceiling, in the rafters, gathering dust and cobwebs?

This desire to entrap is always associated with the men. Brita/Ursilla had no interest in enslaving her selkie lover. She wanted good sex and a relationship of equals. Freud banged on about not knowing what women want, calling us 'the dark continent of psychology' – but he could have asked. Virginia Woolf might have enlightened him, in 'A Room of One's Own'; and so could Brita/Ursilla. When I first read Traill Dennison's story I was frustrated that he censored her real name: I felt he was over-squeamish, disrespectful to the truth of her experience. But maybe her having two names, neither of them her own, is just a sign that she stands in for all of us.

Eight years into our marriage an assault on my name came from a completely other direction. My first novel was about to be published, and the editor told me she felt that it should come out under my initials. 'Men won't buy books by someone called Victoria.' I gaped at her. A truism in commercial fiction apparently, but new to me. 'No specific prejudice against Victorias,' she said, laughing. Women will buy books by men, but not vice versa. My novel had men in it, and swords. Men might well buy it, but not if they knew it was written by me. And when I told her my middle name was Jane she sighed and shook her head again. 'V. J. No, think of something else.' When I pressed her for an explanation she gave her complicit laugh, and squirmed a little, and said it reminded her of *vajazzle*, *vajayjay*. Those words will date this book. I hope. There was a peculiar humiliation in being told by a young woman that my very initials evoked female genitalia and were therefore unacceptable. I felt as though I had been caught on the way to the loo with a tampon poking out of my handbag.

And I wonder: did anyone try that line on Dick Francis?

My middle-aged, battle-scarred, female friends shrugged and sighed and said *go with it, they know the market, what do you expect?* Some tried to console me, mentioning Charlotte Brontë's male pseudonym of Currer Bell, George Eliot… *Hey, it worked for J. K. Rowling!*

But my cousin Thom, in his early twenties, was incandescent with outrage on my behalf. How I love him for that.

It was a strange, prolonged process of alienation of public from private self, first to lose my surname, then my given name, and then even my initials, like being buffeted by waves, dragged and rolled by the undertow, suddenly realizing that this is a rip current and that the water is carrying you further and further away from where you want to be, out into unknown, annihilating seas. I peer through a looking glass darkly, *per speculum in aenigmate*, through the riddling mirror (or maybe the enigmatic speculum), through the accretions of soot and grease: where has that girl gone? What would she say to me now?

Standing on the pier watching the ferry depart, the gap of choppy water widening.

The layer of hardened tissue laid down by repetitive microtrauma, each wounding moment too small to register.

Air temp 14, sea 11 C. Many many curlews flying low over the water. Wave-skimming wing-tips. Coming so close, uncaring whether I am a seal or a rock or a lump of weed. Stiff southerly breeze, palpably incoming tide.

Names and naming strategies are always powerful magic. The name of Orkney itself is a mystery: its similarity to *orca* is haunting, although philologists are sceptical about their having a direct connection. I'm less sure; meaning inheres in the mind, not in the word. Puns and echoes, homophones and folk-etymologies, these all have their own magic. 'Orca' just means 'whale'. Carl Linnaeus, the eighteenth-century Swedish scientist who largely invented scientific taxonomy and the convention of giving species two-part names, called the orca the *Delphinus orca*; in Middle English it had been the grampus, from French for *fat fish*, although of course it's not a fish but a mammal. Linnaeus is said to have pointed that out, definitively, in 1758 when he invented the category of *cetacean*, although Olaus Magnus's map made more than two hundred years earlier shows the *orcha* suckling her calf, right next to *Orcadia*. It hasn't yet become the orcine whale, the whale belonging to the god Orcus: that would happen in 1860, when the Austrian naturalist Leopold Fitzinger redrew the borders of knowledge yet again, establishing the genus *Orcinus* and *Orcinus orca* as its only extant member species.

Like a recurrent motif in a piece of music, like the *Jaws* theme, like the *forever-and-ever-Amen* that closes the rosary, this stuttering heartbeat, this insistent reminder that I am safe: *no wild orca has ever attacked a human being*. Maybe it's my guilty conscience, my fear of being pursued for my broken promises, but the sea's choppiness this morning means that my eye is caught over and over by little dark triangular shadows, shapes and splashes in the water. What was that movement? Just a wave? A shag, diving? A seal's head? Or the stubby recurved triangle of a female orca's dorsal fin, Mousa or one of the others, slicing the surface? Every twitch of my cornea is accompanied by a little thrill, my sympathetic nervous system releasing cortisone and adrenalin, my heart pounding, mouth dry, the blood loud in my ears. We are pareidolic, pattern-making creatures. *Pareidolia*: the capacity for perceiving meaning when no meaning is there. Our brains identify features in abstract forms, the face of Christ in a slice of burned toast, camels and weasels in clouds, killer whales in the waves.

We see what we want to see.

Freud's construct of the *Lustprinzip*, the pleasure principle, the pleasure/pain binary pay-off, is predicated on the idea that when mature and healthy we are rational creatures who can perform a minute-by-minute cost–benefit analysis of the potential outcomes of our actions, and that we choose the outcome which will maximize pleasure and minimize pain, subject always to the further restraints of the reality principle. To do otherwise, to take unnecessary risks, to return over and over to the source of pain and fear: this is neurosis.

The warning leaflets issued by the coastguard tell me only to swim on patrolled beaches; that water this cold is a danger to life within thirty to sixty minutes; that currents are unpredictable and often invisible from the shore. That I should never swim alone.

They do not mention *Orcinus orca*.

I almost always say orca, not killer whale. A friend accused me recently of cutesifying them by using this name: 'That's what SeaWorld calls them. What's wrong with *killer whales*?' Nothing, of course. I agree with him: names matter. But there's nothing cute about the words *Orcinus orca*. Poke beneath the surface and there's a long narrative there of terror, the uncanny, guilt and the fear of the deep.

Who is Orcus, and why does the orca belong to him? I've been teasing out the connections, with the suspicion that there's a lot going on deep under the surface, down in the hadal zone, rather than the sunlit zone where philologists feel entitled to play.

Classical writers called these islands both 'Orkas' (singular) and 'the Orcades' (plural). In Old Norse it's 'Orkneyjar' (plural). (And yet now if visitors refer to 'the Orkneys' we hiss and suck our teeth: it's become a shibboleth that marks the outsider, you have to say Orkney or the Orkney Islands.) Orkney as it stands is a perfectly clear Old Norse word. *Orkn-eyjar* – the Islands of Seals. But the name is much older than the Vikings, and they must have reinterpreted what they found: there are plenty of parallels for such misunderstanding and misappropriation in colonial history. Even during the Viking Age the islands are referred to in Irish sources as 'Innse h-Orc', Orc Islands, and the Picts must surely have called them something that sounded similar. But where did that name come from? Tracing the name back through early medieval and classical writers takes us to Bede and Adomnán in the eighth century and Pliny in the first. We have already met Pliny's contemporary Tacitus, describing Agricola's circumnavigation. Before him there was Diodorus of Sicily, and the trail finally runs into the sand with Pytheas of Massilia in the fourth century BC.

Let's start there.

Pytheas's work is lost, but he is quoted by later writers. Like Agricola four hundred years later, Pytheas came from the south of France and is said to have sailed right around Britain. He describes the island as essentially triangular with three promontories, Cantia (which is clearly Kent), Belerium (probably Land's End) and, the most northerly, Orkas. Pytheas wrote in Greek, as did Diodorus, who picked up his description and passed it on: he too assumes Orkas projects out from northern Scotland. There is no hint here of islands. It's as though they're passing on some ancestral memory of the Mesolithic, before melting ice and sea-level rise turned a hilly plain into an archipelago.

In the first century AD the mental map is redrawn to more accurate specifications. Pliny the Elder, who was killed when Vesuvius erupted in AD 79, rewrites our name as a plural, 'Orcades', and he tells us for the first time that we are islands, 'some forty in number'. Pliny and Tacitus were acquainted, and Agricola, to whose daughter Tacitus was married, was stationed in Britain from around AD 70, so we might suspect a vector of information here, though Pliny had been dead for twenty years by the time Tacitus got round to writing Agricola's biography and describing the subjugation of those Orcades.

Orcus is a Roman god of the dead. There are no myths attached to him, just a festering aura, a shudder: he feasts on the corpses of evil-doers. He has Greek antecedents: a demon called Horkos, one of the sons of Strife, whose job it is to pursue those who break their promises. Whether or not Pytheas or Pliny intended it, the name they perpetuated for these islands, hovering on the extreme edge of their vision, was one with very sinister associations. *Orkas-Orcas-Orkus-Horkos*: that echo must have resonated in the minds of their original audiences. One of Horkos's siblings was Lethe, the goddess of oblivion, who gave her name to one of the five rivers that flow through the underworld kingdom of Hades and stolen Persephone.

Orca is a generic Latin word for whale; it also means *barrel* or *vase*, referring to the animals' sleek, streamlined rotundity. It delights me that Mousa, one of the Northern Isles matriarchs, is named for the best-preserved broch tower in Shetland: they share their lovely ergonomic curves.

How can we be sure what the Picts called Orkney, and why? We don't even know what they called themselves. The likelihood is that they had many different names, community by community, from Shetland down to Fife, and only a very select few would ever have referred to themselves as Pictish. *Picti* is Latin for *the painted people*. Like the demon-redolent Orkas, it's a word that turns up in the works of Mediterranean writers long before we hear the first voices coming directly from these lands about which they were writing. Early medieval elites looked back to the classical world to give authority to their claims to kingship, ethnicity, statehood, some descent from the Roman world. They scoured the works of poets and historians in search of a name that resonated, from whom they could claim succession. Did the kings and clerics of seventh-century eastern Scotland read the Latin poetry that treated of wild Caledonia and the lands beyond the wall, and seize on the name 'Picti' as a label that could both unite these disparate tribes, and grant their rulers legitimacy and classical gravitas? There's an almost indefinable quality that runs like DNA through early medieval identity, this search for Roman-ness, *romanitas*, a link both to the lost splendours of the Classical world and the Roman Empire, and to their present Rome of the popes and glorious churches. The name Picti tells us very little about the indigenous past of the people of eastern Scotland; it's much more informative about their aspirations to membership of the European club of Christian kingdoms: a people who had never been forced into the old Roman Empire but wanting to claim a part of it, nonetheless. Maybe they encountered Orkas, Orcades in old texts too.

The pod of orcas currently feeding in the Flow is a fair few miles round the coast of Mainland from the Sands of Evie, but they could swim those miles in a leisurely hour, and this stretch of water between Evie and Rousay is a good place for seeing them. Not long ago a pod of a dozen was sighted from the ferry that crosses between Rousay and the Mainland harbour of Tingwall, just down the road from here, and the captain turned the helm to follow them along Eynhallow Sound for twenty minutes before going back to his timetable.

Spring and summer are the best time for orca-watching, but they are here in every season. A spate of headless seal corpses has been spotted this winter on local beaches, including one just below the Knowe of Stenso, the nearest broch mound to where I am now, visible just a couple of hundred yards along the shoreline to the west. It's the end of the pupping season for the grey seals, and this is probably the work of rival bull seals, attacking the young who have only recently taken to the water. But orcas could also be responsible: although they're after their winter food of herring at the moment, seals are the meal of choice of the Scottish–Icelandic orca community, and perhaps they have been concentrating on the nutritious brain and discarding the rest of the carcass. Floppy Fin and another young bull from the Northern Isles pod have been sighted a few times cruising for seals right here, off the Sands of Evie.

When they catch one the water flowers red.

Orcas don't mistake people for seals. They're very choosy about what they eat. Even if I looked more like a seal than I do, I'd probably still be safe: orcas don't rely on sight to find their food. Instead, like all toothed cetaceans, orcas use sonar, sending out pulses of sound which they can focus with extraordinary precision, and use to distinguish between very small, and very similar, objects. It sounds like a stick rattling fast along railings. And their sonar doesn't just bounce off the skin: the sound waves go right though the body, skin and fat, muscle and blood vessel, tendon, ligament and sinew, bone and marrow, heart and brain, describing the shape of every internal organ before returning their multi-layered message to the extraordinarily complex brain that sent out the first transmission. Orcas in the Pacific Northwest distinguish between their favourite food, the fatty Chinook salmon, and the other, similarly sized varieties of salmon with which the Chinook swim, based on the different echo-patterns of the various species' swim bladders. The orca that might even now be scoping me out from the sunlit shallows of

Eynhallow Sound understands my body in the way that an MRI scanner would: the information it's garnering about me is the equivalent of thousands of histology slides. The orca already knows me inside out, without having to eat me first.

Orca brains are huge, both absolutely and relative to their body size. They are deeply convoluted, like ours. The areas associated with speech, hearing and emotion in the human brain are massive in the orca's, and the limbic brain in particular is much more complex than ours. Observers of wild and captive orcas emphasize their emotional range, their self-awareness, their ability to intuit the physical and emotional experiences of others, their extraordinary capacity for co-ordination. It has been suggested that an orca's sense of identity lies in the group as much as the individual; that their capacity for emotional complexity, indicated by that limbic lobe, is tied into their echo-locating abilities, that they read each other for information about feelings as well as facts. If the *sensation océanique* involves a sense of unboundedness and the dissolution of the boundaries between self and other, then orcas are the sensation embodied.

The orca knows me far, far better than I know myself.

Back in September I was sitting in the onboard café on the big ferry as it chugged out of Stromness. I was watching the serried houses, tight and narrow, gable-end on to the sea, drop behind us to starboard as we left the harbour, peering idly out of the salt-scratched window at the familiar view, the great igneous lump of Brinkie's Brae looming above the town. There was a black dot in the water, just off the shingle beach at the Point of Ness, below the campsite and the golf course and the path from which Anouk and I had seen Sule Skerry a couple of weeks earlier. A regular Polar Bear swimming place, though not one I go to very often, as it's a chilly twenty minutes' drive back home. It takes a lot to lure me away from the Sands of Evie.

The dot was moving fast, and in a straight line, in the shallow waters under the retaining wall of the car park. The current is strong here in Hoy Sound, strong enough to bring smaller boats heading against the tide to a standstill; the dot was too far away to see detail clearly: I assumed it was a seal being borne speedily along by the water. The ferry rounded the Point of Ness and turned west into the sound. There were no seals hauled out on the skerries. A couple of minutes later I saw the dot again, now much closer. I thought, *That seal is fairly speeding along.* Then, *That seal's head is very pointy.* Then, and with a cold shock of revelation, a rib-tightening adrenal gush, *It's not a head, it's a dorsal fin.*

Now, with a new understanding of what I was seeing, I could make out the rest of the fin beneath the water, and the dark, bullet-shaped cetacean bulk, and the white patches of cheek and saddle. And then I realized there was a second one, just beyond and ahead of the first, zooming along parallel to both ferry and shore, heading in the same direction as we were. I watched, heart pounding although I was high and dry and safe; my mouth hung open. No point in reaching for my camera: that fallible eye would only have perceived dark flyspecks, too far away for interest.

But I did gasp, '*Orca!*' to the elderly Orcadian lady eating her eggs and toast at the adjacent table. She looked up placidly and glanced shoreward. 'Aye,' she said, nodding, 'that'll be them.' And she returned to her breakfast.

The ferry began its turn towards the open Atlantic. The orcas continued parallel to the shore. I watched until their dark fins were indistinguishable from the jerky black shadows of the restless waves.

Air temp 2, stiff easterly breeze, ice on the puddles. I swam at 10 a.m. in pale grey-gold light just as the sun was lifting free of hill and cloud. The sea was contradictory, its different energies all playing different games: a very high and running tide, the choppy swell, a fast current that pulled me over the concealed breakwater before I realized it. Chilly and exhilarating, wrestling the waves. No seals, a smattering of rooks, one circling shag.

The second time I put my head under the water it is just as cold, just as shocking. I surface and gasp, perfectly timed for a rogue wavelet to smack me in the face, dousing eyes, nose and open mouth with brine. My sinuses flood, and I choke and splutter, very glad I am still close to the shore, only just out of my depth. The physiological response to sudden immersion in cold water is very like that of a panic attack, in which your heart pounds, your breath shortens, you are hyper-aware of perceived threat. There are doctors who recommend cold-water swimming as a therapy for patients who present with depression or anxiety. Replicating the symptoms of a panic attack in cold water is a valuable step towards taking back control.

I can feel the cold brine trickling down the caves, hollows and tunnels that lurk above and behind my palate, deep within my skull. The sea, inside me now as well as outside, gives me a wholly new, three-dimensional awareness of my body. In the sea, I realize how limited an understanding of the human body I have, both in terms of my everyday encounters with other members of my species, and also as a result of my background as a specialist in early medieval death, burial and afterlife. In the first capacity I perceive the human body primarily as skin; in the second as bone. The exterior surfaces of the other people whom I encounter in my own, embodied existence; and the excavated skeletons, always elegant, always beautiful, that I meet through my work.

I've never had much cause to ponder the detail of what lies between skin and bone.

But over the last four years of sea swimming I have come to a new appreciation of how much there is, in between, and what some of it does. How a few extra pounds of insulation, subcutaneous fat, blubber – *bioprene*, as cold-water swimmers call it, as opposed to artificial *neoprene* – can make all the difference to my ability to tolerate, even enjoy, the cold. How the body in cold water instantly reroutes blood to the vital organs. I can feel it ebbing drop by rapid drop as the vessels constrict, retreating first from the expendable hands and feet, then calves and forearms, and then from quadriceps and hamstrings, biceps and triceps, glutes and lats, as though it were mapped out for me on an anatomy model. The way that the shivering starts deep in the core and pulses outward. Sometimes when I leave the water I cannot straighten my hands: the little fingers stick out at an unnatural angle because the deep muscle tissue of my forearms is so contracted with the cold. Will I be safe to drive even the short distance home?

And yes, I will.

Or, at least, overconfident with happy-hormones, I believe I will.

Because at the same time as all this is going on my system is coursing with joy, crackling with energy. I feel every little electrical jolt as my nerves high-five across the synapses. The cold-water plunge brings me so close to the pleasure/pain boundary that my body reacts with the painkillers it keeps stowed away for crisis: dopamine, serotonin, endorphins. *Endolphins*: more cold-water-swimmer slang, the happiness hormones that the sea engenders. I can visualize my endolphins so clearly, tiny, silver-blue and bottle-nosed, charging exuberantly up vein and down artery.

Never mind Freud's *Lustprinzip*: the word that comes to mind for this sensation is *jouissance*. Enjoyment, joy, rapture, orgasm. It's a term from Lacanian psychoanalysis, the card Lacan threw down to counter Freud and the penny-pinching accountancy of his pleasure principle. It gets left in French because there is no English word that takes pleasure so close to the edge of the unbearable.

I swam soon after 9 in sinister blood-orange light. Air temp 2 C but no wind. Another very high tide. The sea was much quieter than yesterday but there was still a big rolling surf breaking on the beach, strong enough to knock me sideways. The constant cloud of spindrift around Westness and Costa suggests there's some big Atlantic weather brewing. One snub-nosed common seal showed himself briefly but clearly had business elsewhere. A flock of around 400 curlews streamed low over the waves, giving their swooping cry. I emerged glowing and exhilarated to find all the flooded fields reflecting back the orange light.

The third time I put my head under the water, there is no brain freeze. I am moving into an altered state, at home in the water. I open my eyes and take in the underwater deepgreen for one, two, three long strokes. The world below the surface is blurry because the refractive power of the vitreous fluid of the human eye is almost identical to that of water, but I can still perceive the kelp and thong-weed swaying just below me, and the murky bulk of the breakwater. My heart-rate has slowed. I am more comfortable. Now that my head is as wet and cold as the rest of me, my body is achieving a new equilibrium: all the receptors in my sensory neurons, top to toe, are taking in the same information. After the third ducking my skin and brain and muscles can make sense of what is happening to me in a different way.

Now I can start to swim for pleasure, to stretch out, relax, spend more time immersed. Sea and air are quiet enough that I might swim out to the buoys marking the lobster-creels, not far at all but still something I hesitate to do on my own in the winter. It's swimming out into the bay, rather than entering the water, that often attracts the seals, and I wonder if even now they are watching me, waiting for me to make the first move. 'No place of habitation,' Donne called the sea, 'but a passage to our habitations.' I disagree. Sure, I can't call the sea home as a selkie or an orca would, but how else can I describe this sense of release, this oceanic sensation of settling back into a safe and familiar space?

Familiar, but always capable of surprise.

One autumn dusk I went for a second swim as the bright day was giving way before an ominous wall of grey from the south-west. As I rounded the corner by the old stone hut I was arrested by a flash of brown movement: an otter, trundling across the sand. It climbed on to the breakwater, loped to the far end and slithered into the water. I followed it, swimming cautiously behind. It swam, surfaced, dived, bobbed up again repeatedly, for about ten minutes, maybe fifteen metres from me. Then, a fish flapping silver in its jaws and its head held high, it zoomed for the deserted and darkening beach. I lay prone in the shallows, shivering as my core temperature dropped but unwilling to frighten the otter by emerging, and utterly rapt. The otter ate its fish in neat bites and then groomed itself, lazy and prolonged, lifting its triangular head from time to time to acknowledge me with calm courtesy before finally disappearing into the grass. Not interested in me, not wide-eyed and eager in the manner of a seal, just letting me know that it was aware of me. Probably a young male, recently evicted from the holt and setting out on his own.

In John Heath-Stubbs's poem, 'St Cuthbert and the Otter', the two creatures, man and otter, embody different kinds of love. Cuthbert stands deep in the cold water, eyes fixed on the stars, chanting his prayers, ignoring the rolling shingle that bruises his feet. Afterwards, Cuthbert's otter, even friendlier than my one, comes out of the sea to warm his feet. She is among the numerous creatures that bear witness to his sanctity. As with many saints, and centuries before St Francis, community with the natural world is an index of Cuthbert's sinless condition, like Adam and Eve before the Fall. In Teviotdale an eagle miraculously brings him a fish, and he courteously shares it with her. He chides the ravens who steal the thatch from his Farne hermitage to eke out their nests, and in compensation they bring him a lump of lard with which his guests can dubbin their boots, keeping their feet warm and dry as the otters do for Cuthbert.

For Cuthbert love is harsh and remote. Love may make the world go round, but he encounters it not in pleasure but in numbness and pain. Whether I'm reading Bede's eighth-century account or Heath-Stubbs's twentieth-century version, I get the shivers myself imagining Cuthbert in the cold sea, voicing his wishes for his people. His penitential vigil is a small-scale re-enactment of Christ's sacrifice on the cross, through which the saint hopes to convert his Northumbrian flock. He wants them to abandon their doomed heroes, like Beowulf, for a hero who can bring them redemption. Cuthbert's focus is on the silent sky, not the living sea and its creatures.

The otter knows nothing of Cuthbert's kind of love. She is the embodiment of nurturing, practical emotion, putting the blessings of her body – heat, fur, musk – to immediate good effect. If Cuthbert aspires to be like Christ, then the otter is his comforter, like the woman often identified with Mary Magdalene, who massages Christ's head with precious ointment, wets his feet with her tears, and dries them with her hair.

And she makes him laugh. The otter's concerns are small and petty and animal, and fundamental to all kinds of well-being.

Reading the poem again, I notice for the first time that in fact Heath-Stubbs does not gender this otter, and I wonder what it says about my own understanding of the relationship between love and service and entitlement that I should always have read her/him/it as female. Cuthbert reminds me here of the little mermaid's prince, who cannot see the love and dedication right under his nose. If only Cuthbert would just look down, instead of peering into the unresponsive heavens, he could learn so much about love. But if the otter had any sense she wouldn't be content with him chucking the odd fish-head at her, she'd be streaking back into the sea to do her gambolling and playing with someone who didn't take her love for granted.

I was in the sea at 6.30 this morning. The water feels no warmer – very alive, colder and more stimulating than the Moray Firth where I swam twice last week. North-westerly breeze and an incoming tide. Grey grey grey shifting mists and damps, a little rain, the very occasional silver-water gleam from a hidden sun. One grey seal asleep in the shallows – woke up and came closer to check me out, shrugged ('Oh, it's only her') and went back to sleep. Tern, curlew, eider, raven.

In the Northern Isles winter comes in riding the blast, the snow hurtles through horizontally and while it may adhere to the sides of the buildings it rarely settles, just rattling over the ground before blowing into the sea. My friend Alex, originally from Sweden, is very strict about definitions of snow, and she refuses to accept this Orkney version. 'It's not snow, it's hail. It bounces.' I maintain it is compacted snow; if you look closely you can see it is not ice, it doesn't melt fast in the way hail does. We talk about the crystalline structure of snow, the way that each flake forms around a grain of dust, like soothing pearl around the irritant in an oyster. Scandinavians dislike Orkney winters: the ratio of dark to light may be familiar but they miss the crispness, the glitter, the winter activities. Most years Orkney in the winter is grey and brown, bringing acres of mud and flooded fields, and gales that keep children indoors.

The first two winters we spent in Orkney were seasons of heavy snow across almost the whole of Britain. Even the Northern Isles saw significant snowfall, although when the national press printed satellite photos that showed the whole country like a blank white map they cropped Orkney off because the East Mainland let the side down by remaining obdurately green. But the lochs froze hard, and the hills of Hoy and Rousay and the West Mainland were white for weeks, a *tabula rasa*. No winter has been like that since. The collective desire of the Orkney Polar Bear Club members to behave like the *real* Polar Bear and Walrus Clubs we read about in Russia and Finland, breaking the ice to swim and rolling in the snow afterwards, has so far been frustrated. Although we are on the 59th parallel the Gulf Stream coddles our archipelago.

But it's cold enough, whether on those winter days when sleet and rain and hail vie for supremacy and they're all coming in sideways, or those June mornings when the wind shifts to the north and I stand on the Sands of Evie and inhale the air straight from the Arctic, sharp as a whetted blade. The Orkney year is one in which July has been surgically removed, with spring running straight into autumn, and a new nameless month of dark stitched in between December and January. The last primroses flower next to the first purple bells of heather, and summer falls down the gap between.

Living in Orkney is like living inside the lines of *The Wanderer*: I thought so when I first got off the ferry aged twenty-one, and I think so still, but it is only now that I am middle-aged that I realize what a profoundly middle-aged rant this poem is.

It's a monologue, spoken by a homeless exile, a meditation on loss and grief, written by Anon, some time before the year 1000.

The Wanderer breaks my heart these days in ways that my eighteen-year-old self could barely have imagined. She didn't know what it was to like to hear the voices of dead friends in the cries of the gulls, or to dream about hugging and kissing the dead, sitting at their feet and resting head and hand on their knees. She hadn't been made redundant from a job she loved, sent off to wander the paths of exile. It is a poem of bitter experience. I am not yet quite fifty, but I have no one left of an older generation: grandparents, parents, aunts and uncles all gone. 'Always they swim away,' as the poem says, no matter how I call after them. 'No one wins this wisdom before he has achieved his share of winters in the world.'

For a long time, *The Wanderer* was thought to be a composite: a true warrior-pagan core that some later monkish critic had bracketed with pious mouthings. More recent scholarship sees it as a unity, a wholly Christian narrative about regret and rumination and pilgrimage, full of passionate juxtaposition that makes the reader work hard. I agree, but there is still no easy glossing over that abrupt transition at the end, from the bleak and honest recognition of transience that governs most of the poem – 'Here wealth is on loan, friends are on loan, here man is on loan, kinsmen on loan, all the substance of this earth falls into the void' – to the trite one-sentence solution: 'It's well for him who seeks mercy, comfort from his Father in heaven, where for us all security lies.' The poet hasn't prepared us for the glibness at the end: we are still adrift on the paths of exile, dreaming of the dead when – *voilà!* – he pulls the rabbit of salvation out of his hat with a sudden flourish. How are we supposed to trust him in that final line, when he insists that there *is* a permanent home, after he has spent the preceding 114 lines undermining the idea?

He has thought this dark life through, he tells us, and there is no consolation to be found in any of the things with which we attempt to shore up our sense of self. He doesn't mention sex or the companionship of women: his is a wholly masculine universe, in which physical intimacy consists only of homosocial bonding. It's not that this was an inevitable point of view for Anglo-Saxon men, even avowedly Christian ones. He had options. There's a tenth-century sermon which describes the joys of Paradise – the sun shines every day, the streams flow with honey, and 'you'll have a new bride every night', says the preacher wistfully, 'and she as beautiful as Juno'. But I can't see the Wanderer-poet falling for this Club 18–30 vision. And he would have had little patience with cold-water swimming: in his world, as for Cuthbert, the sea is the locus of fear and struggle, not comfort. Images of the natural landscape, the weather, the birds, the buildings and the bodies of men flow in and out of one another, effortlessly shifting scale. For all the wild weather, the storm and hail, it is a desperately claustrophobic poem. 'Taken under the helmet of night,' he laments, all the joy, 'as though it had never been.' *Nihthelm*, night-helmet, is a word found only in this poem, an imagist condensation: the shadow falling across each face, across the whole world.

Serene winter swim, last before I head south for nearly three weeks away from the sea – sky a uniform silver, sea a pale green-grey-blue that has no name in English (but in Gaelic it would be *glas*). Surface calm, windless, but still a big swell. Shags, plovers and geese but no seals. Yesterday's and tomorrow's storms equally unimaginable in this floating world.

What follows is not exactly a translation of *The Wanderer* (though you'll find one in the Appendix, on page 277), but rather a gloss, an update, an answer. My attempt at picking a fight with a poet who has been dead for over a thousand years.

The Wanderer: A Response

Only the lonely put up with God's mercy.
Why do we take it from Him, the Measurer-of-grief?
I run, fleeing over the ice,
Fighting waves hand to hand.
He drives me out, yet He won't leave me alone.
There's no escape.
Or so says the one who is running,
Mind-crammed with hard memories,
Dragged down by blood, anger, loss.
Cold light before dawn. Alone. Every day.
Perforce. Compulsion. I must voice pain.
But there's no one to hear me, no one alive.
(Nis. Is-not. Why have we lost this word?)

I don't dare speak my mind.
Oh, yes, I know. Keep your mouth shut.
Careless talk costs lives.
Officer class.
Suck it up, buttercup.
But I'm tired of this, the crap He keeps throwing at me.
My heart's too troubled to help other people.
This is wrong.
I've spent too long worrying what they'll say about me,
Keeping my lip zipped, my heart likewise.
Someone like me can't confess to wretchedness.
Being a wretch.
How did I get here? This isn't home.
No habitus, no ethnos, no cognates or agnates:
Their absence ties my hands.
Bosses aren't for burying, but mine,
Shiny though she was, is lost to me
(It seems years ago now); and
I don't know what to do without a leader.
It's cold outside, and I'm on thin ice.
I know there are other jobs,
But I'm on the outside, looking in
(I was Beowulf; now I'm Grendel)
At the shop-talk, the comfort, the friends, the laughter,
The raised glasses. Cheers!
Things you only know if you've been there;
Things you only miss once you've lost them.
Parents, workmates, friends, lovers.
Sense of humour.
Do you remember the fun we used to have?

I don't.
Not till I drift off at last in the small hours
And wake in tears from a dream of your embrace.
The hard, warm body, your hands, your knees, the very
*   smell of you.*
Waking is a plunge in cold water:
Salt-sea drying on my cheeks,
And your face morphs into mist.
Your voice the cry of gulls,
The rattling mockery of hail,
And it hurts more than it did.
I won't do that again.
Fight it. Fight it:
The sense of my body decaying,
Knowing we're all doomed
(You can't say that in a serious voice),
That we're killing our middle-earth.
Why am I still sane?
Things you think you know when you're young...
... but you don't.
I've learned to shut up, the hard way.
No more hot heart, or glibness,
Or slithering out of commitments.
Don't feel too much.
Don't ask for anything.
Don't expect credit for anything you do.
Don't expect promises to be kept.
Why bother?
We're all doomed.
Who'll give a toss in a hundred years?

There's a post-apocalyptic pornographic pleasure
In imagining the roofs off the offices,
Tumbleweed,
Frost on the filing cabinets,
Spreadsheets flapping in the wind.
Look around you, workmates:
Who's for the heart attack?
Who for cancer?
Dementia, or
Death by a thousand strokes?
It's His fault, God's I mean.
The Shaper, He's done it before.
He'll do it again.
Free will? Don't make me laugh.
This dark life: think it through
And see if you're still laughing.
It's your turn next to
Put on the helmet of night.
How many graves do you visit?
Count them. Go on.
There's as much meaning in death as there is
In the sound of the sea battering the cliffs,
The clatter of hail, the north wind
When it goes hunting and whining round the eaves,
Scratching for entrance.
We're all dooooooooomed!
What will last? Money?
No. Mates? No.
Me, my family? Don't make me laugh.
It hurts.

You think I'm a smart-arse? A Cassandra?
I'll take my tray over here, to this table,
The one where no one is sitting.
Keep my lip zipped.
              Suck it up.
At least until I figure out the answer.
Jam tomorrow, always jam to-fucking-morrow?
Don't give me cosy platitudes,
Come on, Wanderer-poet.
You and I, we both know you can do better than that.

Got down to the beach at 16.30, well after sunset. Everything segueing fast through green and blue and purple to charcoal-grey. Sky and sea very quiet, little waves breaking on the beach, the roar of surf from Eynhallow. No birds on the sea, the peeping of plovers and curlews from the shore. One heron heavy-flapping eastward, one shag low over the water heading west, one seal cruising past, a black dot in a leaden sea. Fade to black.

There are other beaches in Orkney besides my familiar curve of sand at Aikerness in Evie. Many, many other beaches, and each one has its own ecosystem and microclimate, its own riff on the blend of sand and slab and shingle, its distinctive combination of shells and flotsam, its soundscape. They may share an underlying grammar, speak a common language, but the message each one conveys is unique.

Newark is in the wild east of Mainland, in the parish of Deerness, almost as far from our house in Evie as it is possible to get. One's perception of time and distance changes after living for a while on a small island. Places more than twenty minutes' drive away become challenging, adventurous, and alien. Kirkwall, the archipelagic capital (population 9,000), re-emerges in this altered consciousness as metropolitan, corrupt, teeming with strangers. To reach Newark I have to drive into Kirkwall and out the other side, past Grimsetter Airport, through the unfamiliar territories of St Andrew's and Toab, and over the last parish boundary into Deerness. But the journey is not yet over. The peninsula of Deerness narrows into a hairline isthmus bracketed by beaches, St Peter's Pool on one side and Dingieshowe on the other, separated by dunes, the road, and a tiny car park and loo-block. A terse sign says *Toilets*.

This isthmus is a low, liminal zone, shifting sand and water. A little sea-level rise, one big storm, and you feel it could be swept away entirely. But it's been here for a long time. This site was used in the Neolithic. The *howe* of Dingieshowe is a broch mound from around 300 BC, and the name suggests that later it became a Norse meeting site, a *thing-howe*, long centuries after the broch had gone out of use. It is also a trowie place, a fairy mound from which Tam Bichan's fiddle can still be heard on those days when the sun stands still and the membrane between the worlds is grown thin. Tam went into the mound to play for the trows, as so many did, emerging in the summer solstice dawn to find a generation had passed and his yamils were now old men while he was still young. He never settled, and in the end he knocked on the mound, fiddle in hand, and the trows took him back again. They say a witch was burned at the howe, and though her charred remains were cleared away her skull keeps reappearing in the dunes. St Peter's Pool, on one side of the road, is a creepy place, sedimentary, like a miniature Morecambe Bay at the southern tip of an enclosed, north-facing firth: a shining expanse of silt streaked with great mounds and banks of cockle shells. The fine, soft sand doesn't abrade the shards of broken glass and china found here, they retain their sharp edges: be careful if you go barefoot.

This isthmus is two-faced, like Janus, looking forward and back. Some fifty yards to the south, across the road and over the mountainous dunes, Dingieshowe Bay is open to the North Sea, wild and exposed. Little glass or ceramic here: instead we find fragments of fishermen's multi-coloured twine, tiny grains and crumbs of wave-pulverized plastic. The dunes that separate the two beaches are always on the move: the cubicles in the loo-block can be knee-deep in windblown sand.

When you meet someone who lives in Deerness, it's the first thing you ask: *Which side of the toilets do you live?*

You're not in real Deerness until you've gone *beyond the toilets.*

I drive beyond the toilets.

Deep Deerness widens out again. This almost-island is rich in the remains of Norse Orkney: an ancient church; an aristocratic stronghold on a near-inaccessible sea-stack; burial grounds from the tenth to twelfth centuries. I rarely venture this far from home outside the summer months: and in my mind Newark Bay is a place of endless sun and sparkling sea. Sometimes the water is even warm. The south-facing bay embraces shallow sand. At the western end there is a concrete pier and a picnic table. But it is the eastern end that interests me.

The sand tails away into shingle and the slabs of old red sandstone, jutting in steps and platforms like the decks of an Art Deco ocean liner. Some are patterned with ripples made in the Devonian lakebed, others with fossil mud cracks mimicking the reticulations of a giraffe, others still spattered with the marks of ancient raindrops: fleeting interactions of water, air and silt preserved for four hundred million years. Behind the beach there is a cliff some ten feet high: a thick deposit of soil, undercut and overhanging, with rocks the size of footballs embedded in the earth and threatening to tumble. Down to the right the rubble and scree show how often this threat is fulfilled, helped by the force of the gale-driven breakers. Today, though, the sea is keeping within its bounds, a steady southerly driving the water into the embrace of the bay. It is spring, nearly summer, though I need my thick coat. I walk along for a few minutes, always aware of the toppling, precarious soil and rubble to my left, the slick surface of wet flagstone under my soles, the hard rocks below. The sea laps and sucks – *clapotis* – and out in the surf a shag bobs. Among the crevices of the rocks are the stems of kelp, water-smoothed limpet shells, ravels of colourful nylon rope, the occasional sun-bleached cartridge case, the pale forms of bark-stripped driftwood.

And then I see what I have been half-consciously looking for: a smooth curve of hard whitish matter that could at first sight also be taken for driftwood.

It is a human rib.

I pick it up and weigh it in my hands: small and delicate, so light I can barely feel its weight. The shape is at once simple and complex, a beautifully modulated arc, like a wind turbine blade. As fit for purpose as a seal's whisker. Ribs have a head and tail: the thick, blunt cranial end; the sharper caudal end, the morphology of an eel. I try to work out which rib this one is, right or left, higher or lower in the thorax. To imagine it flexing with each breath, caging a pulsing heart, part of a matrix of muscle and ligament and cartilage. And that breath supporting a voice. Language. Song. This brittle white stick was part of a mind-body-soul, deeply encultured and embedded in family, community, parish, lordship. I think of the last time it pushed against the intercostal muscles, expelling the death rattle. I'm picturing it as a woman's rib, but only because I'm a woman myself.

I hold the rib against my own abdomen, a best guess, trying it for size between my left breast and my waist, guessing it's one of the floating ribs, *costa fluitans*, with its large head and pointy tail. Probably the eleventh, the penultimate one, as the twelfth is smaller. But I'm no osteologist, and I'm struggling to be sure without other ribs to compare it against.

The last time I was here, there were several skeletons emerging from the striated face of the low cliff, all partial, embedded in the friable red clay. A bowl-like curve of cranium in cross-section. The knobby end of a tibia, coy, half revealed. The bones are deep orangey-yellow when they first come into daylight, not much paler than the soil.

Today, however, I can't see anybody in the cliff face. The winter has done a lot of damage to the sea's margin, scribbling and over-writing, scouring its palimpsest. Tumps of grass overhang my head. Someone – perhaps the county archaeologist, perhaps the farmer – has shored up part of the cliff with sandbags, but they too have been tumbled about by the water. I get closer, always aware of the risk of falling rock. Boulders wobble beneath my feet. The cliff is boldly striped, the top layer nearly black, thick with burned material and shell.

Still cradling the rib in my hands, I gaze at the stratum below the thick top layer of midden, let my eyes drift out of focus; stop looking; start seeing.

First one, then a second skeleton. The first is just a femur and fragment of pelvis. The second is even harder to spot, higher up, on the same alignment as the first but too far away to be part of the same individual. I can make out the ridged ripple of a spine and the snapped-off stalks of the true ribs, squashed into the space of an inch or two between flat stones above and below. Impossible for the imagination to reclothe these skewed, compressed bones with flesh. They are becoming entirely mineral, all collagen scoured from their crumbly honeycomb. Little by little they erode, become brittle with light and salt and air, and the sea takes them.

The Norse cemetery here at Newark was partially excavated in the late 1960s and early 1970s. My PhD supervisor Sid Bradley dug here and told me stories. There was an elderly lady from a nearby farm who used to come and watch them at work. One day he asked her, 'Have you always lived here?' 'Oh no! I only moved here when I married, and I've never really settled.' He was surprised, given her very local accent, and asked where she had come from. She raised her arm, and pointed across the bay. 'There.'

When Sid first told me this story, only a few years into my own acquaintance with the islands, it seemed romantic, wild, charming, primitive. I revisit it now, and wonder whether she wasn't just playing the endlessly amusing game of 'Wind up the ferry-louper'. I've encountered so many anecdotes like this one.

The Orkney Museum store has many containers of material from this site, the bodies of Newark folk who died in the eleventh and twelfth centuries. They could be the ancestors of that old lady. Boxes and bags, some labelled only *Norse Baby Bones*. These were Christians: the chapel at Newark may be one of the earliest in Viking Orkney. Apart from one jet bracelet and a bone comb there are no grave-goods from the cemetery.

Mourners do not bury skeletons: they bury people. These bones have never seen the light of day before. When these folk were laid to rest they were decently clothed in their flesh and skin, and wrapped in lengths of undyed linen.

Among the browny-yellow fragments visible in the soil is a made thing: a slim bone spike, whittled to a point, like one of a set of Victorian spillikins. I've seen things like this before: it's a shroud pin. I reach out a fingertip to it, my other hand still holding the rib. Is there any reason why I shouldn't prise the pin out of the clay and take it home? It's already almost fully exposed, another heavy rainfall or a southerly whipping up the waves, and it will be gone. But I don't, and maybe I can't. Partly because I've internalized the rules about not interfering with archaeological sites. And partly because these days something stroppy in me resists the urge to cling on to and categorize and over-analyse every facet of the past. Why can't we just let things go?

Also, I am assailed by emotion. It takes a moment to trace it back to source. My dear friend Anne, who worked at the museum in Kirkwall, was writing a doctoral thesis on early medieval bone and antler tools, a project her untimely death left unfinished. She used to pass me little objects like this and gently prod me into really looking at them: to notice the organic structure; the marks that indicated which tools had been used in their manufacture, and how; the evidence of wear. I couldn't go to her funeral because it clashed with my father's cremation in London, but *The Orcadian* reported that St Magnus Cathedral was full to overflowing.

I have a sudden image of competent, short-nailed fingers pinching the layered linen of the shroud together above the hidden face, the beloved face, and stabbing the fabric in place, a swift in-and-out-and-in, with this little pin. There's no sign of wear that I can see: it was made for this purpose.

One careful owner.

Another, much older memory assails me as I peer hard at the cliff face, still feeling Anne's approving presence. The pin looks smooth as first, but the sun shifting out from behind a cloud gleams on the shaved facets, and I have a sudden, multi-sensory vision of a baking-hot day nearly forty years ago. Our parents have thrown us in the back of the white Ford Cortina and taken us to Olorgesailie, in the Rift Valley, a couple of hours' drive south-west of our home in Nairobi. It's my first visit to this site, which for a palaeontology-obsessed child like me is up there with Olduvai (where I have also recently been), and Neandertal, and Sterkfontein, as a place of legend. Olorgesailie isn't that old, not compared to Olduvai: it was in use from around a million years ago to around 500 thousand. So it's just *Homo erectus* here, not the much earlier australopithecines who are my real love. It's 1977. Donald Johanson's discovery of a half-complete *Australopithecus* skeleton, Lucy, at Hadar in Ethiopia is very recent. Johanson and my god and hero Richard Leakey are fighting a macho public war over human origins. I have Leakey's autograph, in a copy of his book *Origins* – it's smudged where I stroked it while the ink was still wet. He was Director of the National Museum in Nairobi, where my mother was a volunteer guide – guardian of the stuffed elephant, the racks of Joy Adamson's watercolour portraits of Kenyan tribal people, all those skulls of *erectus* and *habilis* as well as the australopithecines.

But even if Olorgesailie is only Lower Pleistocene, it's still amazing. It's known as the 'tool factory'. We wander the walkways over the site, looking at the thick scatter of Acheulean hand-axes lying apparently *in situ* everywhere, embedded in the yellow-grey soil. We are shown the bones of familiar species, baboon and zebra, with the cut marks of ancient butchery visible to the trained eye. Our guide explains how the site is dated, the layers of volcanic ash coming from Mount Olorgesailie, and the more distant craters of Suswa and Longonot. He tells us how it was found and excavated by Richard's mother, Mary Leakey, in 1942, with the drafted labour of Italian prisoners of war. This is exciting too. I know about the prisoners of war: they built the tiny stone chapel on the road down into the Rift Valley; we pass it often on the way to Lake Naivasha, just north of here, where we keep that little motorboat.

Olorgesailie fills me with a desperate longing. So many hand-axes: do they really need them all? I know that to take even one would be a sin and a crime, but the temptation is terrible. I am still young enough to think that *having* things matters, that ownership is permanent and makes a difference to who you are. I have not yet learned that possession weighs us down. I am ten years old and my ego spans the horizons: I do not understand the folly of thinking that I could *own*, however illicitly, an object which is already nearly a million years older than me. On the way back to the museum I pick up a faceted lump of stone from under an acacia bush and show it to our guide. He has already been laughing at me, and I am not sure whether he is annoyed by my incessant questions. 'It's not a tool,' he says, still laughing. And then he relents. 'But it is worked, look, see the strike marks. Well spotted!' I preen. It's a core, from which many small sharp flakes have been knapped away. 'Keep it,' he says, shrugging and smiling. A core, I think, like an apple core. It fits my hand.

That core was a talisman for years, but somewhere in

the many moves between houses and cities and countries and continents it got lost, and I became less obsessed with human origins.

People laboured at Olorgesailie for half a million years, but they didn't live there or die there. It wasn't until 2003 that the first hominid remains were found at Olorgesailie: parts of a small *Homo erectus* cranium, gnawed by carnivores. It's not the presence of skeletons or even the rawness of the archaeology here at Newark that reminds me of the lithic core from the Rift Valley, but something as slight and transient as that sheen on the facets of the bone shroud pin. Two objects, linked only by me, and my desire for possession. The shroud pin has triggered a tactile memory, somehow encoded in my brain, my nerves, my fingertips, although the intervening nearly forty years will have seen almost every atom of me renewed.

I feel as though I know these people, pinned into their shrouds at Newark nine or ten centuries ago. Under my breath I mutter fragments of the rites that accompanied them into the ground, the Latin prose-poetry of high medieval funerary ceremony: 'Non ei dominentur umbrae mortis... Non tegat eam chaos et caligo tenebrarum... In paradisum deducant eam angeli.'

May the shadows of death not lord it over her... May chaos and the fog of the dark not touch her...

May the angels lead her into paradise.

These people are contemporaries of St Magnus, and his nephew Rognvald Kali, as well as the anonymous author of *Orkneyinga Saga*. It was Kali who lifted Magnus's bones from their shrine in the old cathedral at Birsay and moved them to the new Romanesque church. The person whose rib I have in my hands could have been in the crowd, holding her breath, her ribcage a cradle of longing for the saint. Magnus's bones are still in the cathedral though no longer formally enshrined: they are hidden away, in an ossuary cavity within the pillar to the south-west of the crossing, hidden behind a wall of pale red stone. They came to light and were photographed in the early twentieth century, the gash made by the cook's axe still riving the jarl's skull. And then the bones were replaced within the pillar.

A skull thought to be Kali's was also discovered immured in St Magnus Cathedral, in the north-west pillar, opposite his uncle's: it is assumed that the ossuary cavities in the thirteenth-century pillars were made in the mid-sixteenth century, in some haste, when the old Catholic saints were ousted from the new, reformed, saint-free kirk.

Kali's skull and Magnus's bones have not been seen since 1919, although forensic analysis on the basis of the century-old photographs suggests that both sets of remains are compatible with what we know of the men's appearance and life-story. Uncle and nephew have survived both the ravages of the Reformation and the scientific curiosity of the modern age. Nonetheless, some people think the bones in the south-west pillar are not those of Magnus at all.

We could hoick Magnus and Kali's skulls out of their pillars, subject them to DNA and Carbon-14 and isotope analysis. But I'd rather we didn't: I don't want to know how short Kali really was, or the sorry state of his teeth. Let's hang on to the possibility that Magnus was a real saint, Kali a real hero, both superhuman. Let the mystery remain in the dark of the cathedral as well as here, on this sunny beach at Newark.

This rib that I hold now had near-magical power without any need for imagined sanctity. It's one of the few bones that continue to make red blood cells in the adult body. The only bone that can regenerate: if a rib is taken out of its periosteum during surgery a new rib will form. No wonder this bone was chosen for the making of Eve. The costal cartilage continues to harden in adult life, and is therefore one of the more reliable ways of judging the age of a skeleton, though not the sex. Biological miracles. Forensic miracles.

These bones fray out of the cliff, without the police or the county archaeologist or Historic Environment Scotland recording their presence or their absence. Local people, including several archaeologists, keep an eye, but there are so many eroding coastal sites in Orkney. They can't all be saved. If there's a watching brief here at Newark, or a preservation order, it isn't having much effect. Instead there's just a silent slippage back into constituent atoms. I imagine each molecule of calcium phosphate uttering a little sigh as it emerges finally into the light after a millennium of dark, bursting like a bubble as it goes back to join the main.

And I stand here on Devonian sandstone, peering in at them, intruding on their privacy for the first time in a thousand years, newly aware of the bone-on-bone artic-ulation of my own spine, the jut of pelvis, the flex of rib. In-breath and out-breath, in-wave and out-wave. The bowl of my skull feels as fragile and evanescent as the foam that continually bubbles and fades on the sea below.

I bend down and tuck the rib back into the crevice where I found it.

Evie was white with snow almost down to sea level when I woke but it's mostly gone now. Lots of very puzzled lambs. The sea was like gin and tonic. And, oh, the swallows. I feel they have come straight from Kenya with news of the long rains, and I can smell the wet murram earth in their vapour trail... The puffins are back, too. Now I am waiting for the Arctic terns to arrive.

I need to come out of the water. My hands and feet are numb. I'm not shivering, not yet, but I know my core temperature will fall even faster once I'm out of the sea and into the wind. It's what cold-water swimmers call 'the afterdrop', and needs to be taken seriously. I'm beginning to lose focus. I swim back into the shallower water, in the lee of the breakwater, and stand, looking around me one last time, hoping, always hoping, for another glimpse of a companionable seal.

The sand stretches away from me. The winter sun is lifting slowly clear of the hills to the south, and the sand gleams silver-gilt. Although I know I should get warm and out of what wind there is, I can't bear to leave.

As I linger my way up the beach, my eye is caught repeatedly by iridescent flashes. The gently ebbing tide has left a treasure trove of little shells in roughly parallel undulating lines, the fossil footprints of each last wave as the sea drew slowly back into itself. There are limpets of every size from baby's fingernails to old men's kneecaps; brown and yellow periwinkles; whelks. It's the top shells that are giving off that shimmer in the oblique light, their outer layer abraded to reveal the mother-of-pearl underneath. I don't know any beach round here that treats its shells more lovingly than the Sands of Evie, the coarse calcareous sand gently taking off the outer layer and leaving the inner shell intact. They prompt memories of my mother at the dining table with a rag and a jar of silver polish, cleaning the tarnish off the Georgian silver spoons in which she traded at antique fairs.

There are three kinds of top shells: the largest are the painted ones, beautifully conical and mottled pink. They often lose the tips of their cones, leading to the revelation of their inner spiral, that perfect Fibonacci geometry which underpins all our ideas of what makes for ideal proportion; Robert Rendall saw these ordered progressions as clear proof of 'a Creative Intelligence... a divinely implanted correspondence between the constitution of man's mind and the structure of the universe'. I'm less sure. We are pareidolic animals after all, imposing meaning on random patterns: it's not such a big jump from seeing faces in clouds to seeing the Hand of God in the spiral of a shell. Why should one association be more valid than another? When intact and viewed from above the pinkly painted top shells remind me, irresistibly, of nipples.

Then there are the grey and the purple ones, more squat and bulbous, like navels (and the Latin name of the purple top shell is *Gibbula umbilicalis*), both with tiger stripes. They're all grazers, living on tiny algae. It astonishes me, every time I pick up one of these beauties, to think that the shell is exuded by the body of the little animal that lives inside. I know it's no different, really, from my own endoskeleton, but it still seems extraordinary that these molluscs should have two kinds of shell-producing cell in their mantle, one for the outer and one for the nacreous inner. The nacre protects their delicate flesh from parasites and irritating grit: it entombs the irritants in successive layers of calcium carbonate crystals, woven together with silk-like proteins. Suffering and experience and memory are all charted and frozen within those luminous layers.

The zigzags of the outer layer of the top shell are complex in the way that a knitting pattern is, or the cards of a Jacquard loom, and it's been suggested that they perform a similar function for molluscs: a set of instructions. If the shell is damaged the animal can 'read' the pattern by sensing it with its mantle, and work out where to begin the repair. You'd think the top shells' mother-of-pearl would all be the same, but as I walk along the line of the ebb I pick up shells whose rubbed sheen is variously purple, blue, green, silver-grey. All the cool colours of the rainbow. Palette of sea and sky and hill.

I have a handful of top shells now, pretty enough to be mermaid's buttons if mermaids were fool enough to wear clothes, but as yet I've found none of the shells I'm really always looking for: the cowries, *groatie buckies*. *Buckie* is a Scots word for shell, but no one seems sure what the *groatie* part means. Groatie buckies are common enough to be worth looking for; rare enough that it's always a thrill finding one; said to bring good luck. There are two species in Orkney, *Trivia monacha* and *Trivia arctica*, but only *monacha* has spots on its shell. (I'm told another way of differentiating between male *monacha* and *arctica* is by comparing their penises, *monacha*'s being cylindrical and thin while *arctica*'s is leaf-like and broad, but that's not much use when all you have is the shell, and besides, I feel it would be a little impertinent.) There is such a contrast between the animal, a vivid yellow snail which holds its siphon up like an elephant's trunk, and its home, a cool dove-grey shell with a blush of pink, an intimate, furled little shape that nestles in your palm. The ridges on the back of the shell look like fingerprints, or a ploughed field, or the pattern left in the sand where the water has pulled it back and forth. Turn them over and they're smiling at you. Cute as they are, they're carnivores, night-time scavengers. The shells are much the same colour as the Evie sand, easily missed; the best way of looking for them is not to look, just let your gaze drift over the fragments of bleached coral, the little pebbles and scraps of weed, until the ridge-and-furrow curve snags your consciousness like a half-forgotten face seen in a crowd.

Groatie buckies aren't born with ridges: the babies have smooth white shells, incredibly fragile and much more noticeably spiraliform, which give them buoyancy as they swim. Slowly the shell hardens, gains bulk, darkens, the ridges develop, and the adult settles on the sublittoral seabed. All mollusc shells are designed around spirals, but often you must look at the shell in its earliest stages to see the truth of this.

Trivia are not the true cowries, which belong to the genus *Cypraea*, although they are distant relations. The true cowries have smooth, not ridged, shells. In the garden up the road I have a pile of weathered, faded Kenyan shells, giant clams and textile cones, spider conches and bull-mouth helmets, and several tiger cowries, gathered on the beaches around Mombasa and lugged around the world by my parents, somehow always getting tucked into a box when we were packing up. The name of the tiger cowrie (*Cypraea tigris*) used to confuse me: they're spotted, not striped, but it's another name given by Linnaeus in that first flush of scientific labelling, and in 1756 the distinction between big stripy cats and slightly smaller spotty cats was maybe not as clear as it is today (though surely Linnaeus of all people should have known). Leopards and tigers were both big and scary and far away.

There is no confusing exotic *Cypraea tigris* and our little *Trivia monacha*, though, even if both have spots: the tiger cowrie is not only smooth and lushly patterned but the size of a big lemon, while I've never found a groatie buckie bigger than my little fingernail. The Romans called cowries 'little sows', *porcellae*, which ultimately gives us *porcelain*, from the smooth translucence which both share. *Porcella* is a euphemism for *vulva*, and presumably Linnaeus had this in mind when he called the true cowries *Cypraea*, shells of Cyprus, the birthplace of Venus. In contrast *monacha* means a solitary, though it's still a feminine word. A 'monkess', a nun, an anchorite. It suits these demure little shells, folded in on themselves, self-sufficient as clasped and praying hands.

Linnaeus thought there was only one species of *Trivia*. He was proved wrong by Emmanuel da Costa, who showed that spotty *monacha* and immaculate *arctica* were distinct, and gave *monacha* its name. Da Costa was an eighteenth-century London antiquarian with a free-and-easy attitude to other people's money, but scrupulous where conchology was concerned, and a self-righteous prude when it came to Linnaeus's incorrigible habit of drawing analogies between the forms of molluscs and human genitalia, scattering labels like *labia majora* and *mons veneris* around like confetti. 'Science should be chaste and delicate,' Da Costa tutted. 'Ribaldry at times has been passed for wit; but Linnaeus alone passes it for terms of science.' Da Costa awarded *Trivia monacha* its pious little name in protest against both Linnaeus's predilection and the ancient association between the cowrie and the human female genitalia.

Trivia means commonplace, which seems unfair. It comes ultimately from Latin *trivium*, a place where three roads meet, more than just a fork in the road, not quite a crossroads. Something that's trivial is gossip, the kind of information you might pick up on street corners. But Sophocles had Oedipus kill his father at a *trivium* on the way to Delphi: the three roads embody fate, past, present and future. The Greek goddess Hekate had three faces, personifying these aspects of fate, and the Romans called her Trivia. She's associated with Persephone in the underworld, Artemis the huntress on earth, and Selene the moon in the heavens. Not so trivial, after all.

(I've been chasing up another reference, another Latin name for cowries, *matriculi*. Little matrix, little womb, little mother. It's cited in books on mother goddesses, sea goddesses, the eternal feminine. But the search runs into the sand: I can trace it back as far as a catalogue of Indonesian curiosities published in 1741 by the German botanist Georg Rumpf, and Rumpf says he found the term in the works of Ennius, the Roman poet. Among the surviving fragments of Ennius's work is a poem in praise of seafood, including scallops, mussels, oysters and sea urchins, but I can't find *matriculi* anywhere. As with most quests to return to the womb, this one seems ultimately futile.)

I am so focused on not-quite-looking for the groatie buckie which I feel sure must be hiding somewhere in this litter of shells that I almost miss the shard of sea-washed pottery. It's late-Victorian, kelp-brown transfer-ware, a pattern of leaves and flowers, its curve and incline suggesting that it came from the rim of a dinner plate. Like most of us I find sea-glass and sea-china irresistible. I have a basket of smoothed shards at the house, picked up for their intrinsic appeal, retained partly because they remind me of my mother. She collected and dealt in china as well as silver, in a small way: weekends at the local street market, the occasional fair. A lifelong hobby, acquired from her father, put on hold when we were in Kenya, resumed with enthusiasm once she was back in London. I never paid enough attention when being dragged round Camden Passage or Brick Lane or Bermondsey markets: only just enough to learn how hallmarks worked, or to tell Chelsea from Spode. But something must have sunk in. Invited to dine once at one of the older Oxford colleges I was impressed enough with the attractive dinner service to turn my plate over without even thinking what I was doing, looking for the pottery's mark. From halfway down the long, polished table came a cheery shout: 'Are you from Stoke too?'

In later life, my mother fell in love with restoration: now her quest was for the imperfect rather than the flawless, the Regency bone-china plate that had been valued enough to be badly mended with clunky Victorian rivets. She would soak it, dissolve the old glue, extract the metal staples, reattach the broken fragments and paint over the cracks and any damaged part of the decoration. She learned to rebuild plates with chipped rims and jugs with missing feet. The problem was always the final painting; the colours were never true enough to please her, the restored surface too matte to match the original glaze. And yet at the same time she wrestled with the dishonesty of restoration: she was unhappy with the idea that someone might be misled by her work, put a higher price on it than it was worth. We talked about how the damaged pieces were uniquely valuable, the ones which could tell something of their story, and how her work on them was simply the adding of another chapter to the biography.

After my father died, nearly a decade after my mother, it was time at last to clear the house. Bone china and earthenware emerged from every corner, stacked in the bottom of cupboards, tucked into bookshelves. The unsold stock from the last antique fair she'd ever been to, years earlier, still crated, still wrapped in that distant weekend's yellowing newspapers, with prices attached, and the little notebook in which she recorded sales. Solid brown Doulton jugs, Mason's Ironstone phoenix-pattern plates, huge blue-and-white platters, tiny translucent tea-cups with gilt rims. I couldn't have sold her collection even if I had wanted to: some was valuable, all was precious; much was damaged, nothing matched. I certainly couldn't keep it, though I have hung on to far too much. I could have thrown it away: I had a vision of driving to the sea and tipping the whole lot in with one glorious almighty crash. But in the end I advertised online for people to come and help themselves. I set as much as I could out on my mother's dining-room table, as though for a fantasy banquet. Strangers came and marvelled, and swapped stories, and left as friends. I wept to see the treasures leave, and then I set the dining table again.

When I turn up sea-china in my beachcombing I can hear my mother at my shoulder. Right now she's pointing out a detail I hadn't noticed: the slippage in the wreath of brown flowers where the transferrer, the specialist craftswoman responsible for applying the design, has laid down two abutting sections of pattern-paper slightly askew.

The treasures I find along the Evie shore are quotidian, mundane: even the pottery is mostly very utilitarian, thick shards of cream- and brown-glazed stoneware from the jugs and jars and bottles that were the staple vessels of Orkney crofts. As today, there is the occasional piece of blue or green or brown transferware; occasionally the blue-and-white stripe of Green's Cornishware; sometimes an extra kick of pleasure comes with the discovery of a fragment of Scottish spongeware, thick jewel colours overlaying crackled cream, a pattern of daisies or thistles smudged on. There's always a thrill when a shard has text on it, even if it's only 'Burslem' or 'ade in Engla'.

But somewhere out there in Eynhallow Sound there is a real treasure. Scramble west from here along the rocky foreshore, past the Knowe of Stenso, and the next mound you come to is the Broch of Burgar. There is a tangle of stories about this place, but at their heart is a gold and silver treasure which was found in 1840 by the laird, a Mr Gordon, and – to Gordon's fury – subsequently claimed on behalf of Queen Victoria as treasure trove. Piecing together the different versions of the story is rather like reassembling a pot from worn and broken fragments, but by patient processes of elimination and comparison a shape emerges. The treasure was never drawn, and we only have an amateurish inventory. Silver pins, brooches, chains and bowls, and amber beads: a combination which is only matched elsewhere in Scotland by Pictish hoards. There were silver combs as well, which have no parallels. Gordon is said also to have found two gold arm-rings, which may have been Viking Age. In response to the Crown's claims, he wrote that:

> A private Individual, who chooses, for his own amusement, to be at the expence and trouble, of searching for relicks of antiquity, upon his own property, is not bound to deliver up, for behoof of Her Majesty, what he may find, as 'hidden

treasure', until adequately indemnified for his labour and expences.

Gordon never did give the queen the treasure. He claimed he had already sent it to the Earl of Zetland, and that the 'ancient relicks', which had all fallen to pieces anyway, were worth no more 'than a Groat of Scottish money'. Some bureaucrat backed down in the face of all this bluster, accepting the story and letting Gordon keep the treasure without ever checking with the Earl; and no reference to the treasure has ever turned up in the Zetland papers. Other eye-witnesses muttered that Gordon was lying about the value of his hoard, and after his death stories circulated in Evie that he had gone to the top of the cliff and thrown it into the sea in a fit of self-righteous pique. I am reminded of the closing episodes of *Beowulf*, when the hero enters an ancient barrow and kills a treasure-hoarding dragon but dies himself in the fight. His grieving people enter the chamber and take the treasure; they tip the dragon's corpse over the cliff and raise a mound over Beowulf's cremated remains, together with the dragon's hoard – 'and there it lies', the poet says, 'just as useless to men as it was before'.

I like to think that Gordon's treasure is all still out there, if sea-changed: the fragile embossed bowls remaining defiantly intact despite the force of the roaring rost that tumbles boulders as big as buses; the amber beads rolling in the tug and pull of the water, camouflaged among the golden-brown holdfasts of the kelp; the brooches growing thick and blurred with barnacles. Perhaps one day a rogue wave will roll ashore the silver combs and pins, the natural companion of the mirror carved on the Sands of Evie symbol stone.

What's that gleam, down by the tideline?

I swam this morning at 7. Moon huge in the SW, sea and western sky nacreous, eastern sky a crucible of molten dawn. Air temp 8 C, water 12 C. Much bird activity, four shags ducking and diving, gulls, a flock of turnstones, crows, an endless stream of noisy rooks like smuts blown from a bonfire. Curlews ululating. One common seal, cruising slowly by, curious, diving leisurely with a great arc of dark back. Returning, coming closer, closer, then at about 5 yards from me was startled, vanished in a huge splash, resurfaced amid the shags, who took off in outrage. I tore myself away just as the sun was lifting over the edge of the world.

My mother died on the Tuesday of Holy Week, in 2002.

I just typed, My other died…

'No man is an island…'

'… never send to know for whom the bell tolls; it tolls for thee.'

Just over two years earlier, she had begun to realize that the tickle in her throat was more than the aftermath of a cold. She began, discreetly, to make enquiries, visit specialists. I was finishing my doctorate in York, my sister flying for Air Mauritius. Neither of us was to be worried. Months ticked by. The tickle became a scratch.

I knew, vaguely, she was concerned about whether her voice would be capable of delivering a paper at a conference in Budapest: I said something glib drawn from my own fledgling academic experience. I don't remember what. Make eye-contact, probably. Swallow. Keep breathing.

In the summer of 2000, she was briefly hospitalized with a deep vein thrombosis, nothing to do with the tickle. When a specialist was flicking through her notes, he said, 'I understand you're also being monitored for motor neurone disease.' That was how the news was officially broken to her. But she had been nursing her suspicions for a while: a lifetime in the social services, latterly in hospice work and bereavement counselling, meant that she knew what MND looked like. However, no matter how hard-headed you are, some truths are difficult to confront, some shapes easier to perceive with averted vision. In its early stages her version of the condition, amyotrophic lateral sclerosis, flies under the radar. Who thinks a tickly throat is a death sentence, or for that matter a slight weakness in your grip, or a nasal quality to your voice? She had been letting the idea unfold slowly, but the doctor's moment of indiscretion made her look her terror in the face. She was catapulted in that instant from one side to the other of the professional divide. Having spent many years working with doctors on how to care for the dying patient, she was now that patient.

She was still determined not to worry us. But my sister went to see her in hospital, and overheard another indiscreet conversation, another reference to *motor neurone disease*. Straight home and on to Google.

Rapidly progressive, she read. No treatment. Invariably fatal.

Amyotrophic means the muscles are not being fed. *Lateral* refers to the areas on the sides of the spinal cord where the motor neurons are found. *Sclerosis* is hardening.

Motor neurons look like seaweed, genus *Laminaria*, kelp, tangles, daberlack. They have a sprawling star-shaped head, with dendrites like the fronds and blades of kelp growing out of the cell nucleus at one end, a stipe of the axon coated in its myelin sheath, and the axon terminals, like a holdfast, emerging at the other end. They cling on to the muscle. The task of the motor neuron, like a seal's vibrissae, is to receive information about movement. It then passes the information on, from the brain to the muscles.

No one has yet told me, but I know something's up. Something.

My mother calls a summit meeting: my father, my sister, me. Sitting at the television end of the sitting room in the Islington house, she breaks the news. Steady degeneration. Her voice will be the first thing to go. Then paralysis. Suffocation. Death.

I am shocked beyond speech, beyond tears. *Orcinus orca* has risen from the depths, rammed me, flipped me over into tonic immobility.

I'm a historian, an archaeologist, I deal in stories and patterns and symbols. I'm supposed to be the expert on death and dying. Where can I go, to understand the story of what is happening here?

Amyotrophic lateral sclerosis was first identified by Jean-Martin Charcot, in 1869, and is therefore known in France as *la maladie de Charcot*. Motor Neurone Disease – MND – is too cold and clinical a label for what's happening here and now, to the most important person in my world. *La maladie de Charcot* gives me a narrative, something to grapple with, a way of thinking about the unthinkable. I need ways of connecting this violent alien in our midst with my familiar worlds.

Jean-Martin Charcot was the 'Napoleon of neurology', responsible for the accurate identification of multiple sclerosis and Parkinson's disease as well as MND, and he argued for the reclassification of hysteria as a psychological rather than a physiological disorder. There is a famous painting by André Brouillet, *Une leçon clinique à la Salpêtrière*, of Charcot lecturing on hysteria. Some thirty attentive, black-clad and gravely bearded men stand around taking notes, while Charcot gestures at the subject, a fainting woman supported by another male doctor. She is an island of creamy white in a sea of charcoal-black; the light haloes her pale face, her closed eyes are in shadow, her marmoreal bosom gleams. Charcot's heavy, thoughtful face is turned away from her, towards the room and the men; it's hard to identify the source of the light that falls across his cheek and brow, unless it's the woman's lambent breasts.

Sigmund Freud isn't in Brouillet's picture, but he too was one of Charcot's students, though they disagreed about the causes of hysteria. When Freud was around thirty he bought a lithograph of *Une leçon clinique* and it stayed on his wall in Vienna for fifty years; when he came to London in 1938 he hung it over his couch in his new consulting room.

The hysterical woman in Brouillet's picture is Marie 'Blanche' Wittman, a long-term patient at the Salpêtrière. A recent study moves her from object to subject, showing how she collaborated with Charcot, falling in with his expectations of how a hysterical woman would behave, making a career for herself as his most famous patient and case-study. Blanche Wittman is no longer the blank white page both her name and her portrait imply. Freud's print of Brouillet's painting of Charcot's lecture still hangs above the couch in what is now the Freud Museum in Hampstead, a building my mother knew very well. Compositionally, *Une leçon clinique* is weirdly like that photograph from 1930 of my three-year-old mother looking startled in her short white dress and socks, being loomed over by dark-clad figures, women in cloches and fur-collared coats, Princess Beatrice clutching the flowers, my great-grandfather uniformed and bemedalled, his boots and spurs gleaming.

My mother has been lucky; she is almost seventy-three when *la maladie de Charcot* is diagnosed. It's commonest between forty and seventy, a neurological failure of middle rather than old age. There is a small but statistically significant genetic correlation. When I look at my mother now, do I see my future self?

When is an island not an island?

Charcot Island in the Antarctic was also named for Dr Charcot, by his younger son, Jean-Baptiste, who became a pioneer of polar exploration. When my mother was two, in 1929, a British explorer flew around Charcot to prove for the first time that it was indeed technically an island, although an ice-bridge connected it to the mainland. Eighty years later, in 2009, seven years after her death, that ice-bridge melted, and Charcot could be circumnavigated for the first time. Charcot Island is near the South Shetland Islands, not far from the Inlet of Exasperation and Cape Disappointment.

Microcosm and macrocosm, body and world.

In motor neurone disease, the neurons in the motor nerves die, one by one, breaking the bridge between brain and muscle, between thought and action. The sensory neurons continue to function, picking up information from the world through the skin and passing it to the brain. There's no mental impairment: the brain tries to respond, but the motor neurons have hardened off, and the message doesn't get through. In 80 per cent of cases the symptoms start in the legs and feet: the victim is caught unawares by tripping and stumbling over non-existent obstacles, developing a flat-footed, flapping gait, like a penguin.

In my mother's case, however, the dieback is starting at the top and working its way down. Vocal and facial control will go, then arms and hands, then diaphragm. She has her lawyer and her GP witness a statement: once she is no longer capable of breathing without mechanical assistance she is to be allowed to die.

She jots me down some notes – I have the bits of paper in front of me now, densely covered in blue biro. Her familiar handwriting, just a little shaky, before her hands and arms get too weak. 'Funeral Thoughts', she scribbles. 'Not laid down in talents of stone. Just suggestions. At green burial would like those want to have something to do – write good-bye on coffin? Anything read needs to be simple, familiar…'

No embalming, a cardboard coffin, a green burial site, poems by Kavafis, MacNeice, Shakespeare; music by Mozart and Louis Armstrong. (My mother has also spent years campaigning through the Natural Death Centre for funeral reform.) And 'ashes to ashes, dust to dust', in the old Book of Common Prayer version.

Sure and certain hope of the Resurrection…

MND has been in the news a lot around the time of my mother's diagnosis because of high-profile cases where people with the disease have been campaigning for the right to die, either through a change in the legislation in the UK, or by making it easier for people to travel to a euthanasia clinic in Switzerland. My mother follows these stories with obsessive fascination, but her opposition to the legalization of euthanasia is absolute. She has worked for a decade in an East London hospice: she has supported patients and their families through many different kinds of death, including this one. And she's had a lifetime of sucking it up, coping, not complaining, making do and mending, to prepare her for this end.

She is adamant that legalizing euthanasia will make the old and ill afraid to go to their doctors. That vulnerable people will feel a moral obligation to kill themselves in order not to burden their families, or the state. That most people who want to die are depressed, even if they are also terminally ill, and that the two disorders should not be confused. That the euthanasia campaign distracts attention and funding from end-of-life care. That if there were enough hospices there would be less anxiety about a painful end. That the medical profession needs to stop seeing the death of the patient as the failure of the doctor. That suicide is not an option: it is the end of all options.

That the last, and perhaps the greatest, task of a parent is to teach her children that death is not something to fear.

We talk a lot about her experiences working in the hospice and the deaths at which she has been present. She describes what she sees as the wisdom of the existing legislation, the grey area which means that a doctor can prescribe morphine and advise of safe levels, but the patient can self-administer the kindly drug and choose to transgress those levels. 'We already have euthanasia,' she says.

I don't agree, but I can't retaliate with an ounce of her eloquence, or her experience. She's a wise old war baby, and her story has never been about herself. I'm on the cusp between baby boom and Generation X, and it's me, me, me all the way.

I am speaking in the usual way. She is not. There is a little thing like a laptop in her hands; it's called a lightwriter, and it speaks in a jerky, processed voice. There are two male and two female voices to choose from, all vaguely American in vowel sound and such intonation as they have. The female voices are squeaky, so she's chosen a male persona called 'Paul'. Paul can be programmed with pre-set phrases, and at the press of a button he will croak *Thank you for the lovely flowers*, or *Look at me, being waited on like Lady Muck*. But conversation takes longer, even though the motor neurons controlling my mother's arms and hands have not yet died back and for the time being she can still pick her way across the keys. It's so hard, though, not to finish her sentences for her. In company, everyone falls silent and gazes at her expectantly when she picks up the light-writer; we watch her tapping fingers, and when she presses play it's only to say *What beautiful weather*, or *More coffee?* Her fear of bathos silences her. She's always been a good listener, but now listening is being forced on her. She can no longer support a conversation with the little fillers and prompts that encourage another to keep talking. Her tongue is atrophying into a little hard poky thing; and I find my own tongue is tied. I have to resist the urge to take Paul from her and type my answer; using my own voice feels rude, as though responding to a foreigner by shouting ever more loudly in English.

> '... you must give this voice to me. I will take the very best thing that you have...'
>
> 'But if you take my voice,' said the little mermaid, 'what will be left to me?'
>
> '... have you lost your courage? Stick out your little tongue and I shall cut it off.'

My mother refuses the hospice place that's offered her: it's in her own old place of employment, down the road in Hackney, and in a rare outburst of emotion she is adamant that she will not go. *I don't want them to see me like this*, she makes Paul squawk.

Spent the night in a field full of silverweed, cuckooflower and orchids, with Helen, Donna and other lovely Polar Bears. Swam at 00.09 for the solstice, with the sky still full of light, and sat round the fire eating very fine Norwegian buns (thank you, Ragnhild!), accompanied by drumming snipe. Another swim this morning and sleepily home for the school run.

What gives a ferry-louper like me the right to write about Orkney? The word first crops up in 1661: a woman from the south isles was in court for calling the minister and his wife 'thieffes and vagabonds and runnegatis and ferry loopers'. How I long to know more about her, and the context of her words.

I used to think the 'louper' came from the circular, looping journey of the ferry, endlessly back and forth across the Pentland Firth, but it's an Old Norse word, *hlaupari*. And not a complimentary one. A *dyke-louper* is someone who comes illicitly over the wall, rather than politely by the gate. A *ladder-louper* goes up the ladder to the gallows, to leap off and be hanged. A *land-louper* is a vagrant. So a ferry-louper is a restless soul, someone who behaves suspiciously and may well end badly. It's cognate with *leap*, and an Orkney word for sand-flea, *loopack*. Ferry-fleas, parasites coming over to irritate the natives.

Ferry-loupers are unlikely to stay.

'It isn't the winters that get to me,' another ferry-louper told me when explaining why she was heading south again, 'it's the years with no summer, when you reach late August and realize that there's no more hope…'

The years when equinoctial gales segue into haar and back into gales, and your skin has never once been warm. *Fimbulvetr*, fimbulwinter, the Great Winter in Old Norse religion: three winters in a row, when no crops will grow and the world starves, the winter that presages war, and the end of the world.

Ferry-louper (like *fimbulvetr*) is an Old Norse word, but surely the Norse were themselves the first ferry-loupers. *Longship-loupers*. Those Norse settlers must have come to Orkney with hopes, fears, uncertainties, just like their modern equivalents. Did the Picts smile to the Vikings' faces, mutter about them in corners, cast half-curious, half-baleful glances, say *I told you so* when Knut and Hild upped stakes and went back home to Hordaland after a few years?

Sea a slubby shot-silk in blue-black and jade, embroidered with silver-wire and seed pearls. Sky dip-dyed Wedgwood blue and lemon, tie-dyed peach. Moon a great silver sequin low in the west.

I have gone down to the sea early. No time to swim, I have a meeting in the town, but there are a few minutes in hand. The sun is already high, the tide low and retreating further. A likely time to die, on the ebb of the tide and the waning of the moon. A bad time to marry, in Orkney lore.

Did that proud girl Brita/Ursilla from Stronsay marry her handsome, sulky farmhand on a day like this?

It must have been at this kind of tide, with the strand all gleaming and the rocks on show, that the Thorodale farmer and his wife came down to collect bait in the liminal, inter-tidal zone. I wonder for the first time what that young woman thought about her abduction by the Fin-man. Was she altogether sorry to be snatched away from drudgery on the croft? What was life like on Eynhallow, among the Fin-folk? What did she say to her man when he came to haul her back?

The breakwater is exposed, its slabs of sandstone stacked like haphazard piles of books waiting to be boxed and carted away. Bits of rusty metal, hooks and staples. A length of chain. Colonies of limpets, clinging to their home scars. The various weeds, kelp and daberlack, carrageen and wrack. If you wander up the western side of the breakwater and peer into one of the crevices towards the lower end, the bit that's under water most of the time, there is a surprise waiting. We have a guerrilla artist, who takes smooth pale stones and draws on them in indelible black pen, creating stark zigzags and cells, patterns reminscent of the carved stones from Skara Brae and the Ness of Brodgar, then tucks them into the landscape, balanced on fence posts, camouflaged among the shingle, resting on top of a drystone dyke. One of these anonymous gifts, like a Neolithic Easter egg, lurks wedged and irretrievable in a crevice of the breakwater.

The calm sea has left the pale gold sand smooth, clear of weed and thickly studded with shells. The sand is patterned with tiny wavy lines that run parallel to the ebb, each one marking a fallback, a retreat, the fingerprints of the last fluttering wave to reach this high. A few paces to the west the little burn has cut a ravine through the sand, exposing the underlying slab and shingle, before spilling laterally into a miniature estuary of a thousand interlacing rills that run down into the lapping brine. You lose all sense of time and scale: this could be the Grand Canyon, the Mekong Delta. Great deeds of geology are compressed into a few square metres, the twelve hours between tide and tide.

Everyone reads this beach differently. One friend helps me understand weed; another shells; a third, who's a sailor, talks about the tide and the rosts; another reminisces about her childhood, trudging down here to swim before the council put in the road and the loo-block.

I see this space as a landscape of the dead. A couple of hundred yards up from the beach there is a little walled cemetery, eighteenth-, nineteenth- and twentieth-century graves, Orkney names of folk and farms. There was a medieval chapel here, dedicated to St Nicholas, but it's hard to trace, even though the undulating grass within the drystone dyke has been mowed recently. In the seventeenth century the minister recorded that mysterious lights glowed from within the ruins 'as if torches or candles were burning': explanations have ranged from spontaneously combusting kelp to clandestine Catholic masses. The church went out of use in 1788, though some of the dyke-stones may have come from its walls. An irate evangelist visiting in 1797 noted that 'in Evie there had been no sermon for eight or nine years'.

In St Nicholas kirkyard a different artist has been at work: in among the gravestones of standardized, imported granite there is an upright slab of local sandstone. Unsigned, but I know who made this one: Frances Pelly; she's a well-known local sculptor whose secret stone gifts punctuate the Orkney landscape. It looks like another headstone at first, but you need to lean in close and read the elegantly serifed capitals, up and over and down again, forming a tantalizing sentence-fragment, like a half-heard whisper: 'found the secret of immortality and took it with him to the grave'.

From the Sands of Evie I can see two nesses, two head-lands: Gurness, which forms the eastern arm of the bay, and Westness over on Rousay. There was a Pictish cemetery on Westness, typical Pictish graves, rectangular, stone-lined, unfurnished, east–west aligned, into which the Norse later inserted their own more cluttered and complex burials. Gurness has its Iron Age broch, later surrounded by Pictish houses, and there are Norse burials at Gurness as well, of which one survived largely intact.

The Westness brooch is a famous thing – famous, at least, in the circles in which I move. It's in Edinburgh now, trapped in a glass box set into one of the bronze humanoids by Scottish sculptor Eduardo Paolozzi, in the lower gallery in the National Museum on Chambers Street. The Paolozzi statues are big, assertive forms, part of the Early Peoples gallery, though they themselves are futuristic cyborgs. They're very masculine, they intimidate small children, but this brooch belonged to a woman, part of her grave-clothes. She was buried in the middle of the ninth century together with a baby, newly born and newly dead.

They were wealthy and well cared for, interred in a stone-lined grave. The woman also wore traditional Norse oval brooches to fasten her dress, and a bead necklace, and she was buried with her tools: weaving implements, an iron sickle, a lump of pumice.

The Westness brooch was the most visible and expensive part of her burial outfit, pinning a cloak or shawl across her breasts. Its pin is nearly eighteen centimetres long, the ornamented ring five and a half centimetres wide, made of silver, decorated with gold, red glass and amber. The brooch was already a century old when it came into the hands of the doomed young mother at Westness: it's much the same age as the Book of Kells and emerges from the same artistic milieu – the Kells scribe and the Iona stone-carvers would have been at home with the elegant birds and serpents adorning the brooch, the delicate filigree interlacing, the minute scale at which the artist felt comfortable working. The brooch is full of tricks and secrets: traces of beeswax in the cells that hold the glass insets hint at the adhesive the goldsmith used. The red glass looks like garnet until you get it under a microscope and can see the bubbles. Gold wire was soldered with copper which vaporizes when heated. The finest wires are less than a quarter of a millimetre thick. Examination of the back of the filigree panels shows that the design was laid out by one hand, but the ornament executed by another, and less skilful, one. All the closest parallels come from Ireland, and so it seems likely that this brooch crossed the Irish Sea, though whether it was new or old when it did so is anyone's guess. It could have belonged to a Pictish woman. Maybe she was the loving mother of the woman in the grave. Or the brooch could have been looted from her still-warm corpse. Sentimental, or cynical: make up your own story.

The Westness brooch is a Christian object, although it has no explicitly Christian imagery – no cross, or image of Christ. But that's typical of this art: you find the same ornamental repertoire on the bindings of holy books, on reliquaries, chalices and patens. It's probable that to the informed eye these images encoded messages about the relationship between God, Man and Creation, life and death, time and eternity. The beast-head out of whose jaws the pin protrudes has been compared to a classical sea-monster, a Ketos, the creature who menaced Andromeda and swallowed Jonah, and gave its name to *cetacean*. An image of the devil.

The Westness lady's necklace had thirty-nine beads, three of bone, three of stone, many of Baltic amber. These are all carved natural substances, but the glass beads, of which there are also many, some of which are multi-coloured mosaic and millefiori, represent a different level of investment. Beads are one of the commonest objects in furnished Viking graves, men often have a few, perhaps carried in a bag or attached to a thong; wealthy women have spectacular necklaces. Our Westness lady's is pretty low-key compared to the crystal, carnelian, garnet, gold, silver and amethyst rocked by some of her contemporaries. Still, one of her glass beads, striped blue and white, comes from the Mediterranean or Near East, others were probably made in France or Germany, others still in Scandinavia.

The Arab commentator Ahmad ibn Fadlan, writing in the late tenth century, said of Scandinavian traders on the Volga that they prize green clay beads: 'They will go to any length to get hold of these; for one dirham they procure one such bead and they string these into necklaces for their women.' We don't know why beads were so prized: whether they were status-markers, or souvenirs of travel, or protective amulets. All three maybe.

Women probably accumulated beads over a lifetime. They strung them across their breasts, on strings hooked to the lumpy oval brooches used to fasten their pinafore dresses at the collarbone. I like to think of mothers and grandmothers letting curious babies gum the hard, smooth surfaces, telling toddlers not to tug too hard, answering children's questions.

Mama, tell me a story...

She sighs, and bats away a grubby little paw.

Well... This plain stone disc at the back is the first bead I was ever given, when I was only a little bit older than you. I made this one myself, whittled it from whalebone. Bjarni gave me this red and yellow one when he came back from Norway, the summer before he was drowned. Those amber ones were my mother's; she came from Gotland. The blue glass? I bought it from a trader with dark, smiling eyes who put into our harbour the same year that the dun cow had twins...

Of course, we don't know if the woman buried at Westness with her baby left older children behind.

Among the other furnished graves at Westness, there were two men buried in boats: both vessels were færings, the ancestor of the clinker-built four-oared boats used in the Northern Isles for a millennium, like the yole used by Jeems o'Quoys in Robert Rendall's poem. One of the boats still had a rowlock and a fishing-line runner, both carved from deer antler, *in situ*. The men bristled with weapons, but they had farming tools as well, and the runner, the *vadbein*, suggests they were also deep-water fishermen. Analysis of their bones bears this out: the women were sourcing their food on the land; the men were getting much of their protein from the sea.

Over on this side of the water, maybe a generation later, another woman was buried in the ramparts of the Broch of Gurness, her flagstone-lined grave covered with a low mound. She was buried near a farmstead, and presumably she lived there. Water had seeped into the grave, destroying most of the organic material including most of the bone, except for her skull. Still, we can tell she was wearing a dress of finely woven wool, as the bronze of her brooches had corroded around the fabric before the wool itself rotted away, leaving a perfect impression of the weave in the metal. Around her neck she wore an iron ring with pendants, including an amuletic hammer, which we usually call a 'Thor's hammer'.

I wonder about the relationship between these two women from Westness and Gurness: they could easily have known each other, their lives overlapping in time and space, their homes practically intervisible. A clinker-built boat buries its prow in the shelving sand of Evie; the young man and woman who farm at Aikerness come down to meet their middle-aged neighbour. He's crossed the dangerous rosts to ask them to a funeral: *They were both doing so well, but then she sickened with a fever. We tried the baby on cow's milk but they died on the same day.* The young bride at Aikerness keeps a solemn face. Every older woman she knows has a corner of the farm where some of her children are buried. She has no children herself; she's only been married since Yule. And yet at the same time she has a flash of malicious satisfaction. *That bitch, always lording it over me, flashing her jewellery. Much good may it do her now.*

There's a beautiful Ministry of Works pen-and-ink drawing of the Gurness woman's burial in excavation, by J. S. Richardson, dated 15–16 August 1939. It shows the stone-lined grave from above, and in section, from the side and from the foot. Her skull has fallen to the right, and though the other bones are gone apart from a scrap of tibia, a length of femur, her possessions still map out the shape of her body: oval brooches above her breasts, her sickle at her waist. Richardson has added little details that vividly evoke the setting: the short grass growing around the excavation, cross-hatching on the stone slabs. Looking at the drawing, I can hear the terns shriek in the mid-August sky. It's the time of the County Show; the puffins will be leaving their burrows and heading back to the *haaf*; winter is just around the corner.

Thor's hammers are seen as blazoning paganism. But they only become popular when Scandinavia is teetering on the brink of conversion to Christianity, and maybe they develop as a backlash, an assertion against the talismanic power of the cross. Overwhelmingly, they turn up in women's graves. There is a comic poem from the *Edda*, about how Thor's hammer was stolen from his bedside by a giant whose outrageous ransom demand is the hand in marriage of Freyja, goddess of sex, gold and war. But without the hammer the gods will not be able to fight against the forces of darkness in the battle at the end of time. So Thor dresses up as Freyja, with a thick veil to hide his beard, and goes off to the wedding. When the phallic hammer is brought in and placed on his lap to hallow the bride, he seizes it and attacks the giants, with predictable results. So it's not only a weapon, it's a fertility symbol. Thor means *thunder*. The woman buried at the Broch of Gurness may have been given the Thor's hammer amulet at her own wedding, for rain at the right time, good crops and healthy babies.

How pagan were these people? Hard to tell: the evidence of cult practice and ritual centre, the big buildings, the huge burial mounds, the evidence of sacrifice found in Norway, Sweden and Denmark is largely absent from Orkney's archaeological record. If the colonists brought other gods with them, such as Freyja and Odin, they did so in fugitive materials such as wood, textile and leather, and in their minds. For an understanding of their world-view we have to turn to Iceland's medieval literature. The pagan world-view constructed by Old Norse poetry is brutal, relentless. The best death is the death in battle, and the chosen warrior will live on in Odin's Slaughter-Hall, Valhalla, only to fight again and lose in that last battle of gods against giants, when all creation goes down into darkness. Winter in *The Wanderer* is a sign that our true home is elsewhere than on this earth: the Norse pagans thought the end of the world would be heralded by fimbulwinter. Their world is every bit as fickle as the Wanderer-poet's, but their afterlife only offers ultimate defeat. There is a deep suspicion about human motives, the petty and self-seeking impulses that govern action. No one is given the benefit of the doubt.

Harshness, ruthlessness and pragmatism govern the conversion of the Norse world to Christianity, too. The only recorded miracle of Olaf the Holy, Norway's patron saint, was to turn bread into stone. When King Olaf Tryggvason required Jarl Sigurd of Orkney to convert in 995, the only other option offered was death. *If you refuse, I'll have you killed on the spot, and I swear that I'll ravage every island with fire and steel.*

In *Hávamál*, a poem of Odinic wisdom which survives in a thirteenth-century Icelandic anthology of old poetry, there are many unforgiving nuggets of advice, including:

> *Cattle die, and kinsmen die,*
> *And so one dies one's self;*
> *But a noble name will never die,*
> *If good renown one gets.*
> *Cattle die, and kinsmen die,*
> *And so one dies one's self;*
> *One thing now that never dies,*
> *The fame of a dead man's deeds.*

The Old Norse refrain, 'Deyr fé, deyja frændr, deyr sjálfr it sama' is very close to the Wanderer-poet's Old English:

'Her bið feoh læne, her bið freond læne, her bið mon
læne…' 'Here cattle/wealth are on loan, here friends are on
loan, here *mon* is on loan…' Old English *mon* is tricky to
translate here – yes, it means *man* but it also means gender-
neutral *human being* and can be used as the impersonal
pronoun *one* (as in German). Here, I'm tempted to translate
mon as *oneself* – you don't own yourself, you're on loan,
but from what? God, family, the cosmos…

There's a common currency shared by the Old English
and Old Norse poems, as revealed by the pairing of
transient *friend* and *fee* (which means both cattle and
money); a shared cultural tradition, and yet such a different
conclusion. For the Christian Anglo-Saxons, the transience
of the world is a perverse, paradoxical guarantee of the
permanence of heaven. For the pagan Norse, you only
live as long as others choose to remember you. The two
snatches of poem are so close, and yet the slippage of
meaning creates a yawning gap between.

Historians talk about *conversion* and *Christianization*
as though these are finite processes. I've just been writing
glibly about the Christian Picts and Anglo-Saxons, the
pagan Norse. But the truth – as any priest will tell you –
is that every human soul is a battlefield, and conversion
begins again in every generation. Early medieval historians
debate whether Orkney was converted to Christianity
under the Picts, or the Norse; but in the summer of 1797
the visiting evangelist James Haldane observed that 'The
islands of Orkney, by what we actually witnessed, have
been as much in need of the true Gospel of Jesus Christ,
so far as respects the preaching of it, as any of the islands

of the Pacific Ocean.' This was less than twenty years after Cook first set eyes on Hawai'i and exactly twelve centuries after the death of St Columba.

A friend of mine, a girl on the edge of adolescence, one of the youngest Polar Bears, a brilliant musician and talented athlete, an aspiring cosmonaut and one of the most life-enhancing people I know, is suffering existential anxiety. It's not so much that *she will die*: what eats away at her is that *she will be forgotten*. Her mother and I have no words of consolation. Yes, sweetheart, you will be forgotten. And even the tiny minority of us who are remembered at all survive only as symbols, distorted reflections in the riddling mirror, empty shells, the puppets of history, verbal tics, fossils. We still say *mesmerize* but who remembers Mesmer? Rich lives are reduced to mute ornaments of bronze in a glass case, mirrors on which later generations can speculate. At times like this the consolation offered by Christianity seems most alluring: not just eternal life, but eternally being valued. Every quirk of my individual personality, every perceived flickering fragment of *Now*, all filed away and curated – *cared for* – in God's moth- and rust-free museum.

My mother's younger sister Barbara outlived her by over a decade. She was an observant artist and poet and my godmother as well as my aunt, and she moved in to a nursing home towards the end of her life. While she is sorting and discarding, preparatory to the move, she says to me, 'There's something upstairs I'd like you to have.' We go up, her on the stairlift and me keeping pace on my legs, and in the spare bedroom she shows me a little chair, balloon-backed, under a faded and frayed cover with a pattern of fruit. The purple upholstery fabric below is pristine. 'This is very special,' she confides. 'It came from Osborne House. Queen Victoria gave it to your great-grandfather.'

Where is the truth? I look back across the chasm to my mother and my aunt on the other side. Down into the widening crack between us there sifts a continuous dust of memories, conversations, ephemera, worm-riddled wood, powdery rust, half-remembered gestures, the inflection of a familiar, beloved voice. My mother wore Chanel No. 5, and so did I, for years, until I finally acknowledged it didn't suit me. But a whiff of it bridges the chasm, throwing me back into the safe warm space of her lap. When I hear her voice on an old recording I'm astonished by her clipped, fronted vowels – her accent is beginning to sound archaic to me, a ghost from a vanished world. Sometimes the floating spirits are so close, sometimes so very far away.

I leaf through the old photo albums, two little girls in monochrome building sandcastles on a beach – are they me and my sister on Diani in 1974, or my mother and my aunt on the Isle of Wight in 1932, or my grandmother and my great-aunt at Margate or Whitstable in 1904? My grandmother died just before we moved to Kenya: if she had still been alive my mother would never have felt able to leave the UK. I remember little more than a presence, a capacious lap (but I was very small), her voice reading Beatrix Potter. Have I imagined the smell of talc? In photographs she is a formidable figure: upright, broad-shouldered and strong-jawed, staring the camera down whether in white satin and feathers for Court or sturdy shoes and tweed on Scottish grouse moors, or in uniform as a senior figure in the Girl Guides. But there was more to her. 'Ma always regretted not having driven in the Paris–Dakar rally,' my mother said once. And my aunt wrote this:

> My widowed mother
> skied down the Parsenne run
> aged sixty. Drove alone
> in a wonky car through the Masai Mara
> wearing her drip-dry blouse
> from Marks and Spencer. Took
> a donkey to the rose-red city,
> a camel to Samarkand. A magic
> carpet to a far horizon,
>
> and then came home again.
> What did you see, Mother? we asked her
> So much, she said.
> So much to tell your father.

What are people for? *Friends die, kinsmen die, a woman dies herself*, our names die too, in the end, despite the contrary assertion of *Hávamál*, and there is no heavenly foundation. Hold your beloved dead close. People are for each other, and that's all there is.

Tide and surf high, moon low, westering and golden. Lightning flashing against blue-black clouds in the southern sky. Big swell crashing over the breakwater, hard to keep my footing, smack in the face, rolling over, salt water rush through the sinuses. Waves in such high peaks and low troughs that the seals – many seals – and I couldn't see each other until we were almost on top of each other. Last swim for a week – glad it was such a sensational one.

Seal Lullaby (Rudyard Kipling)

Oh! Hush thee, my baby, the night is behind us,
> And black are the waters that sparkled so green.
The moon, o'er the combers, looks downward to find us,
> At rest in the hollows that rustle between.
Where billow meets billow, then soft be thy pillow,
> Oh weary wee flipperling, curl at thy ease!
The storm shall not wake thee, nor shark over-take thee,
> Asleep in the arms of the slow swinging seas!

The events of the last few years have forced me to reframe and reclaim the concept of depression. I had internalized the idea that it is an illness, a chemical imbalance, that you cannot blame the person who is depressed, to the point that that I had become incapable of seeing how this is only part of the story. It is my kind and wise GP who tells me that everyone is different, that there is a spectrum, a complex interdigitation of personality ('call it chemistry if you want to'), experience and environment. 'I'm not depressed,' I said to him. 'I can't be. I'm a happy person. I'm strong, full of positive energy. Maybe I'm a bad wife but I'm a good mother. My sister calls me a force of nature. I cope. I'm creative. Yes, I'm stressed, but who isn't? I deal with it, meet deadlines, speak in public. I eat well, exercise, box, run, swim...'

He just looked at me, this rangy man in blue shirt and chinos, who has been announcing his intention to retire as long as we have been in Orkney, and yet somehow is still here today to meet my eyes and call me out on the crying, the not-sleeping, the erratic behaviour, the hair-trigger temper, the longing to swim out into the dark and drift, let the cold take me, go into that happy place where the endolphins swim in my bloodstream and welcome me home, where my orca comes to find me, and none of it matters any more.

'Do you ever think about harming yourself?'

I nod, and put on my listening face, and reach for the form he offers me. It's a way of deflecting attention. He wants me to talk, not listen, but I'm reticent.

A lot of what he is saying makes sense.

Nonetheless I reject his diagnosis. Leaving the surgery, coming out into Orkney air, the fierce joy of the sun and wind on my face, a packet of pills in my hand, I can't accept this as depression. And even if it is, I am wary of medicalizing powerful emotion. But he's the man in the white coat, metaphorically if not literally, and I'm the good girl who tries to please. I read the list of possible and probable side-effects.

Nausea – sea-sickness. What about *sea-wellness*, instead?

Sleeplessness, headaches. I've got those already, thanks.

Loss of libido. I do not want a drug that will take the edge off pleasure as well as pain.

Can you get swimming on prescription? It would have to come with a warning of the dangers of addiction.

It occurs to me that I do not know anyone who has started sea swimming and then given it up.

Whatever it is I am feeling, it is like the weather – powerful, external, sweeping over me. However hard it is to face, I don't want to cower indoors in my duvet. I want to ride the blast.

I think of my father, diagnosed with depression and prescribed SSRIs because his grief, two years after my mother's death, was still so acute, and the various health professionals who took an interest – GP, district nurse, social worker – didn't know what else to do with him. No one listened when I said angrily that my mother had been an extraordinary woman, that two years of grief seemed the least tribute my father could offer her. He was bereft, homeless, treading the paths of exile. Outside in the overgrown Islington garden the lilac and lavatera were in bloom but for him, as for the Wanderer-poet, the night-shadow thickened from the north, sending harsh hail to men on earth. All was wretched there.

He tried to kill himself, putting a plastic bag over his head and fastening it with a belt. He was found by his cleaner, Mary, as I learned when a call from the paramedics summoned me out of a seminar I was giving at Birkbeck on the Lindisfarne Gospels. When he was asked why, he said he'd been feeling lonely and fed-up. His discharge summary calls him *eloquent, frail...* His consultant noted, 'Apparently suicide was a rational decision.' Seven more years of steady deterioration followed, the insults of stroke after little stroke, progressively degenerating maculae leading to near-blindness, repeated bouts of pneumonia putting him in hospital, repeated courses of ever-more obscure antibiotics hauling him back from the brink. Food and drink were banned, and he was fed by gastric tube, enduring the further indignity of nappies. They used to call pneumonia *the old man's friend*, because it put a swift end to the struggle, but not any more. This was my father's fimbulwinter, his year after year of winter which could only end in defeat and darkness.

Allow us to grieve. Allow us to be aware of the dark as well as the light, and to see death as a friend. Life is too short and too absurd to do otherwise.

They talk about endogenous and exogenous causes of depression. I cannot comment on the former. It's outside my experience. But when I was doing my PhD, researching the poems and stories and sermons about death that survive from England in the ninth and tenth and eleventh centuries, looking at site reports from churchyard excavations and the treatment of the body in the grave, a common response from others, including Sid the supervisor who had dug at Newark, was 'Isn't it a depressing subject to work on?' Inevitably, I was called Dr Death. My students gave me a ring adorned with an open coffin revealing a skeleton within, like a mourning ring made at the height of the cult of melancholy that prevailed during the sixteenth and seventeenth centuries. I began to accumulate other mementoes: a bracelet of skulls; a whole slew of Mexican Day of the Dead cavorting skeletons; a pendant mirror into which a beautiful woman gazes, her elegant, naked back to the viewer – but peer at her reflection, meet her gaze, and there's a shock lying in wait: a skull grins out at you. Around the mirror is engraved 'Omnia mutantur nos et mutamur in illis' – 'All things change and we must change with them'. But these reminders of death make me happy, and I'm ready to bet that keeping a skull on the bedside table had the same effect in the sixteenth century. Look death in the eye every morning on waking. Say, *Hey, don't I know you?*

I didn't lay out my mother's body. After she died we rang the National Hospital for Neurology and Neurosurgery and they took her body away, and then Roz the undertaker collected her from the hospital. My mother's brain and spinal cord had been removed, in accordance with her wishes. They survive as histology slides, the material embodiments of her consciousness dispersed into numerous fragments like the True Cross or the relics of St Columba. I wanted to help with her body, but Roz asked me, 'Did your mother look peaceful when you last saw her?' I nodded, and she patted my arm. 'Let's keep it that way.'

Kipling's 'Seal Lullaby' comes from *The Jungle Book*. After the Mowgli stories, he goes on a brief northern excursus before returning to India to explore narratives of mongooses and elephants. It's the story of the little white fur seal, Kotick, growing up in northern Canada. There are mortal threats that Kotick and his kind can cope with, like orcas:

> Now and then he would see a thin fin, like a big shark's fin, drifting along close to shore, and he knew that that was the Killer Whale, the Grampus, who eats young seals when he can get them; and Kotick would head for the beach like an arrow, and the fin would jig off slowly, as if it were looking for nothing at all.

And there are other dangers, which the seals have no way of dealing with:

> Kerick said, 'Let go!' and then the men clubbed the seals on the head as fast as they could.
> Ten minutes later little Kotick did not recognize his friends any more, for their skins were ripped off from the nose to the hind flippers, whipped off and thrown down on the ground in a pile.

It's a story about a little hero, an outsider, who goes on a quest and becomes the saviour of his people, leading them to a promised beach, 'a sea where no man comes'. Kotick is the Moses of the northern marine mammals. A visionary, like Columba leading his band of monks to their new home on Iona. Kipling isn't a fashionable writer these days, but his animal fables are so much more than a modern Aesop pointing a moral, a Disneyfied world of humans masquerading in animal form. He is tough and unsentimental, and yet his animals are complex and individual. I have a complete edition of Kipling, taking up almost a whole shelf. Their flaking red leather is embossed with gold elephants, each volume has its silk bookmark; they belonged to my mother's father, and then to her, and now to me. My grandfather bought one a month with his first salary from the army, when he was still a teen-ager. Some look almost new, but *The Just So Stories* and the two *Jungle Book* volumes have been read almost to destruction.

In 'Seal Lullaby' the sea is a cradle of safety, a place of habitation, a substitute for a mother's embrace.

We gave my mother the funeral she had asked for, on a bright day in early April. The cardboard coffin had been decorated inside and out with snatches of poetry, family jokes, children's handprints. It was taped shut: I couldn't see her, but Roz assured me that my mother was wearing her red cotton Marks and Spencer's pyjamas and shrouded in the multi-coloured Afghan blanket that she had crocheted some time in the 1970s. In the coffin with her was the edition of *Pride and Prejudice* from which I had been reading to her over the days before she died. We had just got to Netherfield Ball, when Lizzie Bennet is flirting with Darcy for the first time – that undercurrent of sexual excitement sparking the sharp, self-aware dialogue. '"Perhaps by and by I may observe that private balls are much pleasanter than public ones..."' I looked out of the window to see the district nurse's car arrive, and finished Lizzie's speech. '"...But now we may be silent."' Two hours later she was dead.

Between her death and her funeral the garden comes alive with forget-me-nots.

We played Mozart, as she had requested, and Louis Armstrong singing 'What a Wonderful World' on a battery-powered cassette player; I read Kavafis's poem 'Sailing to Ithaka', in which the island destination is only important because it gives you the journey.

When she is excavated from her chalk hillside in Hampshire there will be no coffin, no blanket, no book, no pyjamas, no fossil imprint of Mozart or Louis Armstrong or Shakespeare or Kavafis – just bones and little red plastic buttons, and maybe an organic stain. In the writing of this book I contacted the National Hospital, asking for details of how the brain and spinal cord were removed. I wanted to know if their extraction would have left any signature on the skeleton, but no one got back to me. Although my mother was born in Broughty Ferry just outside Dundee she spent her youth in Hampshire: analysis of her collagen and stable isotopes will point to her growing up not too far from her grave. Would anyone find evidence of the middle age spent so far away, in the volcanic landscape around Nairobi?

On the underside of the lid of her cardboard coffin I wrote a verse from a seventeenth-century monument she and I had once read in a parish church in Exeter. St Martin's was built by that same Bishop Leofric who bequeathed the Exeter Book with *The Wanderer* in it to the cathedral in 1072. We'd been to the cathedral, she had dutifully admired the rather plain manuscript, we were looking for somewhere to have tea, we drifted into the church as we did so often on our expeditions.

This, is my dwelling: This, is my truest Home.
A House of Clay, best fits a Guest of Loam!
Nay, 'tis my House. For, I perceive, I have
In all my life, been walking to this Grave.

They may find her bones and her buttons, but the rest of her is gone, burst like a bubble, or leached out through the chalk into the River Meon and out to the Solent, the sea around the Isle of Wight, atoms that were part of her washing up on the beaches where she played as a child, foam on the crest of the waves. Swinburne, a writer whose lush, sensuous *fin-de-siècle* verse is possibly even less fashionable than Kipling, wrote (in 'The Garden of Proserpine'):

From too much love of living,
*   From hope and fear set free,*
We thank with brief thanksgiving
*   Whatever gods may be*
That no life lives for ever;
That dead men rise up never;
That even the weariest river
*   Winds somewhere safe to sea.*

If my mother lives, she lives in memory.

After she died, her colleague Ngozi said to me, 'You know, I think Sheila did more to bring black and white social workers together than anyone else in London.' I just gaped at her. I had had no idea. Right to the end, she had been my mother. Never, quite, a name or a person in her own right. 'You can't die,' I sobbed to her once, 'because nothing I do will matter any more if you're not there.' I had had a sudden shocking vision of pausing in my song-and-dance routine, looking out over the footlights and realizing that the auditorium was empty. When will I finally move on from being that bouncy, attention-grabbing child whose ego spans the heavens? Look at me! Watch me swing on the monkey bars! See my name on this thesis!

Perhaps you can only really know a person when she is dead.

I feel I've ticked all the obvious boxes, writing this book. My own version of Orkney Cliché Bingo. The wind. Selkies. Groatie buckies. The martyrdom of St Magnus. Let's just riff through old tropes, shall we? I've mentioned a chapel built by Italian prisoners of war, but it's not the one in Orkney. I'm pleased about that.

And, reiterated though they are, these themes wind their way differently through everyone's story.

What's more, we need new stories. Orkney is changing, just as my beach is different every time I pick my shivering course across the sand. The way we understand the landscape is changing: we are learning new things, even as old ways are being forgotten. Renewable-energy engineers are paying close heed to the shape of seals' hydrodynamic whiskers. Researchers in nanotechnology are fascinated by the way that the molluscs who inhabit top shells exude their nacre, so flexible, so resilient, so tough. Limpets' teeth, with which they fasten on to their home scars, are the strongest biological substance on the planet. There are many lessons here – not just for the nanoarchitects and the designers of wind and wave turbines. Hang on in there. Bend, don't break. Go with the flow...

My life has changed, too, while writing this book. My husband and I have agreed to go our separate ways, and in the last few months my daughter and I have left Orkney – for how long I don't know – and washed up like flotsam in Easter Ross, on the Moray Firth.

A little later my furniture followed me south in a van, many of my possessions inherited from my mother, thick with recent dust and neglect, overlaid with greasy fingerprints and bad memories. I'm wiping them and waxing them and polishing them: a Georgian chest of drawers, bedside tables, Regency dining-room chairs, silvered mirrors and foxed prints in wormy frames, both those little balloon-backed chairs. A mismatched pair of Wakamba salad servers, one carved with an elephant, the other with a lion. Soapstone chameleons and a malachite egg. I'm looking at the tapestry chair-seat embroidered by my grandmother, all those wild animals circling the sturdy Kikuyu woman in her blue dress, shouldering her burden of firewood, smiling, smiling, smiling. I'm thinking, I'll dismantle the chair, have the tapestry off and frame it – it feels wrong, plonking my arse down on that indomitable little figure – and I can hear the reproving voices of my ancestors, loud and clear.

Hush, I say. *Come on, you can do better than that. I've got enough to carry without you dumping filial piety on top of the load. I want to live my life, not curate it.*

And while we're about it, the green balloon-backed chair badly needs re-upholstering. I might choose mossy velvet again, but I might fancy something else. Neon flamingos – why not?

Swimming here in Easter Ross is quieter, the water more sheltered than in Orkney; the beach at Shandwick is surrounded by houses, the bird life is less varied, the seals are fewer. But dolphins are much more common. And only weeks after I got here some of the Northern Isles orcas (including matriarch Mousa) were sighted a few miles from here. They don't often venture down the east coast of Scotland; they have never before been recorded so far south; and though I didn't see them their fleeting presence feels like a blessing.

The Sands of Evie were scintillating this morning, sparkly-choppy in a light northerly. My first Orkney swim for about six weeks, my last till God-knows-when: the water was ice-champagne. Blue sky hazing over, the scream and flutter of a tern proving that it really is spring. Stayed in until I was almost immobilized with cold. Worth every shiver.

When I was pregnant I prepared for labour with a hypnotherapy CD, lying in bed with door and eyes closed. It took me down into a deep meditative state by asking me to imagine I was on a favourite beach, and the beach to which I always went was one where we often used to holiday in Kenya, self-catering cottages on a little cove south of Mombasa, built of blocks of coral and thatched with *makuti*, the fronds of the coconut palm.

I close my eyes and wind my way down between the leggy doum palms and the squat baobabs. The wind hushes in the casuarina trees whose needles and spiky cones litter the path; the white shell sand is soft and flaky between my toes. It is half-light, and the beach is deserted apart from the pale pink ghost crabs scuttling along the tideline. A few hundred yards out to the east the surf breaks gently on the coral reef. I settle into the warm sand and let the soothing voice on the CD describe the experience of giving birth in affirmative, comforting language, no mention of *labour* or *pain*, just a powerful reassurance that this is my body doing what it was designed to do. The hush-hush of the waves is indistinguishable from the beat of my heart. I press a switch and go down to the beach, every night, for months, happy and alone.

But the last time I do it, when I wake soon after midnight on my daughter's due date with contractions that tell me quite clearly she is on her way, and I settle into the familiar, soothing narrative of hypnosis, I go down to the beach at Capricho to find that my mother is there already, waiting for me. She and I sit companionably side by side, sometimes talking, but mostly in easy silence, watching the rhythmic play of the water. After a while, she says, 'You're allowed to be Demeter, you know, as well as Persephone.' When at last I return to the surface and breathe the air of the waking world again four hours have gone by, and I am primed for the most exciting day of my life.

Demeter as well as Persephone. The strong mother as well as the needy daughter.

Swimming in the sea has helped me rediscover myself. It has opened Orkney up for me, and made me understand the strengths of my body, as well as its limits. It has been fundamental in healing my feet, but, more than that, it has allowed me to fall in love with being embodied all over again. With being alive. I have finally lost a lot of my self-consciousness: there's nothing like trying to wriggle out of a wet swimming costume on a darkening beach in a Force 7 with a lot of other giggling idiots for knocking some sense of proportion into you. And then there are the seals – the orcas, too, but mostly the seals. The human face of the sea. The shape-shifting selkie offers me a narrative that makes sense of my tangled life when nothing else does. Swimming out into their space gives me the release I seek, beyond the line of surf. A different way of being human, a freedom unavailable on land.

Xenophon tells a story of a Greek army who had been fighting the Persians and were struggling their way back westwards and homewards overland, lost, starving and disorientated, until at last they stumbled down to the eastern shore of the Mediterranean. With one voice, they shouted in joy, 'Thalassa, Thalassa!' *The sea, the sea…* It might not have been their own particular stretch of salt water, but it was the sea, and once they had found the sea their way home was clear.

I swam at Shandwick in silver light, the sun already high in the sky at 7 a.m., a running swell with a few white horses herded by a steady easterly. There was one vocal tern hovering overhead, reminding me of Eleni's wonderful paper on *The Seafarer* at Leeds. A seal bobbed in the shallows – neither of us in more than four feet of water – swam around me, treading water and stretching its neck up to see better. Sea swimming: like having a finger on the pulse of the world.

APPENDIX

The Wanderer: My Translation

The lonely man often abides God's mercy, even though, careworn, he has to stir the freezing sea with his hands, walk the paths of exile. Fate is fully determined! So said the wanderer, mindful of hardship, battle, the fall of kin.

Often, every dawn, I have to voice my cares alone. No one now lives to whom I dare clearly open my heart. I truly know it's a noble habit in a man that he keep his thoughts fast bound, hold his secrets, no matter what he thinks.

The weary spirit can't withstand fate, nor can the tired soul seek help. People eager for renown often bind sad thoughts in their breasts; so I, wretched with care, deprived of my native land, far from my kin, have often fettered my spirit since long ago I buried my gold-friend in an earth grave, and I went hence in wintry mood over the surface of the waves; sad for the lack of a hall, I sought a treasure-giver – somewhere, far or near, where I might find the man to comfort me in mead-hall, friendless as I am, to bring me joy.

The man who's been through it knows how hard a companion sorrow is to him who has few dear friends: lonely paths, not twisted gold; a cold heart, not the joys of earth. He remembers men in the hall, treasure-giving; how in his youth his gold-friend weaned him on to feasting. All joy passes: he knows that, the man who has to forgo the beloved wisdom of his lord, his *friend*. When sorrow and sleep join forces to bind the wretched wanderer it seems to him that he hugs and kisses his lord, and rests his hands and head on his knee, just as he used to in the old days when he enjoyed favour.

Then the friendless man wakes again and sees before him the fallow waves, the bathing seabirds with their outspread feathers, the driving frost and snow mixed with hail. Then his heart's wounds are heavier, yearning for the beloved.

Sorrow is renewed.

Memory of kinsmen passes through him; he greets them joyfully, eagerly scans the men. Always they swim away. The floating spirits do not bring the familiar songs.

Care is renewed, over and over, for the man who must send his weary spirit over the bound waves.

I don't understand why my soul doesn't darken when I think through the life of man, how the proud warriors so suddenly departed the hall, just as this world of ours each and every day rots and withers. No one wins this wisdom before he has achieved his share of winters in the world. A wise man must be restrained: not too hot-hearted, nor too outspoken, nor weak in battle, nor faint-spirited, neither fearful nor joyful, nor greedy, nor boastful, before he comes of age. A man must endure, when he makes an oath, until his spirit truly knows which way his heart's deliberation will turn.

The wise man knows how ghostly it will be when all the wealth of this world stands waste, just as we now see here and there across the landscape the wind-battered walls upstanding, frost-shattered, the buildings dilapidated. The halls rot, the ruler joyless, the warrior band all cut down, once proud by the wall. Battle escorted some on their road out of here; others carrion birds took to a high island; others still were dealt death by the grey wolf; and some the sad-faced survivor hid in their earthen graves. The Ancient Creator has so handled us that the dwellers in this city have no joy. The ancient work of giants, abandoned.

The man who meditates on this world and this dark life, wise in spirit, often calls to mind the many dead of long ago, and he has this to say:

Where is the horse? Where is the man? Where is the giver of treasure? Where is the table set for the feast? Where the joys of the hall? Alas for the bright cup, alas the mailed warrior, alas the pleasure of the lord. How that time has gone, taken under the helmet of night, as though it had never been.

Now in the place of the beloved warband there stands a wall high with wonder, patterned with worms. The spear-strength, the bloodthirsty weapon, notorious fate: these have taken the men.

And the storms batter the stone-cliffs, the driving sleet binds the earth, winter's wailing, when darkness comes. The night-shadow thickens from the north, sending harsh hail to men on earth. All is wretched here, shaped by inexorable fate: wealth is on loan, friends are on loan, here man is on loan, kinsmen on loan, all the substance of this earth falls into the void.

So spoke the wise man, who sat apart in thought.

He's a good man who keeps his word, never over-hastily revealing his heart's anger to men: not till he both knows the solution and can put it into practice.

It's well for him who seeks mercy, comfort from his Father in heaven, where for us all security lies.

GLOSSARY

Bioprene – subcutaneous fat

Bonxie – great skua

Craigs – cliffs

Cruisie – oil lamp

Daberlack – winged kelp, *Alaria esculenta*

Dunter – eider duck

Endolphins – a pun on endorphins, the morphine-like chemical
   produced by the body

Grimlings – twilights

Haaf – deep sea

Haaf fish – grey seals

Haar – fog

Pickie-terno – Arctic tern

Rost – tidal stream

Scarfie – shag

Selkie – grey seal

Simmer dim – night around the summer solstice

Tang, tangle – seaweed that grows in the inter-tidal zone

Tang fish – common seals

Trow, trowie – supernatural creature, fairy

White maa – gull

Yamils – age-mates

A NOTE ON THE COVER PAINTING

Tressness Sand Dunes, Sanday (in the collection of the ACE Foundation), Julia Sorrell 2016

JULIA SORRELL RI, RBA is an artist living and working in Norfolk. In 2015, she was awarded an ACE Foundation TravelArt Award to produce exhibitions of paintings and sculpture based on the landscape and archaeology of Orkney. She has works in many public and private collections in Britain, Europe and the USA. Julia has also written many articles and given talks about herself and her artist parents Elizabeth and Alan Sorrell, and has recently completed a book on her father commissioned by Oxbow Books.

Also by Victoria Whitworth

DAUGHTER OF THE WOLF

'A beautiful, rich tale about a young woman in
Dark Ages Northumbria who takes over her
father's domain when the king sends him on a
mission to Rome. There is a slow-burning plot
about a rival clan and plots against the king,
but the deep joy of this book is in its portrayal
of everyday life in a harsh time. The heroine,
Elfrun, grapples with how to wield power,
while the fascinating characters over whom
she rules face their own dilemmas. Gripping
and highly recommended.'

THE TIMES

Turn the page for an exclusive extract from
Daughter of the Wolf

Her scalp was smarting from the tugs of her grandmother's fine-toothed antler comb, her face and hands were glowing and abraded from the coarse linen towel, even her fingertips stung from the gouging Abarhild had been giving her nails. And dressing her down all the while, listing her seemingly endless faults of morals and manners while Elfrun squirmed under her grandmother's glare and the interested regard of the other members of their party.

Especially Saethryth's. The eldest daughter of the Donmouth steward, she had been roped in to dab the mud off the blue dress, and Elfrun still felt hot at the memory of the other girl's disingenuous cornflower gaze, directed alternately at the spatters of filth on the wool and at Elfrun herself, fidgeting in her linen shift under her grandmother's litany of shame. It wouldn't have been so bad if it had been any one of the other girls, but Saethryth's angelic fairness always had Elfrun feeling angular and grubby. And Saethryth's talent for well-aimed and malicious comments was second to none.

Elfrun had hardly had another moment to wonder why the king might want her.

Now, her grandmother chivvying her as she might a wayward ewe, they were walking as fast as Elfrun's stiff leather shoes would allow her on the dewy grass to the thronged open area outside the king's tents. To her great relief her father was there already, seated on the bench nearest the entrance to Osberht's tent. She could pick him out from any crowd in that blood-red cloak. A gift from the king only a few days earlier, and far and away the gaudiest thing he owned, he was wearing it over the much more characteristic wolf-grey tunic which was the last thing her mother had ever woven, soft and light with all its worth in the fineness of the weave. His only glitter came from the silver tags weighting the woven bands that fastened the cloak at his shoulder.

But, plainly dressed though he might be, in his daughter's eyes Radmer of Donmouth shone brighter than any half-dozen of the more gaudily clad dish-thanes and riding-men who hovered wasp-like around the king's court, bullion glinting silver and gold at shoulder and wrist and throat, and on the sword-belts they insisted on wearing even if the swords themselves were packed away.

No weapons in the king's presence, not at spring and harvest meeting. Stakes were too high, old feuds always simmering too close to over-boiling. Northumbria might have been at its fragile peace since Elfrun was little more than a toddler, but she had heard the threats chewed over and spat out in the hall often enough. Internal dissent, brooding exiles, sea-wolves and the warlords of Mercia and Wales, Pictland and Dumbarton. The king's cousin, Alred, banned from coming south of the Tees since his rebellion seven years earlier. She knew fine well there were stories of disloyalty and over-leaping ambition attached to some of the faces she could see here, too. But she found it difficult to take any of the hard-edged talk seriously. With her father at the king's side, what could ever come to hurt them?

Radmer was gesturing to the bench beside him. No smile, but the lack of a frown was enough to fill Elfrun with relief. She knew only too well the drawn brows – worse than any spoken reproof – that would have greeted her if she had arrived in her former muddy and tangled state, and she felt a burst of still half-sulky gratitude to the old lady stomping along beside her.

Abarhild lowered herself on to the bench in silence, back straight and mouth still clamped.

'Mother.' Radmer bowed his head, still fair rather than grey in the spring sunlight, and she nodded.

Radmer looked beyond her, at Elfrun's demurely bowed head, the neat, pale parting in her rich brown hair. 'Daughter.' She came to stand in front of him, hands folded, gaze still lowered. 'The king has summoned me,' he said quietly. 'And he said you should come too. Something to our advantage.' Radmer set his hands on his knees. 'Well, I've been here for a while, and still waiting. There are legates come from Canterbury, and Archbishop Wulfhere is with them. But Osberht's steward said he'll see us next, whatever it is.' He reached out his hand and gave hers a brief pat. 'How have you been amusing yourself? Not frowsting in our tents, I hope, not on a day like this?' She lifted her steady brown gaze to his, and he smiled reassuringly.

Elfrun could feel the auger gaze of her grandmother boring into her. 'Watching – watching Athulf with the horses. Racing.' Not quite a lie, even if truth fell down through the crack between her words.

'Did he win?'

She wished suddenly, passionately, that her father had seen her ride. Radmer might have been – no, he *would* have been – angry, but no one had a better eye for horsemanship. And she was as good as Athulf, she knew she was. Better. The way the wretched boy had been sawing at Apple's mouth… 'He – I—'

'He did well,' her grandmother said. 'The other boys were older.' She shot Elfrun an inscrutable look. 'And he was riding Apple, not Mara.'

'Athulf.' Her father sounded thoughtful. 'Now your uncle Ingeld's home from York, it's time he took that lad in hand. Promising boy, but he's been left to run wild for far too long.'

'He should be trained for the Church.' Abarhild's tone was flat, uncompromising. Elfrun stared at her grandmother. Sulky, whining Athulf, a cleric?

And it seemed her father shared her incredulity. 'That puppy? Less fitted even than his father.'

Elfrun braced herself for the blast. But Abarhild had set her withered face hard, the lines between mouth and chin deep and oppressive. 'The boy is our responsibility. What's the alternative? Will you make him your heir?'

'Promise him the hall?' Radmer turned on his mother with a swiftness that startled Elfrun. 'Ingeld's brat? I'll be damned first.'

'Why not? Who else is going to take over Donmouth after you?'

'Don't bury me, Mother.' Radmer glanced from his mother to his daughter, and then turned his stare back to the king's tent. 'I'm not dead yet.'

'Radmer! Don't ignore me. You need to do something for Athulf.'

'Why?' Her father's voice was flat and hard as stone. 'Ingeld got him. Let Ingeld look after him.'

Abarhild levered herself to her feet and stalked away, her very shoulder blades eloquent of disapproval.

Radmer was drumming his fingers on his knee. 'As though I haven't done enough for Ingeld already.' He bared his teeth, white and strong in the silver-blond beard, but there was no smile in his eyes. 'Sit down, daughter, and learn the virtues of a king's good servant from watching me.'

'What are they?' The bench stood on uneven ground, and it lurched a little as she sat.

Radmer snorted. 'Obedience. Patience. Anticipating every need. And never asking questions.'

It sounded very like Abarhild's standard lecture on being a good granddaughter, and Elfrun wanted to say as much, to see if she could make her father smile. But Radmer was no longer paying any attention to her. His whole body had stiffened, like a wolf that scents the hunt on its heels. She followed his gaze across the thirty feet of open grass that served as an antechamber to the royal tent, but she could see nothing.

Just men.